G000145905

Grand Hotelier

The World on a Plate

By the same authors

Grand Hotelier

Inside the Best Hotels

Salute, London, 1998
ISBN 0 9532737 0 9

Gastromania!

Smith Holliman, Newport, Pa, USA, 2000
ISBN 1 931318 00

GRAND HOTELIER:

The World on a Plate

Ronald and Eve Jones

Line drawings and illustration Ronald F. Jones

Salute 2004

First published in 2004 by
Salute
London EC2Y 8BN

© 2004 Ronald and Eve Jones
Illustrations © Ronald and Eve Jones

A catalogue record for this book is available from the British Library

ISBN 0-9532737-1-7

Ronald F. Jones OBE and Eve Jones's rights to be identified as the authors of this work have been asserted by them in accordance with the Copyright, Designs and Patents Act 1988.

All rights reserved. No part of this book may be reproduced by any means, electronic or mechanical including photocopy or any information storage and retrieval system without permission in writing from the publisher.

Typeset in Times

Printed by Ashford Open Learning, Ltd., Southampton
www.ashfordopen.com

This book is dedicated to the memory of Bill and Patsy Abell of Chevy Chase, Maryland. They were, and are, part of every journey.

We gratefully acknowledge *Caterer & Hotelkeeper* and Reed Business International for permission to quote freely from 'Travel Log'. And the *New Orleans Times Picayune* for permission to quote freely from 'Going All the Way', 'Venetian Holidays', 'Swiss Bliss No Laughing Matter' and 'Amblin' Santa Monica'.

Front cover photograph:
Image Photo Services Inc.

Back cover photograph:
Bruce Morgan, Louisiana State Tourism Office

Cover design:
Ashford Open Learning Ltd.

ACKNOWLEDGEMENTS

They won't believe us, but we truly *are* grateful to Millie Ball Marshall and Dr. Keith Marshall for providing the 'Madewood Experience'. And for their generosity in allowing us to paint this 'warts n' all' picture of our sojourn in the Deep South. Most of all, for their continuing friendship. MOPS will prevail!

Bruce Morgan, Director of Communications, State of Louisiana Office of Tourism, has been a treasure trove of information over the years, and worked hard to keep us on tracks with the facts.

Warm thanks to David Warren and Michael Brooks for reading, editing and suggesting. And to Millie Ball Marshall – again – for being an editor in a million.

A few stalwart Cunarders deserve a round of applause: John Duffy, ace hotel manager, Colin Parker, best-ever cruise director, I.T. officer Brian Martin, and Mary Thomas for all her invitations to come aboard.

To the friends we made around the world at sea and ashore; the aspiring hoteliers and clients who asked – and sometimes heeded – our advice; and to our friends and family who have put up with our peregrinations and still been here for us to come home to.

Thank you all – you know who you are – from the bottom of our hearts.

INTRODUCTION

The notice was pinned to the wall of a Polish GP's surgery in Richmond-upon-Thames.

Retirement Kills!

He must have been eighty-four himself, but had the clear-eyed, fresh-skinned look of a younger man. Feeling tired? Out of sorts? Not sleeping? His remedy was simple. 'You walk every day four miles. And one day each week eat nothing – only two pounds of apples.'

I recalled the good doctor's maxim when I retired from Claridge's, where I had been Director and General Manager for ten years. I was about to enter my seventh decade in robust health, good spirits, and looking forward to a new challenge.

The small consultancy my wife had set up ready for my 'change of direction' was producing assignments in the UK and overseas, and I was gratified that still there would be work. I love it; it has always provided solace in it in difficult times, fulfilment in good ones.

In a rewarding career that spanned over half a century (chronicled in our book *Grand Hotelier: Inside the Best Hotels*) I had been associated with eighteen of the UK's 'grandest' hotels. Claridge's – at that time – was the jewel in the crown.

Leaving, I felt a little like the staff officer in *Henry IV* venturing into the field. Only I was hanging up my 'uniform' of tails, waistcoat and striped trousers and exchanging five-star hotels for the battlefield of bar stocks and below-par kitchens, under-trained staff and customers whose demands there might be only myself and Eve, to satisfy. No brigade of waiters, no luggage porters, no support team of assistant managers and department heads.

The change of direction would afford the liberty of choice and the luxury of spontaneity. But I learned that saying no is harder than you think. At the back of the mind of the freelance is the thought that if you say no you might not be asked again! Nobody understood this better than my wife Eve, a freelance journalist, lecturer and wine tutor. One of the happiest aspects of our new direction is being able to work together. Not all married couples can, nor would they choose to, and we thank God every day for the good fortune of having each other.

It has been a joy, travelling the world this past decade, to see young men and women I helped to train, now general managers, managing directors or owners of their own grand hotels. It has been a privilege to be invited to advise new and established businesses. And pure pleasure for my wife and me to spend several months each year as guest speakers on fabulous cruise liners. Thanks to 'the happiness business' we have enjoyed – and are still enjoying – the world on a plate.

Ronald F. Jones London, October 2004

CONTENTS

Foreword by Len Deighton   xiii

Part One
Louisiana Spring   1

1   The Incomers' Tale   3
2   The Cook's Tale   15
3   The Caretakers' Tale   23
4   The Cops' Tale   33
5   The Caterer's Tale   43
6   The Cat's Tale   57
7   The Car's Tale   65
8   The Consultants' Tale   75
9   The Congregation's Tale   89
10   *Lagniappe*   97

Part Two
'The Captain's Sober. We Sail at Midnight...'   107

11   Have Tales, Will Travel   109
12   Going All the Way   119
13   Sybarites at Sea   131
14   'Two Dozens of Mangos as a Token of Love'   141
15   Half the Fun is Getting There...   151
16   Salute to the Queen   161

Part Three
A la Carte   171
17   After Claridge's   173
18   California Dreamin'   187
19   The Wizardry of Oz   197
20   Wait Awhile   209
21   Skirtless in Switzerland   215
22   Venetian Winter   225

LEN DEIGHTON

Ronald Jones and his wife Eve have one over-riding motive in writing this account of their adventures. If, says Ronald, this book persuades people about to retire that the world is a wonderful place and there is a great deal to do, then the book will be a success. It is only too easy, he says, to accept retirement as the end of a working life. As you will discover in this book Jones and Jones don't have a spare moment in any day. Their energy is wonderful and inspiring, and so are their ideas.

Ronald Jones was for many years the manager of the illustrious Claridge's and that wonderful Piccadilly hotel the Athenaeum. It says everything about Ronald and his 'can-do' attitude to life that so many of the hotel clients became his friends and his career was celebrated when he received the Order of the British Empire from the Queen.

Before the glory of London's Mayfair Ronald had made a name for himself as a miracle worker. Aged only thirty he had taken over hotels that were losing money and transformed each of them. Turning a hotel into a profitable concern is not like putting up the charges for water or gas. To make a hotel work you have to create a contented and highly motivated staff and have clients who come back again and again and recommend your hotel to their friends and business colleagues.

This skill is not something you can learn at a school no matter how important schools have now become in the administration of the international hotel business. A good manager has to have the eagle eye of the detective and the heart of a saint. You must have energy galore because the job never stops night and day. In Ronald's words: 'A hotelier worth his salt ... sleeps in his own beds, never visits the kitchen without a tasting spoon, and looks at the building inside and out with the eyes of a first time guest. He surrounds himself with talented young people – the hungrier and more ambitious the better – and gets rid of yes-men.'

So when Ronald and his wonderful wife Eve faced retirement they didn't blink. They decided to become consultants. But first there came the trip they had promised themselves. They had enjoyed previous visits to Louisiana and the time warp wonders of the Deep South and its ante-bellum world. Sitting on the 'gallery' of Madewood, a plantation house acknowledged to be one of the twelve most beautiful inns in America, they looked at the cypress trees and the sugar cane that long ago provided so much of the wealth of the old south, they enjoyed a southern breakfast and adjusted themselves to the idea of returning home to England. But the owners of Madewood recognised a unique opportunity. If Jones and Jones were hotel consultants how would they like to revive the fortunes of this lovely old home? As an inn it was only just paying its way.

That was the start of an adventure that is recounted in this book. Cockroaches are nothing new to anyone who has worked in a hotel but these were extra large ones. And what about snakes, mosquitoes and the armies of fire ants that locals said were known to consume a whole cow?

It was not an easy job. The fundamentals of business had to be applied. Should prices go up? If so when and by how much? How much more should be spent on staff, food, improvements and maintenance? With a rather fragile building of historic importance the fabric of the old house was an ever-present concern.

'If it ain't broke don't fix it' became the Jones motto, but they were surprised one day to see a small crowd of guests staring up at the ancient damage to the hall's high ceiling. Some plaster had fallen to leave a gaping hole. But the octogenarian staff member who sometimes conducted visitors around the house was saying: 'see here? This all has been kept just as it is, all the paint and plaster removed so you can see the original structure and building materials used in the house.'

Eve says he was deeply disappointed when funds became available and the damage was repaired.

But improving this historic plantation house (without disturbing its original magic) was only part of the post-retirement adventures of Jones and Jones. As part of their consultancy work they began writing articles and lecturing. Eve specialised in wine and wine tasting. Ronald talked about their time running grand hotels and they talked about the great hotels of the world in which they had stayed. This proved to be a controversial subject, for many in the audience had their favoured hotels and were prepared to fight for them. Soon Jones and Jones were persuaded to take their lecturing skills to sea and became popular speakers on some of the world's most luxurious cruise liners. This in turn was to provide them with more material for their talks and writing.

Eve and Ronald are an inspiration to young and old. Their previous book, Grand Hotelier, is not just a gripping account of life in a grand hotel. It is a splendid example of logical thinking and business management, and shows what can be done when talented and energetic managers are prepared to take their coats off and get their hands dirty. To be with Eve and Ronald is delightful and galvanising and their plans are terrific, as this book will show you. Stand by for book number three.

Madewood 1998.

Part One

Louisiana Spring

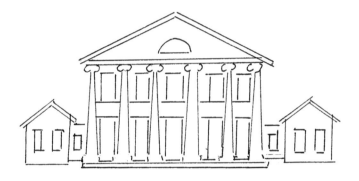

The Incomers' Tale

Love at first sight? Of course it was. You drive about ninety minutes north west of New Orleans, past the small town of Napoleonville. Meandering along just out of sight on your right is Bayou Lafourche, on the left a scattering of small homes with neat lawns. The road bends to reveal a lone pine surrounded by cypress, live oaks and pecan trees. Then, without warning, there is Madewood, 'Queen of the Bayou'. Set back from the road, vast pediment supported by six Ionic columns, dazzling white by day, now almost iridescent in the setting sun. Named one of the twelve most beautiful inns in America, the plantation house is a National Historic Landmark, one of the finest remaining examples of Greek Revival architecture of the antebellum period.

In Britain we'd call Madewood a country house hotel. There, it's a B&B or an inn. We called it home for one unforgettable spring. The mansion stands like a sentinel on Highway 308, between New Orleans seventy miles to the southeast, and the State capital Baton Rouge to the north. Two miles outside Napoleonville, a few more from Labadieville, and seventeen from Thibodaux, the nearest town of any size. It faces Bayou Lafourche and is part of Assumption Parish. This is Cajun country.

Nothing could have prepared us for the place, the people, the pleasure or the occasional pain of our Louisiana spring. At the approach of the long and steamy summer we were sad to leave, eager to return – and thankful we didn't have to live there.

The people who do are as unique as their Deep South homeland and their multi-cultural heritage. Louisiana – especially southern Louisiana – is unlike any other state in the Union, seductive as satin and guaranteed to produce the unexpected.

Native American tribes were the only inhabitants until in 1682 French explorer Sieur de la Salle named his new-found-land *Louisiane* in honour of Louis XIV. For 120 years Europe played musical chairs with what seemed a pretty remote and inhospitable territory. It 'belonged' first to France, then Spain, then Britain, then Spain again, then France again. In 1803 Napoleon sold it to the US for fifteen million dollars (a transaction financed largely by Barings Bank of London) as the 'Louisiana Purchase'. It became the eighteenth State of the Union in 1812.

With such a heritage, you can imagine the exotic mix of people who live there. Not so much cultural melting pot, more cultural gumbo. Descendants of the original settlers, the Spanish, the French-speaking Creoles. Today Creole is commonly used to denote mixed race, but the word comes from the Spanish *criolla* meaning 'born here'. Into the mix came the British; slaves from Africa; Irish and German immigrants; Acadians, refugees from religious persecution in Nova Scotia, then known as Acadia, during *le grand derangement*. The Acadians were French-speakers too, but with an alien dialect and a different way of life from the sophisticated Creoles. Acadians were boat-builders, shrimpers and fishermen, with their own culture and music. They were Cajuns. In the wake of the Louisiana Purchase, an influx of Americans arrived from the North to seek their fortune, ill prepared by their Puritan background for the fun-loving Creoles and their European lifestyle.

You'll hear talk of *lagniappe* if you visit New Orleans. Roughly translated it means 'a little something extra'. For 'Jones and Jones', partners in the small consultancy we call Hospitality in Focus, it dished up a double helping of *lagniappe* all over our *lagniappe*. It turned Ron back into a hands-on hotelier and transported both of us back to the basics of life-before-Claridge's. It provided an experience unequalled in half a century in 'the happiness business', and our most bizarre and rewarding assignment.

Our ties with Madewood grew along with our friendship with its owners. Friendship has been behind most of our adventures in New Orleans and Louisiana. Eve first visited in 1978 as the guest of Albert and Nancy Aschaffenburg, owners of the historic Pontchartrain Hotel on St. Charles Avenue. We returned together (as Ron promised we would when he proposed) two years later, making so many friends along the way that we became regular visitors to the city known to tourists and jazz lovers as the Big Easy. Mayor Sidney Barthelemy made us Honorary Citizens in 1986.

While Ron was general manager of the Athenaeum Hotel in London, then director of Claridge's, we visited New Orleans to promote the hotels, introduce them to a wider audience, and pay court to the many regular guests who lived in the city: Jimmy and Minnie Coleman, co-owners of the Windsor Court Hotel and close friends of the late Princess Margaret; Bernice Norman, Jimmy and Mary Koch, Mildred Ball and Gladys Jurgens, all Claridge's regulars. The city's top travel professional Leonard Parrish, distinguished US Air Force Col. and Mrs. Albert Wetzel and the Aschaffenburg family had been loyal guests since Athenaeum Hotel days, and society columnist Nell Nolan and Robert Young honeymooned at Claridge's. There were so many friends among the citizenry of New Orleans that we felt thoroughly at home.

We met Millie Ball Marshall, whose husband owns Madewood, on the last day of our visit in the late 1980s. It was Sunday morning, an hour before we had to leave for the airport. Millie was a feature writer for the New Orleans Times Picayune newspaper. She had returned from vacation the day before and asked to interview us in our suite at the Pontchartrain. It was not an auspicious start to the friendship. Millie was a terrier of a journalist. She would not be told that Ron couldn't disclose information about the Royal Family or any of the 'haughty and the naughty' among our famous guests. In desperation Eve, herself a journalist, thought of some of the great stories of guests throughout the hotel's hundred-year history, and said: 'You can talk about the *dead* guests, darling.'

And that, in large black type, was the strapline on the article that appeared in the New Orleans Times.

Still, we took to Millie and she to us. She and her husband Keith, a dashing art historian and Anglophile, had already stayed at Claridge's, as had Millie's mother Mildred, a lady whose Southern charm won her no end of friends wherever she travelled. By the time the family paid their next visit, our friendship was cemented. Millie came with Keith, then the two of them with her mother, another time with Keith's mother Naomi, and on one memorable occasion, with *both* mothers. Millie became travel editor of the New Orleans Times Picayune, and Eve an occasional contributor of travel features.

At the conclusion of one business trip to New Orleans, we joined Millie and Keith Marshall for a weekend at their plantation house deep in the heart of the bayou country.

The four of us lingered over breakfast on the sunlit gallery outside our bedroom. Nothing fancy, just the local blend of deliciously tarry black coffee and chicory, with warm croissants and homemade preserves, all of us relaxed and surrounded by the Sunday papers. Millie and Keith wondered if one day, when Ron retired from Claridge's, we might return for a longer stay. We had not planned an imminent retirement from the day job, and certainly not on future consultancy quite so far afield. But Keith can be very persuasive. He's had plenty of practice right alongside another American known for his way with words; he was a Rhodes Scholar at Oxford with Bill Clinton. He remembers the two of them standing on a bunting-draped balcony of the Royal Orleans Hotel waiting for their final interview. His companion grinned and waved at a group of pretty girls in the street below, and as they waved back Clinton joked, 'It's just like being President of the United States!'

Now Keith unfolded the story of Madewood's history, as plantation house, Marshall family home, and its latest incarnation as a B&B.

Once the heart of a thousand-acre sugar plantation, the mansion was built by Col. Thomas Pugh in 1846. He commissioned Irish-American architect Henry Howard to build the most magnificent plantation house in the State. The competition was tough; the region already boasted numerous homes that could lay claim to the description. But Howard, most would agree, fulfilled his brief. Between them, Thomas Pugh and his two brothers owned eighteen plantations, three million dollars, and two thousand slaves. While a few of these looked after the family as house servants, the majority were field hands and craftsmen. There was no shortage of labour to make the bricks and to cut, season and fashion the estate's homegrown timber. It was named Madewood, the jewel in the family crown.

Col. Pugh died before the house was finished, leaving his widow Eliza to oversee the completion and raise their five sons. Eliza loved to entertain (and with two hundred slaves still at her command, why not?) and the mansion's forty-eight foot ballroom was the scene of lavish parties to introduce her sons to all the eligible young ladies from miles around.

In those days there were no inns or lodging houses along the length of the Mississippi; entertaining meant virtual open house, hospitality to strangers as well as friends and relatives escaping from the humidity and disease of New Orleans. Plantation homes like Madewood and

Nottoway, Oak Alley and Destrehan were bastions of lavish hospitality and almost unlimited wealth.

The Civil War put an end to that. Only a few of the plantation houses of the south survived war damage, sequestration or abandonment – sometimes all three. Most were destroyed or left derelict. The end of the Civil War in 1865 and the abolition of slavery made it impossible for planters to enjoy the lifestyle they had become accustomed to

Madewood's fortunes ebbed along with the rest, but while the plantation's acreage dwindled, the house survived and remained in private ownership through the first half of the twentieth century. By the time Keith's mother Naomi purchased Madewood in 1964, it was sadly lacking the attention it deserved. Caretakers occupied only one side of the house; birds roosted in the attic, by then open to the elements, and rodents inhabited the basement. A substantial acreage of sugar cane, on the other hand, continued to be farmed by the former owners.

Naomi Marshall, a businesswoman prominent in fine arts circles in New Orleans, was the daughter of a family that had lost its own plantation house during the Civil War. She didn't tell her husband she had bought the twenty-one-room mansion and twenty acres for $75,000 until it was a done deal. He was aghast, but she had an ally in her older son Keith, who loved the house as much as she did. Restoration took seven years, and thirty-five years later, was still ongoing.

Madewood was not alone in its need of a restorative dose of TLC. Lack of funds, escalating costs of repair, maintenance and taxes had their effect on all the surviving plantation houses. Faced with the same problems, each had sought different solutions. Some were taken over by state or local preservation societies and opened to the public. Others were bequeathed to similar bodies on condition the owners might continue to live there and allow occasional access to visitors, not unlike the arrangements our own National Trust has with numerous historic houses. Some became conference or music venues, hotels and inns, and a few remained in private hands. Most fell into dereliction with no immediate prospects of being saved. You can still see these handsome ghosts reaching out to the wealthy incomer who might prove their salvation.

The Marshall family was determined to keep Madewood what it had always been – a family home. At the same time, as hospitable Southerners, they were eager that as many people as possible should experience the glories of Madewood. Even in its pre-commercial days the house and grounds under the Marshalls' stewardship became known throughout the state as a venue for the arts. The family organised opera festivals, concerts and exhibitions of paintings by local artists. Candlelit Christmas suppers with costumed carollers became an annual event.

Inside, the house retains a keen sense of period and the interiors and furnishings reflect its 19th century origins. During the years he lived in the UK Keith, an ardent Anglophile, collected antique furniture and artefacts. With his mother's encouragement he branched out into Europe and shipped some fine pieces from France and Italy.

By the late 1970s the cost of upkeep of the mansion had escalated almost out of control. Keith, already running two businesses in New Orleans, sat at his desk at Madewood one sultry Saturday evening, head in hands, wondering how on earth he was going to pay the $450 increase in the latest electricity bill. The telephone rang. A friendly gentleman with a mid-West accent asked if Madewood did bed and breakfast.

'We are three couples planning a tour,' he explained. 'We're also going to a football game in Baton Rouge and we'd really like to stay overnight in a plantation house.'

Keith looked down at the bill on his desk and with only a moment's hesitation said,' Yes we do!' Decision made, he was on a roll.

'You will be met on arrival and invited to join us for wine and cheese in the library before sitting down to a four-course dinner by candlelight. Coffee and brandy is served in the parlour. In the morning we will bring coffee to your room, and you can enjoy a plantation house breakfast and a tour of the house before you leave.

'The price?' Fingers firmly crossed, Keith regarded the bill on his desk, did a quick mental calculation and divided by three. 'That will be $150 per couple.'

Madewood's new incarnation as an inn had begun. Almost twenty years later, when we arrived on the scene, the cost was still only $185 per couple, with dinner and breakfast.

As Keith now confided, Madewood had done well enough taking in paying guests while remaining the family home and weekend retreat. But it couldn't just pad along indefinitely, barely making ends meet. Wouldn't we, he suggested, whenever we did decide on a change of direction, spend some time with consultants' hats on and share our views on the business and the direction in which they ought to be heading. Wouldn't we just!

So it was that early in March of 1998, after one or two brief return visits, we abandoned London's wintry cold to embark on our Louisiana spring. We went for two weeks. We stayed two months.

Our tedious trans-Atlantic flight touched down in Houston, Texas at the same time as six others. The welcome from grumpy, power-crazed immigration officials took the form of ordering us to the back of the long line to fill in a form different to the one we'd been handed on the plane. We made our short connecting flight to New Orleans with minutes to spare. Keith was there to greet us, looking quintessentially British in Prince of Wales check suit, beaming that signature smile of pleasure in the moment. He clutched a bouquet of red roses for Eve and a short length of red carpet that he spread on the ground with a flourish worthy of Sir Walter Raleigh!

We headed north-west past Lake Pontchartrain towards Napoleonville, and before long were driving alongside the byways of the Mississippi River known as bayous. Dusk falls swiftly in the Deep South. Birds still exotic to us took flight from wetlands and trees. The sky was shot through with rose madder and apricot, orange and yellow, then turned the vivid purple of a new bruise. In an hour and a half we were alongside Bayou Lafourche in a world that while only a day's journey from home, would soon feel like a separate universe.

It was a relief to climb stiffly from the car at Madewood, where Millie waited with outstretched arms to welcome us to the inn in the country. She and Keith insisted on carrying our cases. Had we but known it, they would be the last cases we wouldn't carry ourselves for a long time. The night wrapped itself around us, aromatic, warm and still. The sound of crickets and cicadas reverberated across the grounds, and we breathed in the aromas of warm, damp vegetation. Heaven, right then, was to sit in white wicker chairs on the 'family porch' screened against the flying fortresses that were Louisiana's mosquitoes, moths, daddy-long-legs and other creatures that fly silently in the night eager to feast on a tasty new dish of pale northern flesh.

The wildlife trekking and flying through Madewood's twenty acres was to become a constant source of discovery, though not always of joy.

Between our cottage and the main house lurked more predators than we imagined existed in the civilized world – winged, multi-ped, four-legged and two-.

We appreciated the musical background provided by crickets and cicadas. We became accustomed to the strange calls of Louisiana birds. We never did get used to the other creatures of the night; miniature translucent green frogs that attach themselves to windowpanes as though with rubber suckers and could be unstuck only by scraping with a palette knife. And little hairy brown caterpillars that sting in the spring. They found Ron irresistible and inflicted a series of painful rashes when they dropped down his neck from trees and bushes. Geckos, lizards and skinks were nothing compared to cockroaches the size of model T Ford motorcars. Every morning before Eve would get out of bed, Ron had to perform roach patrol and dispatch. He tried every known remedy and in the end resorted to the one that worked best: a rubber sink plunger to suffocate the *cucarachas* and knock them off the wall. He would then send them to their reward with a shoe – and an audible crack-crunch before counting the corpses (eighteen on a 'good' day, if you must ask). All had to be disposed of before Madam arose.

These great crawling – sometimes even *flying* – roaches were invaders from the outside world. They would be there to greet us at night, too. Eve cringed and pointed out 'the hugest cockroach I've ever seen, darling. It must be three inches long. DO something.' Ron pointed out that the giant beastie was actually two cockroaches playing mummies and daddies up the length of our bedroom wall. There was a patent remedy we'd heard about but didn't quite believe. It was advertised as:

ROACH MOTEL
They check in but they don't check out!

The contraption was like a giant matchbox, the theory being that the roaches were attracted by bait at the open end, and couldn't escape from the closed end. But nobody, it seemed, told our Louisiana cockroaches, and they were too smart to fall for it.

There were nests of fire ants, identifiable only by a small hump in the grass every few metres that turned crossing the grounds into an assault course, especially hazardous in the dark. Step on a nest and the furies of hell would be let loose on your feet and legs. We have it on good authority that an army of fire ants can consume a whole cow. Snakes too, quite small but requiring swift and final dispatch with a shovel. Only one person at Madewood volunteered for snake patrol – and it was neither Jones nor Jones.

At least the occasional alligator had the good grace to confine itself to the bayou over the road. And the mosquitoes, though a nuisance, at this time of year were not at their worst. The gnats made up for them.

That first night, blissfully unaware of the creature discomforts that lay ahead and too tired for hunger, we were fed cups of chicken and *andouille* (spicy sausage) gumbo with cornbread and salad. And a glass or two, or three, of cold white wine. We could have chatted late into the night, but caution and experience told us to retire before midnight. Our friends showed us to the cottage that was to be our home. They were sorry we could not have the slave cabin, now converted into a guest suite, as promised. That, they went on delicately, had a rodent problem, which they hoped would be dealt with shortly.

They had spent three days and nights preparing the clapboard cottage for our arrival. It had been the home of a manager who hadn't stayed long. Neither did the light bulbs, shower poles and curtains. The house had been painted with muted colours chosen by Keith from the range used by the National Trust. Great thought had gone into selecting furniture that would make us comfortable – chintz-covered sofas and armchairs, a TV with cable service and a king-size bed with Colefax & Fowler linens. We wondered, that first night, if we would have time to enjoy all this home comfort. There was a study, and the kitchen, though small, had an enormous fridge and a four-burner stove that we predicted would not see much action. A diet of ham and cheese sandwiches and the three-day Madewood menu cycle would become our staple fare. Or rather, fuel, as we would burn up enough energy to counter whatever we had the time to ingest. 'Our' cottage, as we would soon think of it, was close but not too close to the 'engine room' of the main buildings.

We slept a jet-lagged sleep, waking throughout the night, talking, making plans, surfing the TV for old movies. Soon after six we had an alarm call from the sun shining wetly through our bedroom curtains. Rain had fallen during the night, leaving a crystalline flat, green landscape. Within minutes we were jogging the track through the sugar cane fields behind the house towards a pink sunrise. Instead of the English dawn chorus of sparrows and blackbirds, we were accompanied by the foreign jabbering of mocking-birds, cardinals and redwings.

Our only human encounter was a cheery wave from a grizzled farmer spraying the sugar cane from a rusting tractor that looked even more antique than its driver. In typical Louisiana contrast, on the other side of the track a trio of cropduster aircraft awaited the call to duty from the planters. By 7.30 am we were dressed for work and back in the main house for our first look-round. As always with a new assignment, rarin' to go.

While Millie slumbered on inside, Keith joined us for breakfast on the porch. We talked to him of the future and were joined by Joe, a friend who helped out from time to time. The Marshalls encourage input from everybody and the world and his wife, it seemed, had plans for Madewood – improvements, innovations, systems. Our job would be to input our own plans for turning an enterprise that had worked amazingly well *without* professional help, into a business that would not over-stretch resources but would generate sufficient revenue for maintenance and improvements. The Marshall family had worked hard to make Madewood the success it was; now it was time to work smart.

We knew from our previous visits that Madewood offered a once-in-a-lifetime experience to overnight guests. That was part of the problem; most of them looked upon it as a one-night, once-in-a-lifetime experience, and too few returned. (Given the vast distances some had to travel to Louisiana, this was more understandable than it would have been in Europe.) The property was beautiful, bedrooms comfortable, food wholesome and traditional.

The mansion had a spacious guest suite on the ground floor, the Lee bedroom, usually referred to simply as 'down', in addition to the owner's suite and another used by Millie and Keith. Upstairs there were four bedrooms and suites, all with private bathrooms though not all en suite. Each room was furnished with 19th century antiques and artefacts, in keeping with its character. 'The nursery' had a canopied child's bed, antique doll's pram, Victorian toys and half-tester double bed. Antique cotton and lace nightgowns were laid over the beds. 'The girls' room' had feminine drapes and flounces, with nineteenth century crocheted lace gowns laid ready as though for their next wearer. 'Mrs. M's room' was more elegant, and a portrait of Naomi Marshall hung outside. The master bedroom had its own balcony, approached through a floor-to-ceiling window and furnished as an outdoor sitting room. On the wall, a portrait of Millie. Elsewhere around the house were photographs and portraits of three generations of the Marshall family, one showing Millie and Keith at twelve years old when they were king and queen of the Children's Carnival Club ball in New Orleans.

'Millie was a guest at my birthday party when I was three,' explained Keith. 'We were married at Madewood thirty-two years later. We've known each other all our lives.'

On display in the parlor are portraits, engravings and mementoes of the families that called the mansion home, as well as 'before' and 'after' pictures of the house's restoration. Outside, in a far corner of the grounds, is the Pugh family cemetery, headstones testifying to the lives and deaths of Madewood's original occupants.

There is additional guest accommodation within the grounds. Charlet House, the home of a nineteenth century sea captain, had been bought by Keith, transported on flatbed trucks and deposited facing the back of the mansion across the lawn and connected by a gravel path. Charlet provides three additional guest suites, including the honeymoon suite, and a banqueting facility that could cater seated meals for sixty, with its own kitchen beneath the raised ground floor. In addition to our own, two cottages awaited conversion if and when funds became available, Marquette House to provide guest accommodation and Rosedale, hopefully destined to become the Marshall's retirement home. An elegant coach house was used as storage and workshop space. Then there was the cabin. Every plantation home has at least one of these former slave cabins, wooden shacks with tin roof. In the nineteenth century these might have housed a family of seven. Today many are adapted for use as guest suites complete with air conditioning. A few house small museums devoted to the history of slavery.

Madewood has two working kitchens – three if you count Charlet House. One at the back of the house behind the office is used for preparing food for parties or for freezing should a nice consignment of fresh crawfish or shrimp arrive. The other is next to the dining room for day-to-day food preparation. The mansion's original kitchen, known simply as 'the old kitchen', was built as a separate structure at the back of the house for fire protection, a common practice in plantation house architecture. This, we found, functioned half-heartedly as a small museum and gift shop, displaying a few dusty nineteenth century cooking implements and paintings by local artists.

Many historians believe it to be apocryphal, but legend has it that between the original kitchen and the dining room of the plantation houses there was a 'whistlin' walk', where servants carrying food to the dining room were obliged to whistle all the while, so those inside knew they could not be stealing food.

We understood from the outset that guests who chose Madewood were not looking for the staff or the service of a five-star hotel. They were invited to join a house party as paying guests, but in what is still a family home. Staff, we discovered, possessed a laid-back (OK – sometimes *too* laid-back) Southern charm. The experience the Marshalls had created was a highly individual one and the formula worked well. However, if we were to increase room rates and revenue, some tightening-up was essential.

Up till now Madewood had enjoyed modest success more by luck than judgement. As a B&B it had, more or less, simply evolved. Business in the city prevented Keith from meeting the challenges of the hospitality business on more than a weekend basis. He lacked time and his commitment needed to be backed up with a tougher approach. Our brief, as he saw it, was to:

- Help him identify the niche Madewood was to occupy within the market.
- Set goals and targets for the short and long term.
- Clarify the responsibilities of the owners.
- Implement and oversee some fine-tuning of the operation.
- Help the staff develop, bearing in mind that some long-service staff might be resistant to change.
- Encourage some of the younger personnel to improve dress and grooming standards, and to develop a more friendly attitude to the guests.
- Look closely at expenditure and cost control.
- Examine ideas that had been proposed and identify those that might work.

All of this without changing the things that worked well. Our motto was to be 'if it ain't broke, don't fix it.' But just as Madewood had many unique qualities and seldom failed to please guests, there was still plenty that needed fixing.

2

The Cook's Tale

It was time to meet the staff.

There would be an informal get-together at 2pm. Most of them turned up – a compliment in itself, we realised later. Thank heavens we made the most of it while the honeymoon lasted.

The housekeeper and the cook had been with the Marshall family for half a century between them. Framed portraits of each of them hung on the wall of the library. Clem, the housekeeper, had been ill and was undergoing chemotherapy, but gave no sign in all the time we have known her of being so much as under the weather, insisting on coming to work when most of us would have been only too glad to take time off.

The office manager Janet, who would prove to be Eve's ally in getting to grips with the business end of Madewood, was a pretty lady who looked too young to be mother to three grown children and grandmother of two. Few callers could resist Janet's husky southern drawl as she closed a reservation. 'Ma'am, you-all surely are welcome.' There was nothing Janet wouldn't turn her hand to. She was the chief peacekeeper. She enjoyed working with the other women to prepare breakfast, serve lunch, or cook dinner for special parties. She ran the office single-handed with weekend help from Keith. And she was not averse to jumping in her car and driving the seventeen miles to Thibodaux to do a mammoth shop whenever late payment of bills resulted in a temporary withdrawal of credit facilities from suppliers or when the cook ran out of supplies.

Janet's two sons were roped in to mow grass, help with minor repairs, or act as chauffeur if required. Her pretty teenage daughter helped out as waitress at special parties.

The team of general assistants were soon to become familiar to us, and could certainly be described as familial to each other. Karen and

Tammy are Clem's daughters. Yvette had been the partner of Clem's late father, thus making her Clem's putative stepmother despite Clem being twenty-five years her senior. Another is Clem's niece. Danielle would later wed Carolyn's son. Carolyn's family had been at Madewood since slavery times, and once lived in the cottage we were now occupying. In fact, she was born in 'our' cottage.

The in-house tour guides were two young mothers informally job-sharing. Gladys, a septuagenarian Cajun lady, came in to do the ironing and guide the occasional tour for French-speaking visitors. The other part-time guide was T-Boy, a spry eighty-something who had been a translator for the US in France during World War II. T'Boy liked nothing better than to tell tall stories – in English or in French depending on his audience. We would learn not to interfere while T-Boy ('I was the littlest in the family – *petit* boy is what we Cajuns say, and that was shortened to T-boy') entranced his gullible audiences. Once we overheard him as he gently cradled a ten-dollar pressed-glass milk jug, tell them 'this here is one of the antique treasures of the Marshall family. Priceless now, just priceless.'

Fourteen staff plus casuals seemed a lot for a property with less than a dozen letting bedrooms and suites, but most were part-time, and they worked parties and small tour groups as well as looking after overnight guests.

We outlined why we were there and what we planned to do – which was first of all, look, listen and learn, and always with the proviso 'if it ain't broke, don't fix it'. The Madewood experience worked well; we wanted to polish the diamond, to enhance the product and make it available to a wider audience who would, we hoped, pay a little more for it. Ron emphasised the somewhat pressing need to increase both occupancy and revenue in order to finance improvements and repairs. The business could not survive indefinitely as things stood, and their jobs as well as the house's future depended on the improvements we could make together. Whatever solutions we came up with, we would need the help of the staff to make them work. Naturally we would value their input, as did the Marshalls. The ladies mostly looked at their feet and said little, but at the end Clem sweetly welcomed us.

'I guess Madewood is a family and that you-all now are just a part of our family,' she said, and promised their support. They would not go as far as calling us by our Christian names, but compromised on 'Mr. Ron' and 'Miss Eve'!

Most of the assistants were large young women who took their time. Adapting to work with them after teams of well-trained hotel staff was to sorely try our patience. They were not to blame. We were ill prepared for the differences imposed by the climate of the place – meteorological, social and cultural. When the temperature reaches the nineties and it's barely even spring, and the humidity soars to match; when mosquitoes zoom like kamikaze pilots off the bayou; when the air around you barely stirs from dawn to dusk, you begin to appreciate just why the work ethic of London or New York is an irrelevance.

Work is a means to an end. It puts food on the table and clothes on the kids. In their own way, the staff liked their work well enough, and in their own way they were proud of Madewood. One of them even told us, 'I don't mind the guests!' But there were limits beyond which they would not or could not go. One of our hardest tasks would be to encourage them to go the extra mile, to use their eyes and their initiative, to see when they looked around, what needed to be done, and *do* it.

If anybody was going to adapt, it was likely to be us. Others may call it a learning curve; to us it seemed more a learning parabola.

Madewood offered tours to the public between 10am and 5pm, so we joined a handful of visitors on Marilyn's tour of the house. This we found minimally informative and formulaic. She came across as a fragile young woman, eager to please, but with dark circles under her eyes and a nervous manner. Lucy's tour was different but that, too, could sound scripted. Both had a way to go to make the tour more interesting and personal, and to radiate more genuine interest in the visitors. To respond to friendly enquiries such as 'Hi, how are *you* today?' with 'Fine, just fine. How are *you*?' rather than 'Oh, not so good, y'know?' or 'I've had a *terrible* day.' They needed to learn, too, to see every chance visitor as a potential overnight guest

Madewood operated a three-day menu cycle. Most guests stayed only one night, a few for two, and very few for three. On day one, dinner was shrimp or chicken pie, made in bulk in the back kitchen behind the office and warmed and crisped in the oven each evening. They were delicious, and we were still enjoying them ourselves after having them for at least three meals a week over two months. There just wasn't time to think about cooking for ourselves. Before the pies there was good Louisiana gumbo made from chicken and *andouille* sausage and thickened with okra. This was served with fresh-baked cornbread (from a mix) and followed by a 'dinner salad', a small salad of mixed greens and tomato with house dressing.

The guest's pie of choice was served with green beans (frozen) and pumpkin Lafourche. We considered this an unacceptably sweet mush of (canned) pumpkin mixed with brown sugar and apples, and thought it should be banished from the menu. The staff protested and a quick poll of the guests and the Marshall family backed them up. Everybody loved it. Americans don't, or didn't before the dawn of the twenty-first century, have the same resistance to canned, packaged and pre-mixed food that we do. If the pastry was frozen, the vegetables out of a tin and many things from bread to gumbo to lemonade made from a mix, that didn't bother our guests in the least. In all the time we were at Madewood, we had only two mild complaints about the food; one from a vegetarian who hadn't let us know she would require special meals. And the other from a couple who arrived at 10pm after being told dinner was served at seven. At least they fared better under the current regime than they would have with the previous manager. He used to let late arrivals drive a thirty-mile round trip in search of a late supper. We dissuaded the staff from looking with pursed lips at their watches and pointing the way to Thibodaux! Now, late arrivals would be offered at least a bowl of gumbo and a salad.

Pudding on the first night of the menu cycle was bread pudding with whiskey sauce ('whisky' being reserved for Scotch. This is bourbon and rye country). This was a specialty of the cook's, one she made entirely from scratch, and we've yet to hear of anybody who could resist it.

Guests staying an extra night could feast on the wonderful Louisiana specialty crawfish etouffée, a seafood stew served with rice. The 'appetiser' that night would be corn chowder, the dessert pecan pie.

We felt sorry for new arrivals when there were people staying a third night, because if the newcomers were staying only one night they would miss out on the shrimp or chicken pie *and* the etouffée. Their evening meal would be catfish. We considered it an acquired taste, a bottom-feeding scavenger fish much loved in the South. The smell of it being deep-fried seemed to permeate the house. Catfish was served at Madewood with potato salad, though more traditionally with 'hush puppies' (not shoes, but little fritters made from cornmeal). Precursor to the catfish was, alas, potato and parsley soup, and dessert a spiced apple cake. The visitors seemed to relish every morsel, happy to be introduced to the specialties of the region.

Guests rounded off their stay with a generous plantation house breakfast of seasonal berries and juices, fresh-baked muffins (from a mix) and hot biscuits (scones to us) to accompany the main course of sausage and egg puff or bacon and Louisiana sausages and scrambled eggs. And of course, the ubiquitous *grits*. This mis-named Southern specialty has been anathema to us ever since our first taste in Texas in the 1970s, shocked to discover they were just not – well, *gritty*. More like unsweetened semolina, tasting of absolutely nothing. Worse, the Madewood specialty 'cheese grits' had grated Monterey jack cheese added. This has about as much taste and texture as the grits. Everybody we know in the United States loves them. Maybe Brits and grits just don't go together.

Millie and Keith did their best to encourage the cook and the assistants who helped her to branch out and be more adventurous for special parties and longer-stay guests. They even brought in their friend, award-winning food writer Connie Snow, a comfortable, cheerful lady who introduced a few simple but delicious recipes and demonstrated how to cook them. Connie and her husband Ken are formidable cooks, and we used to look forward to their occasional weekend visits when they would bring a side of salmon and prepare it in their portable smoker for a Sunday evening picnic after a game of boules on the lawn. Alas, once Connie had gone, the staff 'lost' her recipes and without supervision, lapsed back into their three-menu routine.

When we first arrived we made a point of dining with the guests, eager to experience Madewood through their eyes. We slept in each of the bedrooms, too. However, Millie had warned us that we might not want to join the guests for dinner every evening, and she was right.

'When Keith and I are there,' she explained, 'the focus tends to be on us, whereas if the guests are left to their own devices they focus on each other.' This was sound advice, and while we continued to host the wine and cheese reception, we dined with guests only if there was just one couple whom we sensed might want company (which they invariably did), or two couples who showed signs of not getting along. Americans being the social animals they are, this was seldom a concern.

The cook's Southern fried chicken was the best we'd ever tasted. She cooked it for all of us one quiet afternoon, great platters of battered succulent chicken with potato salad on the side, and a few 'biscuits' warm from the oven and dripping with butter. Pity it was whipped butter, an aerated invention of the devil but the only kind that seemed acceptable to Americans. Nowadays, we were pleased to hear, only 'regular' butter is used.

Yvette, who later became the senior assistant, made Southern fried chicken that ran a close second. She 'fixed' hers at home and brought it in to celebrate a birthday. We thought it a pity that one of those fried chicken dishes wasn't on the three-day menu cycle instead of the catfish, but it *was* one of the most popular choices for luncheon or dinner parties. Otherwise party menus didn't deviate much from the menu cycle, though baked goods would be brought in to augment the sandwiches served for an afternoon tea (*iced* tea, of course...)

It came as no surprise, therefore, to find fried chicken on the menu along with cook's famous bread pudding, for the annual lunch of the Baptist Senior Citizens. This was held in the Charlet House function room, a friendly but frugal affair served picnic style with disposable plates and utensils. Ron welcomed the party of forty seniors and left them to the ministrations of the staff. He was called back to deal with a complaint from the head Baptist.

'It ain't fittin',' he admonished, wagging a stern finger at Ron, 'to serve bread puddin' with whiskey sauce at this affair. Baptists do not hold with alcohol.'

He was right, of course, and this should have been picked up when the menu was planned. Fingers crossed behind his back, Ron apologised and assured him and the Greek chorus now lending their support, that only the merest tad of whiskey was added to the sauce. 'You will hardly be aware of it, sir.' Ron thought he would be on safe ground, since cooks are apt to work on the principle of 'one for the sauce and two for the cook'.

Just to be sure, he retreated behind the serving counter and tasted the sauce. Sod's law in action. Cook had excelled herself. This was the most generously laced whiskey sauce he had ever tasted. The pudding had already been served and Ron crept past the rows of tables hoping for a discreet getaway, to be assailed by waving hands clutching spoons and several senior citizens of the utmost respectability *clamouring for more*.

'Why, this sauce is dee-licious' enthused one.

'Finest bread puddin' I can recall, sir,' claimed another.

'I declare! We would surely like to have the recipe,' pleaded an elderly lady in a flowered hat.

Seconds were served until the bread pudding ran out and left some very disappointed churchgoers.

We found the staff liked to work in threes: three to cook, three to clean a room, three to serve dinner. They all turned a hand to whatever needed doing. Even Janet, the office manager, liked to take her turn helping with breakfast and special parties, as well as putting in a 7.30am to 5pm day in the office. They worked well together and appeared to be friends. We got the impression they came in when they liked, clocking on as early as 6.30am or as late as 8am. They would work on through the afternoon or not, returning in the early evening for dinner duty. Rotas tended to the informal. Breakfast, at least, was never late, nor was dinner. During busy periods some appeared to be working sixty-five hours a week, which should have been unnecessary.

It didn't take long to realise that most things about Madewood worked well in spite of rather than because of any definite plan. Ask a question and the answer would usually be one of two: 'I dunno' with a shrug, or ''Cause that's just how we do it...' Things were casual, the approach relaxed. Why look under the carpet if the carpet itself looks OK? In a corner of the hall, dampness had caused the plaster to fall from the ceiling eighteen feet above and paint to peel off one section of the wall. Swathes of ancient, dusty brown velvet had been pinned to a small scaffolding frame to conceal the worst of the damage. (T'Boy, our octogenarian tour guide, was deeply disappointed when funds were eventually made available for repairs to this section of the house. It had made a great story for the visitors. 'See here? This all has been kept just as it is, all the paint and paper and plaster removed, so you can see the original structure and building materials used in the house...' Surely an early exponent of the art of positive spin.)

Never mind if the Louis XV sofa was propped up on wood blocks, the music room chairs too fragile to sit on, the occasional stench of drains – or worse – only partially masked by a score of scented candles and basins full of pot pourri. If dinner was late and morning coffee cool, bathrooms not en suite and the front porch decking treacherous, all that could be forgiven. The atmosphere was exactly what most guests hoped for; the food tasted good; fellow guests were congenial. And Madewood is magnificent. Why, Miss Scarlett, for special events some of the staff could even be persuaded to dress in Gone With the Wind costumes!

3

The Caretakers' Tale

Madewood had been without a manager for some time. Millie and Keith spent the working week in New Orleans, Keith looking after his art supplies business and Millie at the Times Picayune. Many of the staff had been with the family for years, and the office manager was efficient and responsible. While things were quiet, the place *almost* ran itself. But there was no one in overall control, no one who could oversee growth and development, and the enormous unexploited potential. A head honcho was badly needed.

The Marshalls reckoned they had found one, at least temporarily. A forty-something lecturer in geography and history at Louisiana State University in Baton Rouge, he was working on a doctoral thesis on geographical tourism. He believed the manager's job at Madewood well within his capabilities and thought it would give him a unique insight and hands-on experience. He could give eighteen months to two years to the job so long as he was free to write his dissertation in the quiet summer months. Like us, he had fallen under Madewood's spell, and while he had no hospitality experience, he *would* have the former director of Claridge's to give him a swift grounding in rudimentary hotel-keeping.

Michael had intelligence, charm, and a firm grasp of the essentials. He had one other quality that endeared him to us – he was practical (hadn't he worked his way through college as a janitor? Hadn't he built his own house in Maryland? All music to our ears.) He could turn his hand to anything from plumbing to planting to painting. Madewood had planners and would-be planners a-plenty. The house needed a handyman more than it needed a consultant or even a manager. Michael had ideas about the direction the property might take, but he was just as understanding about the indoor and outdoor jobs too long neglected. We agreed with the Marshalls that he could be the ideal man.

But there were problems: until the end of term, still two months away, Michael would be available only from Thursday or Friday night to Monday morning. That, alas, would coincide with our two months at Madewood. He was also agonising over a career decision. He had been short-listed for a good academic post in another state. If this prestigious post were offered to him, he would be hard put to decide between the two jobs: a sabbatical to gain the practical experience of running Madewood? He felt that he and Madewood were made for each other. Against that, turning down the academic post could slow down his long-term career prospects. For ten long days we, the Marshalls and Michael spoke almost daily as we awaited the outcome. Michael was offered the other job. He could not make up his mind. Millie counselled him, Keith counselled him, and Ron counselled him. Given the American tendency to discuss life's most intimate decisions with all and sundry, no doubt all his friends were counselling, too. In the end an ultimatum was issued. Michael put us all out of our misery and said yes to Madewood.

His arrival, even for just two or three days a week, made a huge difference. He would drive up late on Thursday night or Friday morning in a battered wreck of a car overflowing with papers, litter, cigarette packets and rust. Come to think of it, he looked a little rusty himself. He had the slight stoop of the academic, ruddy complexion, red beard, russet-coloured tousled hair and bloodshot blue eyes, all of which lent him the appearance of a backwoodsman. He wore hairy tweed jackets over unpressed check shirts open at the neck, and corduroy pants. He was also generous and warm-hearted and took to bringing us home-cooked curries, casseroles and dishes of Italian meatballs to give us a break from our daily round of Creole and Cajun cuisine.

He was eager to learn and soaked up everything Ron could teach him about the day-to-day running of a hotel. The staff took to him. He was easy and affable, one of them. We did suggest it would be desirable long term *not* to be one of them; rather to be 'leader of the pack'. However, the formula would work for a while, and he would learn as he went along.

In the early mornings we would find him pensive in the garden, hose in one hand, mug of cold coffee in the other, overflowing ashtray at his feet. At odd moments during the day he could be spotted climbing ladders to inspect the guttering, hauling replacement lavatory pans into guest bathrooms, or whitewashing the outside restrooms. He had boundless energy and before long the improvements could be seen around the house and grounds. In the evenings he scrubbed up to join us in hosting the wine and cheese gatherings, changing out of work clothes into jacket and tie, unruly hair slicked down with water, transformed into a genial and charming host. The guests enjoyed his company as much as the staff responded to his affability.

However, with only a two-day-a-week manager and without the input of Millie and Keith for several weekends for reasons nobody could have foreseen, the consultants had to buckle down and get their hands dirty. There was too much to be done for us simply to take a relaxed overview and observe. In any case, both of us were happy enough to get back to the basics of hotel-keeping.

There can be few more beautiful houses to work in. With the massive cypress front door and the more-used back doors open at the same time, breezes swirled gently through lofty rooms built around a central hall. Polished wood floors were covered with oriental rugs, Waterford crystal chandeliers suspended from high ceilings. The lingering aromas of wax polish and a century of candlelight transported visitors back to the antebellum South. There can't have been many who resisted the temptation to stand at the foot of the cantilevered walnut staircase and declaim the closing lines from 'Gone With the Wind'.

'Tomorrow is another day' indeed!

The furniture was in keeping with the house's Victorian origins. While the nineteenth century is by no means our preferred style of interior décor, we can live with and admire anything provided it is (a) genuine, which it was, and (b) well cared for, which much of it was not. Too many copper and brass containers hadn't seen the threat of polish for years. Beautiful silver candleabra and dining pieces were dulled from lack of care. Antique furniture needed attention.

Eve naively decided to set an example, following the credo of never asking anybody to do something you would not do yourself. She got hold of a couple of brass containers dull and green from years of neglect, and spent an entire Saturday afternoon burnishing and polishing until they gleamed. She showed the staff at every stage exactly what she was doing, what she was doing it with, and encouraged them to have a go. At the end she showed off the results of her efforts *pour encourager les autres*, an example of what could be achieved with a little good will, elbow grease and old-fashioned methods. The staff smiled politely, made admiring noises and, we're convinced, had a darn good laugh at those silly foreigners who worked so hard when they didn't even *have* to!

Worse, some of the once-fine furniture was on its last legs. Literally in some cases. In the music room polite notices asked visitors not to sit on the fragile French chairs. After dinner, as guests lingered over coffee and brandy in the parlour, we cringed when three or four at a time lounged on the handsome Empire sofa. Had the unsuspecting visitors troubled to take a peek behind or beneath the sofa they'd have spied the wooden blocks and struts that were keeping it (and them) from complete collapse. The humidity of the Louisiana climate, too, had left its mark on furnishings and fabrics, some of which looked worn and tired (as we would, ere long…).

A closer look at the outside of the house and twenty acres of grounds, beautiful as they appeared to the uncritical eye, revealed areas sorely in need of attention. The back porches and the wicker furniture needed painting. The outside 'washrooms' for day visitors' use required a complete overhaul. Not expensive and barely more than a day or two's work. The floorboards of the front porch seemed in imminent danger of sending someone crashing through to the ground below. The plumbing creaked in agony if more than one or two showers were used at one time. Banana palm trees almost obscured the driveway entrance. The dumpster needed more frequent emptying.

We saw all this. We were looking for it. But we needed to see it with the eyes of a first-time visitor. To the staff, Madewood looked as it always had. To the Marshall family, it was their home and the faded elegance made it none the less so. The guests saw only the beauty of the house and the relaxed ambience of their very own plantation house party. Were we expecting too much?

It was no wonder the guests were happy with the Madewood experience. It was the best bargain in the United States. More than two decades after its birth as an Inn, couples still paid less than $200 a night including dinner, wine, brandy, room and breakfast and taxes.

We were impatient to hike up the price. Keith and Millie argued that increasing the rate would attract the wrong kind of guest.

'More sophisticated people,' Millie explained, 'who *will* see all the things that are wrong with the house, who might expect five-star food and slick service. The guests we have now are exactly right for our style of operation. People paying more might not be so forgiving of

Madewood's shortcomings.

'And besides, we don't want to price it beyond the reach of people who are not rich and who dream of staying in a place like this and find it affordable.'

There was no avoiding the fact, too, that the Marshall family still saw themselves as inviting guests – albeit *paying* guests – into their own home. 'Houseguests' have less high expectations. 'Houseguests' on the other hand, don't pay.

The potentially Catch 22 situation was averted by Anglo-American compromise. The rates *would* be increased, but by less than we advised. An eight percent hike that year, rising to fifteen percent over the next three. It was still a bargain.

Before they left Madewood, overnight guests usually joined the 10am or 11am tour of the property. At noon during the tourist season a mini-bus or two would disgorge a bunch of New Orleans tourists for a show-round and lunch. Although Madewood had recently acquired a liquor license, no attempt was made to sell liquor – or even soft drinks – to visitors. The potential for increased revenue was obvious. It was the same with conferences, business dinners, ladies luncheons and other social and business functions: unless beverages had been specifically requested and quoted for in advance, nobody was asked if they would like something to drink other than iced tea – which was free.

We discovered a serious health problem common to many Americans. That is, the ubiquitous 'bad back'. We made a point of meeting and welcoming every guest as their car scrunched over the gravel driveway. Ron would offer: 'May I help with your bag, sir?' (To which only one replied 'No – she can walk in...') The others had a standard response. The wife of those thirty- and forty-somethings would pile cases around Ron and say: 'Oh yes please, my husband has a bad back.' Then they'd watch *this* septuagenarian husband, arms reaching further towards his knees with each passing day, struggle indoors and up the cantilevered staircase, a suitcase in each hand and, often as not, a dress bag over his arm. He would silently thank God for the landing halfway up where he could pause to show visitors their 'outdoor sitting room', the upper-storey balcony overlooking the grounds.

As they were escorted to their rooms, visitors were asked, 'For main course this evening would you like shrimp pie or chicken pie?' They were invited to meet their fellow guests over 'wine and cheese' in the library at six o'clock. We enjoyed this part of the day (though we often traded the white wine provided for the guests for a couple of Ron's extra-dry martini cocktails). Background music was provided by the Claridge's Quartet on CD. Americans are the most naturally gregarious people in the world; they loved being introduced to fellow-guests, dining with them, comparing stories and lifestyles over coffee and brandy. By the time they left, friendships had been cemented over breakfast, addresses exchanged and promises made to keep in touch. They were all eager to know what a pair of proper Brits like us might be doing in a southern Louisiana plantation house. This gave us a splendid opportunity to mention our newly published 'Grand Hotelier', copies of which were strategically placed around the room, opened to pictures of the Queen Mother and Princess Diana. Better than any bookshop exposure! Several of those early guests still write to us, and a few have visited us in London.

We made a point of memorising (though a tiny notebook could be called into play) visitors' names so we could greet them by name as they arrived in the library, and introduce them to each other.

Crystal decanters of chilled white wine were refilled as required, though most guests were remarkably abstemious. The staff set out silver trays of cheeses with black and white grapes, crispbreads and biscuits. By the time Ron, playing to the gallery for all he was worth, announced: 'My Lords, Ladies and Gentlemen. Dinner is served,' the atmosphere was convivial; visitors were intimate as old friends, ready to dispose themselves around the polished oak table in the dining room. It glowed with silver candleabra, crystal glasses and bonhomie. Following Madewood tradition, Ron would appoint a king or a queen for the evening – usually the oldest lady or a bride on her honeymoon, sometimes a lone child. Their job was to ring the little brass hand-bell at the end of each course to signal the staff to bring on the next.

Wine was poured at dinner, too, at no extra charge, for those who wanted it. We proposed that should stop immediately, in the interests of producing more revenue. In any case, the $185 per couple included wine and cheese *and* after-dinner brandy. Madewood was the bargain of the age – and it had to stop.

At the end of dinner, double doors to the parlor were pulled open and the house party continued there over coffee and brandy.

Now and again people would volunteer to sing, tell stories or play the piano. Or somebody would suggest a parlour game and everybody joined in charades or word games. More than once during our stay a professional musician volunteered to play: Eileen was a flautist from New York on her way to play for a wedding ceremony in New Orleans. She brought her recently adopted daughter, a tiny glorious child named Hannah Joy. After dinner Eileen played duets with a lady piano teacher from Nebraska. On another evening a handsome young Broadway actor kept us entranced for an hour when he sang songs from the shows, accompanied on the piano by a fellow-guest who was a church organist.

On one of our most unforgettable occasions, the talk and laughter and sheer joy emanating from two families meeting for the first time left us feeling humbled. The two fathers had met before – in hospital six months previously when each had had a kidney transplant. One in his late thirties, the other mid-forties, one with three and one with four children, both had been given only a few months to live without transplants. Now they came to Madewood so that each could meet the other's family and celebrate their new lease of life.

Our guests (for within a week of arriving we had begun to think of them as 'our' guests) were a wide-ranging assortment of honeymooners, retired people, families, amateur historians, professional people, businessmen, and ordinary folk eager to explore this unique area of the United States. Most were from within the US – almost every state in the Union was represented. But we had our fair share from Canada, Europe, particularly France and Belgium, countries with historic or linguistic connections to Louisiana. Mostly couples. Fire fighters, musicians and schoolteachers; lawyers and police officers. The owners of one of America's most successful casual-wear designer labels visited every year. An eminent West Coast heart surgeon handed Ron his business card and said. 'I hope you never will, but if ever you *do* need medical attention when you're travelling in the US, please give me a call. I'll make sure you get the best.'

We made a point of asking every guest, while they waited for the wheels of Amex or Visa to 'grind exceeding slow' on the elderly credit card machine, or as we exchanged a farewell word or two while they (or Ron) loaded their luggage, not just how they had enjoyed the Madewood experience, but what they believed made it special, and how we might do better.

To ask them to fill in a form would have spoiled the intimacy of the experience. The house operated largely on an 'honour' system. Guests could help themselves to extra drinks at any time and tell us what they had consumed. Bills were not given until asked for – not as obvious as it sounds, because the office was hard to find and visitors were on their honour to find it. Anybody could have walked away from Madewood without paying. Nobody ever did. In fact, we asked one lady if she had 'anything to declare' before we totalled her bill and she 'confessed', 'Yeah – sorry but I stuffed the gorgeous silver candleabra in my luggage.'

'That's OK,' Ron reassured her. 'Just as long as you polish them before you bring 'em back.'

The visitors appreciated being asked in person, and we believe they were honest in their assessments. Almost without exception they opted for the 'house party atmosphere' as being the most special attribute. Some were even kind enough to specify 'the Joneses' as their best memory! Further encouragement to 'share' revealed that what got them down was the antiquated plumbing and temperamental shower arrangements. There were a few minor criticisms, but on the whole feedback was positive and complimentary. Where we saw faded drapes, they saw faded elegance. Where we saw Jiffy baking mix, they saw home-baked cornbread. And where we saw staff who could be sullen and had never heard of the 'six-foot rule' (nobody passes anybody, staff, guests or any other visitors, without a greeting) they saw local character.

The way *we* saw our brief, then, was a little different from Keith's.

- To make a manager out of Michael
- To prioritise, after a review of the business, the house, the grounds and the staff, those items that warranted immediate attention
- To make a three-month, one-year and five-year plan for other essential maintenance and improvements
- To increase occupancy and revenue
- To make fuller use of meeting and banqueting facilities
- To oversee food quality
- To keep the house and grounds clean and well maintained
- To motivate the staff to become more efficient and productive
- To prepare a report for the Marshalls setting out our proposals.

Complications nobody could have planned for lay in wait. Millie Ball Marshall's beloved mother was gravely ill. Instead of joining us on our first weekends to discuss progress, Millie and Keith would stay in New Orleans to be with Mildred. She died two weeks later.

Nor could anyone have predicted that Keith was about to experience health problems that would prevent him from as much involvement at Madewood as he had planned.

The cook with over thirty years service, recently widowed and, we feared, possibly seeking solace in the cooking whiskey, would walk out the day before the biggest dinner of the season, having done no preparation, leaving the others to shop, cook and serve. But didn't her portrait hang in the library? Firing a family retainer was not an option.

Then there was the po-lice.

4

The Cop's Tale

Two of the assistants, strapping young women both, were being pursued by a pair of local police officers with anything but the law on their minds. Good news, or so we thought. The patrol car parked outside late at night was a comforting sight for hoteliers in such a remote spot. Nice for the girls, too, to have a lift home after working late. If it struck us as odd that uniformed cops in marked patrol cars could take time out for a little spooning, well – this was Louisiana.

Our sense of security was a false one. Our friends Jim and Pat Chandler flew over from Dallas to spend the weekend. On their last night, instead of joining the other guests, we arranged supper for the four of us in the music room, taking care to remove the 'please do not sit on these chairs' notices from the fragile and valuable antique furniture. There were only a few other guests; the two members of staff on duty could easily (we assumed in our innocence) cope with the simple service of plated meals in two rooms. The walnut table glowed in the candlelight, crystal glasses sparkled, and the first-course crab and sweetcorn chowder still tasted delicious, even to us, at the umpteenth time of eating. Salad was served without mishap. Then there was a gap that seemed too long despite the animated conversation of four good friends.

Ron went to investigate and found one young woman busy serving the main course in the dining room, with Michael lending a hand. No sign of the other. The first had no idea where she might be, merely grumbled under her breath at being left to cope alone. Ron looked in the ground floor reception rooms, outside on the family porch, even peered around the darkened grounds with a flashlight. What made him look in the bedroom of the owner's suite we still really don't know, except there was nowhere else to look.

Spread-eagled fully clothed across the imperious Mrs. Marshall's canopied four-poster bed was the other assistant. On top, a young police officer in full uniform. He was very tall and very thin. She was not. Ron's first thought when he saw the long, skinny policeman clenched between those elephantine thighs was that he might not live to issue another speeding ticket. His second thought was that this was an odd way of assisting the po-lice with their enquiries. The third was to find a witness – quickly – while they were still oblivious to his presence. He got hold of Michael, now helping in the kitchen, and told him to throw open the French windows from outside while the visiting British hotelier entered through the door.

Like two actors in a French farce they timed their entrances to the second. 'What do you think you're doing?' Ron barked at the couple. Without seeming in any way disconcerted the policeman stood upright and without hurry adjusted his clothing. The young woman slowly and with apparent lack of concern slid off the bed and got to her feet. 'I didn't even ought to be here tonight,' she muttered, 'I only came in to help out'.

Next morning before he left for his teaching job in Baton Rouge, we made sure Michael agreed she would have to leave. He as manager was the one who must tell her – if indeed she had to be told – and sign papers to satisfy the Labor Board requirements.

The young woman, on cue, called us later that day and told us she'd be filing for unfair dismissal.

'Fine', she was told. 'That's your right. But there is nothing unfair about dismissal for that kind of behaviour in a room you had no right to be in and at a time when you should have been serving dinner.

'Not only that, but if he's a friend of yours, you might think of that young police officer's career. Nobody has reported him yet, but if we do, then we're looking at dereliction of duty, trespassing, behaviour unbecoming to a uniformed police officer – how much more do you want?'

Michael later sheepishly confessed his initial reluctance to deal firmly with the culprits. He had already had one or two tickets for driving his rustbucket of a car that had ignominiously failed the local equivalent of an MOT. He was afraid that if he made a case out of it, the local police would harass him off the road.

After her initial threat, we heard nothing more. The ex-employee asked a co-worker to pick up her wages. The co-worker left, too, the next day. The same pair had walked out without notice a few months before to take jobs elsewhere. They had asked for their jobs back and were re-hired. This time, it would not be an option. Now we were left with a smaller but we could only hope, more effective team than before.

Despite Janet's fears to the contrary – and Janet could be a real Job's comforter – it was not difficult to recruit new staff. She predicted the hasty departure of two assistants would only mean more work for the remaining staff. But there were five applications within forty-eight hours for the two jobs. One lady arrived dressed in her Sunday church-going best; white hat, lace gloves and a smile that set our hearts dancing. She had been on welfare for two years, had four children, and was eager to work. She would be happy to do '*anything*! I guess I'll clean or cook, even wait table if y'all can train me, 'cause I don't know how,' she beamed. She lived two miles away and had no transport, had walked to the interview and insisted she would gladly walk to work if she couldn't get a lift along the way. We suggested a month's trial.

True to her word, Lisa showed up for work on time and with that same smile, every day from then on. Most days she managed to hitch a lift, sometimes one of the other staff would pick her up en route, but when that didn't happen, she walked. And still smiled. Now and again she would blurt out. 'I love it here. I just love this job,' and turn her hand to whatever she was asked to do. Her welfare officer called, as was the custom, after the initial interview and again after a week or two to check on her progress. Janet was able to assure him Lisa was doing a great job and we all hoped she would stay. When we visited Madewood three years later, she was still there and still smiling, had bought a small home and an old car, and was still volunteering for extra work!

A second local lady was hired for a trial period, but she took on more than she bargained for. Annette was a tall, slim brunette, divorced mother of a three-year-old girl. She arrived for interview on the day before Madewood's starring role in the Great Romantic Movie That Nearly Never Was.

Madewood was no stranger to the movies. It had already featured in 'A Woman Called Moses', 'Sister Sister' and others. Even more significant to many guests – Brad Pitt had visited while filming in the area, and a life-size colour poster of the star hung inside the walk-in wardrobe of one of the suites in Charlet House.

Eve had been talking for some time to a TV producer in New York, a tough Manhattan female who explained they were making a series of programmes on the most romantic locations for lovers. We were delighted they wanted to feature Madewood and just one other plantation house in the area, and agreed to co-operate in any way we could. The New Yorker, daily becoming Eve's new best friend, kept her informed of the camera crew's progress southwards as they visited other romantic locations en route. They would get to us in a few days if all went according to schedule.

It didn't. Does it ever, in movie making? On Monday she called to say they were dropping one location and would come to us Tuesday evening, stay overnight, and film on Wednesday. 'They' were a director, cameraman and sound recordist. We would hardly notice they were there. It shouldn't take more than an hour or two. Could we, she asked, select a pair of overnight guests and persuade them to be the loving couple they needed?

Now, we had been down this road before and knew there was no way a three-man film crew would do anything in an hour or two, or without leaving havoc and disruption in their wake.

There was one other small problem. We had no guests booked in for the day of the filming. Don't worry, Eve's New York friend assured her. 'Something will turn up. It always does'.

Experience has taught us that in these situations *mise en place*, preparation, is everything. Nothing must be left to chance. 'Something' does not always turn up. With that in mind, if you can't do it, you fake it. The important thing is to maintain control. The moment you let an outsider take control of events, as film and television crews are apt to do, you are in danger of losing the plot.

Chad, the son of our office manager, was a handsome young man of twenty-four and we asked his mother if he might take half a day off work. He would have no lines to speak. We just needed his profile enjoying a romantic dinner in the dining room. 'I'll ask him,' said Janet. 'He's home right now anyway, so he might do it.' What she neglected to mention, and we found out an hour later when Chad untangled himself from his four-wheel drive, is that the lad had his left leg in a cast from thigh to ankle as the result of a car crash.

Might his brother Ed stand-in? That worked out, and though Ed was a little younger than the average Madewood guest, he would look great.

All we needed now was a partner.

Enter the unsuspecting Annette, looking for a job. We'd forgotten she was coming for interview and when she walked up to the porch door we all but hugged her. She was perfect. Not only that, but she'd known Ed at junior school and they hadn't seen each other for years, so had plenty to talk about while they waited around for the film crew to set up their shots.

It wasn't the job she expected, but she agreed to a day's filming at the same rate as a general assistant's. We volunteered to baby-sit her three-year-old. Next day she could begin her regular month's trial.

The crew arrived just in time for dinner with the timid elderly couple who made a last-minute booking and were our only residents. The movie-makers were a congenial threesome and we knew we could work with them. We were all up at dawn next day. We wanted to make sure everything in the house was gleaming and everything in the garden – well – rosy. Wasn't it lucky that Keith and Michael and Ron had gone on a mammoth plant-hunt two weekends before? Up till then the gardens had been virtually empty. Now, to augment the existing few roses, there were giant impatiens, pansies, marigolds, herbs and all kinds of bedding plants already lush and spreading. You can almost watch things grow in the rich alluvial soil and the humid climate of Southern Louisiana.

For the first few hours it was our turn. Eve, in smock and floppy sunhat, clippers in hand, cut long-stemmed red roses for the house (and the camera). A year later, a friend who saw the programme in California, wrote to us: 'you were bending down, not very flattering, and we wondered why you were doing the weeding...'

Then the two of us, perched precariously on the edge of the fragile French sofa, outlined the history of Madewood and confided to camera, not only what made it such a romantic location but also what we two romantic Brits were doing there!

The cook had walked out a few days before. We persuaded Clem to stand in as cook while they filmed her preparing 'the most romantic dinner for two' with occasional comments from us as to why crawfish etouffée was truly the food of love while Madewood's pecan pie just might be the greatest aphrodisiac of all time.

In the dining room Annette and Ed, who had been waiting around all day for their fifteen minutes of fame, sat down at one end of the polished table haloed in the shimmer of candlelight, crystal and silver. The etouffée, garnished for the first and only time with fresh flowers, was placed before them by a waitress in smart black dress with a white linen serving cloth over one arm. The couple leaned in close to each other and on cue raised their wine glasses in a toast. They turned their attention, as directed, to the food.

'And **action**!' called the director.

Smile bravely glued on her face, Annette gazed at the rapidly cooling etouffée. 'Jeeze', she breathed through clenched teeth. 'Don't you just hate this fancy mucked-about food? You couldn't *pay* me to eat this.'

Filming over for the day, the 'gang of three' accepted our invitation to spend the night and return to New York next morning. The sound recordist in fact lived near New Orleans, and over pre-dinner drinks confessed to being a passionate gardener. His apartment block had a tiny plot that he looked after, but having seen the grounds at Madewood, his life would be complete if he could only come and garden there at weekends. For nothing! We would have jumped at it, and couldn't understand why Michael never took him up on such a generous offer when there was so much garden work to do.

Annette worked at Madewood for the rest of the year, and she and Ed began dating.

Adhering to the principles of Sod's Law, the house was full almost every night for a couple of weeks after the filming. Most days there were luncheons or private parties, too. Clem reported a serious backlog of laundry. Not that she needed to. We had noticed the mounting pile of sheets, pillowcases, towels and table linen on the floor of the back kitchen, a few scant feet from where cook prepared the food for parties. Staff just stepped around it.

The two washing machines and dryers were running throughout the day, and Eve said she'd help out by continuing to load, wash and dry during the evening, leaving the laundered linen ready for pressing each morning. Gladys did this, perched on a stool by the window facing the sun-drenched lawn as she tearfully related the progress of the various sick and elderly members of her extended Cajun family. One after another had passed away during the past few years, leaving Gladys bereft and almost alone. At one point she seemed to lose heart even amidst the family atmosphere of Madewood, and the Marshalls had wondered if taking on T'Boy to help out with tours might upset Gladys even more. Instead, his presence seemed to encourage her, and together, with a combined age of 150-plus, they added an inspirational dimension to the Madewood family.

Even with Eve's and Gladys's daily help, the staff couldn't keep pace with the growing piles of linen. Beds were made and towels hung in bathrooms sometimes minutes before guests arrived. Eve was loading the machines at midnight, and back to start over again at 7am. The machines were extra slow because, we discovered, the water supply was reduced to a trickle. If the assistants had noticed it in the past few days, they hadn't shared it with us. A load that should have taken an hour was taking twice as long. The plumber couldn't get to us for days. Despairing of ever seeing the end of the laundry mountain and red-eyed from midnight vigils over the dryers, Eve asked where the nearest laundromat might be. Nobody seemed quite sure if there even *was* one in Napoleonville.

A chance remark from one of the help about some missing cleaning materials found on the shelves of 'the laundry room in Charlet' caused Eve to prick her ears up and march across the lawn to investigate. There, in a back room behind the honeymoon suite – and accessible only through its bedroom – she discovered a large and none too tidy storeroom. In one corner – joy of joys – an industrial-size washing machine and dryer, hidden under more piles of linen *and in perfect working order*. Gritting her teeth in an attempt to keep her cool, Eve asked why the machines were idle. There she was, for the past three nights up until the small hours to push through load after load in the machines in the back kitchen when there was a perfectly good room full of laundry equipment standing idle across the way. The assistants shrugged and looked at their feet. 'I don' know.' It was the answer we had grown to expect.

A good lesson, we conceded when we cooled down. Never assume. So, we had asked about local laundromats. And received an answer of sorts. Means nothing. Check, check and check again.

Taking a look one morning at the banana palms almost obscuring the main gates, we noticed the stench from the garbage dumpster before we could see the cause. Household rubbish and food waste bagged in heavy-duty polythene were overflowing the dumpster, preventing the lid being rammed down. Enquiries revealed that garbage was collected at most three times a week. If payments to the disposal company were in arrears, collections dwindled to twice weekly, and on one occasion during our stay, just once. With the temperature in the eighties this was not only bad news but also a danger to health. Like most companies, the garbage disposal people were more eager to do business than to lose it, and we came to an arrangement whereby in return for a regular cheque each month, Madewood's rubbish would be disposed of thrice weekly. Now we only had to convince staff that the dumpster itself would need frequent and regular hosing out with disinfectant.

With the help of Keith's friend Joe, the overgrown banana palms were whittled down and pruned so they no longer overhung the entrance. Alas, within days the southern Louisiana climate had worked its magic and the palms sprouted new growth that once again dominated the approach to the driveway.

One Sunday a Japanese car company hosted a lunch to introduce their latest model to local dealers. They had requested a Zydeco band to play on the back porch. This gave us the opportunity to find out the difference between Cajun music and Zydeco. They sound alike to our untrained ear, but the bandleader explained that Zydeco is mainly black music, upbeat and rocky; Cajun is the music of the French-speaking Acadians who were expelled long ago from Nova Scotia, and is often more melancholy and slow.

Then he said, 'Lemme ask *you*-all somethin'. Why do the Brits call the French 'frogs'? Eve explained as tactfully as she could that it was because the French *eat* frogs.

'Is that really all it is?' Heaven only knows what sinister overtones he had ascribed to it up till then.

After lunch we took a break to sit on the back porch chatting with Keith's mother Naomi and T'Boy, listening to the last of the music, feet tapping. We were sorry when the band packed up their accordions and fiddles and took their leave. In the still afternoon air, the smell of burning reached Eve first. It always does. Her wine tutor's nose is sharp as a bloodhound's.

'Burnin' garbage over to the cane fields,' T'Boy offered. Eve agreed. It was that kind of stench. We got up and took a look around just to make sure it was nothing around the house or the grounds. The smell dissipated, but in a few minutes was wafting back again. We looked at each other:

'Barbecue?'

'Yup,' agreed T'Boy. 'They cookin' meat.'

'Strangest meat I ever smelled,' Eve said (the verbal shorthand of Louisiana is catching.) 'Kind of fishy. Leathery. Burnt. Not clean. Not beef or lamb or anything I recognize.' The smell drifted to and fro for another half hour. Eve said 'If that's barbecue it should be well done by now.'

We had another look round, joined at last by a couple of staff who said they could smell it way over the other side of the building.

Eve jumped up. Clear off her rocker (one might say...). 'Smoke! There's smoke.' Right there on the porch, not a metre from where we were sitting. Blue-grey, not much of it, but definitely smoke. Swirling around the blue light of the electric mosquito 'zapper'. Now that everybody had stopped talking, we could hear an ominous 'zzzzz-zsss-ssh-tt'. Longer and louder than the usual short, sharp 'zzt' of mozzies on death row. Closer examination showed the source of the smoke, the smell and the 'zzzz-zsss-ssh-tt'. A whole bunch of lizards and mosquito hawks (flying insects as big as a queen bee) had indeed been 'barbecued' during our quiet hour on the porch.

Now we'll take zapped lizards any time over *snakes*. At Madewood they were mostly the small, harmless variety, but occasionally could be more dangerous species that demanded fast and final dispatch. Volunteers were few and far between. Carolyn, born at Madewood, had dispatched one or two that threatened Millie in the past, but Janet, the chic office manager, was the unofficial designated snake-killer. We may never forget the sight of her, serenely stepping on to the lawn, rusty shovel clutched in dainty hands, bringing the business end smartly down on the snake's head as the rest of us stood back and cringed.

It was Janet, too, who unearthed the source of a foul smell in the house. We noticed it slightly one morning and hoped it would pass. By day two, it was worse. One of the assistants was sent into Napoleonville to rummage around Ace Hardware and buy every scented candle and bag of pot pourri in the store. These were placed strategically around the ground floor public rooms. The smell seemed to be centred on the passage leading from the music room to the ballroom. We all racked our brains, and the best we could come up with was a dead rat in the basement. Rodents large and small found their way into the house from time to time from the sugar-cane fields. T'Boy had put poison down the week before, so this seemed the likeliest cause. We sent him down to check, but no, the poison was still there, as was the feral ginger tomcat that had taken up residence in the basement and was deemed official rat-catcher.

All that day and the next we attempted to sniff out – literally – the source of the problem. It was certainly the smell of decay, too strong for mice, and if it wasn't a rat, maybe we needed to excavate further underground. Or the attic? Nobody wanted to mention the word 'corpse' but the guests were beginning to notice. Pest controllers were summoned to investigate. Before they could get to Napoleonville, Janet came in from outside, wiping her hands on a cloth. 'Found it Miss Eve,' she grinned. 'It's the sewer.' Without saying a word or asking for help, she had gone outside to the far end of the garden, hefted the manhole cover off the drains, and taken a look inside. The burst in the pipe was clearly the source of our problem.

The plumber couldn't get there until the following day, so the scented candles burned day and night, augmented by aromatic oils and hastily ordered fresh flowers.

'How romantic,' sighed the guests.

5

The Caterer's Tale

At the first glimpse of Madewood, any hotelier would think first, 'What a glorious house!' quickly followed by, 'What a venue!' A fairytale backdrop, inside and out, for special events. The ballroom, scene of the Widow Pugh's nineteenth century soirées to introduce suitable gals to her five eligible sons, was perfect still for seated lunches or dinners and dancing. The dining room, music room, library and parlor could accommodate elegant gatherings for between four and twenty people.

Beneath the raised ground floor of Charlet House there was banqueting space with its own kitchen, equipped to serve seated meals for up to sixty and cater for buffet receptions, conferences or meetings for more.

In the earlier days of the Marshall family's stewardship, these spaces had been put to good – and charitable – use when the family hosted music and opera festivals, concerts and art exhibitions. Now, as Naomi's health obliged her to take a less active role, and Keith became further embroiled in business affairs in the city, these had dwindled. When the occasion demanded it 'Miss Naomi', redoubtable octogenarian that she is, could still pull out all the stops and display an energy and imperiousness that put younger people to shame. During our stay she organised an exhibition of paintings by Louisiana artists. Elegantly flamboyant in hand-painted silk, Naomi spent an entire day supervising the installation of the pictures and other works, and then personally manned the sales desk. We were, I think, the only ones to be surprised by how many paintings she sold that day.

We had a more personal demonstration of Naomi's skills soon after we arrived at Madewood, and an invaluable experience of being on the customer side of the fence. Keith had asked Ron to give his presentation

'Revelations from a Life in Grand Hotels' to an invited audience of forty-five prominent local people, hoteliers and travel professionals from New Orleans and Baton Rouge. Keith suggested a Sunday afternoon tea and sent out embossed invitations.

The event would provide an opportunity to promote the new edition of our book with several chapters on US hotels. We announced a book signing after the presentation and it was a great relief when the second, replacement batch of books arrived by Fed-Ex barely twenty-four hours before the signing. The original consignment from the printer had had eight pages of photographs missing.

We looked forward to meeting our new neighbours and hospitality industry colleagues in such a sociable setting. Fate, however, cast a shadow over that special day. Millie Ball Marshall's mother was gravely ill. Keith called on the Saturday morning to warn us that he and Millie might not be there for our presentation. Mildred Ball, he explained, was not expected to live through the night. A telephone call on Sunday morning brought the news that she had died peacefully.

We rolled up our sleeves, literally and metaphorically, to help Clem and the staff prepare afternoon tea leaving Michael, the new and still part-time manager, to set up the ballroom with chairs, projector, screen and lectern. All of those would have to be tested before the guests arrived. As for the tea, Ron suggested we keep things simple (though insisting on what they called 'hot tea' as well as the ubiquitous iced tea) with sandwiches and pastries.

At noon, Naomi arrived with a lady friend, and frail as Naomi was, they swept in and galvanised the kitchen into action.

She called for 'proper English afternoon tea' and in plenty of time for the arrival of an unexpected sixty-five guests, scones were baked, cucumber sandwiches prepared, and enough silver teapots and best china to serve an army brought out and buffed up. The presentation and the book signing were enormous fun, we made many new friends and the tradition of English afternoon tea looked set to be a Sunday favourite at Madewood.

It also convinced us that with the right management and a more pro-active approach to marketing, the property could become better known as a venue for functions and special parties. For the period we were there, several weddings were booked, and a number of annual events, business meetings and small private gatherings. But it was not being exploited to anything like its full potential.

The house and grounds provided an idyllic setting, especially for romantic events, and they were able to offer 'full service weddings'. Couples could have the ceremony in a local church, the registry office, or in the Madewood grounds. Some booked a half-day just to have the wedding photographs taken with the mansion as a backdrop, under the live oaks, or in the small rose garden behind the house. Up to our arrival, this service was practically given away for a token charge; we urged the Marshalls to increase it to a more realistic level.

'Our' most memorable wedding had been booked several months before, and through a characteristic slip or two, nobody had confirmed final details in writing, or taken a deposit. The wedding party was to take over all the rooms in the house for the bridal couple and overnight guests. They would provide their own disco until midnight.

The day before, we were still waiting for the bridegroom to confirm vital details including the timing of events, the final number of guests, and to hand over via his credit card the deposit agreed on long before. He, newly flown in from an overseas business trip, was crusty and in no mood to haggle. He would pay half the agreed deposit, with the full amount to be paid on the day. He also informed us the disco would go on until 2am, and denied having agreed to a midnight curfew.

Since they were also bringing their own alcohol, we were concerned not only about the noise, which echoes around this flat, empty landscape, and the possible nuisance to our neighbours, but about potential damage to the house and its contents. They agreed not to take any alcohol into the house, and we compromised on a finish time of one o'clock.

It was Michael's management weekend 'on' and it fell to him, several times during the evening as the tempo and the decibels rocketed, to party-poop by asking them to keep the noise level bearable. When he reminded them at 1am that time was up, they did start to run down the disco, and it was all over by 1.30. No damage was done. The litter in the grounds was as bad as we anticipated and though the groom had volunteered his guests to clear up next morning (to keep costs down), the job fell to the staff as it usually did. Fishing cigarette ends out of the ornamental sugar kettle where they floated alongside the flower petals, one of the assistants remarked: 'Can y'all explain *why* it takes all that liquor and all them cigarettes and all this *mess* just to get a ring on a gal's finger?'

The next wedding came to Madewood from Dansereau House, a town house hotel in Thibodaux without a garden of its own. Madewood only had to provide the space in which they would pitch a pink and white striped marquee. Their banqueting manager Kelly was a svelte, elegant blonde. Her motto, she told us, was *'Never let 'em see you sweat!'*

She would provide kitchen staff and the equipment they would need, plus waiters and bartenders. They would do the initial food prep in their own kitchens, set up in the marquee and grounds, and do the final food preparation in the basement kitchen of Charlet House.

Old hoteliers' habits die hard. Several days before the event Ron insisted on a thorough inspection of the Charlet House kitchen, used only a few times a year. It was a disaster area. Stoves and equipment encrusted with baked-on grease. Old dishwashers, freezers and other appliances – some in working order – were in need of a good clean. Behind a pinned-on 'curtain' of old bed sheets, underneath the long expanse of worktops, burst a cornucopia of disgust. Kitchen equipment rarely used was rusted by the humidity and thick with grime. The candles of Christmases past had melted in the heat of Louisiana summers, all over crumbling cardboard cartons into which miscellaneous items had been tossed. Your shoes stuck to the floor. Walls were 'decorated' with anonymous dirt. Rodents, cockroaches and God alone knew what other forms of local wildlife from the cane-fields had visited box after box of equipment before poison had been put down. Our own health inspectors would have closed down the entire operation.

The task that confronted us before the smart Danserau House wedding was daunting. We recommended calling a contractor for an all-over steam clean. That proved too much of a strain on the budget, and impossible to arrange in the time available. In any case, we reasoned in our innocence, there was no shortage of staff who might be glad to earn some overtime. No way in the world would Ron let a fellow hotelier use a kitchen under his – albeit temporary – direction in its present condition. He invited the staff on duty to sit down with us and asked for their help. Reminded them that while it was the cook's job to clean the stoves after each use, perhaps as a matter of pride in Madewood as well as to help out a co-worker, the others might lend a hand. They looked at us as though we were *hallucinating*. What was *wrong* with the kitchen? *They* weren't using it right now. Why should it be specially cleaned because somebody else was going to?

There was a lengthy silence before the cook walked out not to be seen again for a week. The following evening there was to be a dinner for sixty, and she had not begun to prepare. We considered our options and once again reminded ourselves she had been a family retainer for three decades. Only then did we learn that Janet often took time out from her office duties to clean the stoves in the main kitchen, tidy the food storage cupboards and shop at a moment's notice for forgotten items because the cook seldom remembered to order anything in advance or made a note of what was likely to run out.

Right now there was a kitchen to be deep cleaned. A wedding and an outside caterer imminent. The staff regarded their shoes.

Ron set an example by volunteering to make a start on walls and floor. He drew the line at cleaning that stove. Eve said she would turn out the contents of the dirt-encrusted boxes. Janet smothered an air of martyrdom as she offered to do the entire job herself in a characteristic effort to restore peace and harmony. It would be easier, she reasoned, than 'causing bad feeling'. The youngsters said nothing. Carolyn, the older remaining member of the 'team', reluctantly agreed to help out. 'I always,' she complained, not without justification, 'end up doing jobs nobody else want.' Carolyn was the willing horse who would take on tasks the others refused, provided she was asked nicely, and preferably by the owners. She transferred some of this allegiance to us, content to help out so long as she could work at her own pace and without interfering too much with her established routines. Porch floor mopping, for instance, was a Wednesday job, and muddy footprints were not excuse enough for a Friday repeat.

Clearly the consensus was that we were crazy. For one thing they failed to recognise that a dirty kitchen was a problem: if they used it, then somebody else could, too. For another, if these crazy Brits were willing to roll up their sleeves and work just to set an example, then they could set up their stall in easy street. This was exacerbated by the temporary absence of Clem, the dependable housekeeper, for chemotherapy treatment of the illness she was fighting so bravely and successfully.

Perverse as it may sound, there was some satisfaction in spending the next two days on hands and knees and seeing the spacious, useful kitchen come back to life. Carolyn had taken on the disagreeable job of cleaning the stove, slowly and with frequent stops to rest. On day two she reported a recurring 'sore arm' and had to take up light duties. Ron got stuck into his self-appointed task of scrubbing the dirt and grease off the walls and scraping the carpet of ground-in dirt from the floor. Worktops untouched for who knew how long, had to be tackled before he could even see what lay beneath and behind them. He was proved right in one thing: that when they saw we were prepared to roll up our sleeves and get stuck in, at least one or two members of staff would feel guilty enough to help out!

Eve mucked out the contents of long rows of shelving behind the old sheets. It was an entire day and then some, in elbow-length industrial rubber gloves, before she had help. She hauled out boxes overflowing with candles and their wax-encrusted holders, unwrapped legions of battered paper cups and plates, plastic utensils, sieves, pots and pans, serving platters and trays, decorations, dishes and lanterns. She stacked bits and pieces of barbecue equipment that should have been discarded years before. The garbage dumpster was already overflowing and not due for its thrice-weekly emptying. She filled the back of Joe's pick-up truck with debris, and Joe spent an afternoon ringing round to find a garbage dump where he could deliver it. Janet and Eve did tell him there was one open about seven miles away, but Joe wasn't one to miss out on a bit of additional research.

The former director of Claridge's grit his teeth and looked inside the fridges and freezers, but shut the doors again on discovering a load of muffin pans encrusted with something mummified – which he was assured was 'only rat poison'

There was in that kitchen, or so it appeared, enough equipment to cater a thousand meals. As Eve hauled out still more, Ron washed and stacked it, scrubbed out cupboards and washed the worktops before replacing anything re-useable in some sort of order.

For the next day or two we had the help of a local handyman to move furniture and equipment and clean the fridges and freezers, all of which had been switched off and stuffed full of bits and pieces. We discovered a perfectly good dishwasher that had been carted off to languish in Charlet House after the staff decided they preferred to wash up by hand. Eventually the Madewood staff, like those children 'unwillingly to school', helped finish off the great kitchen clean up.

Weeks later we learned from a resigned Keith that we had chucked out a valuable (albeit dirt-encrusted, rusting, broken-glassed) Victorian light fixture he had been hoarding until he found a place for it. We may well have discarded other treasures, but thankfully nobody remembered what they were, and Keith was too good-natured to chide us. Perhaps they're still finding – or rather, not finding – treasures they could have sworn were stored under the worktops in Charlet House kitchen.

Our reward came when the glamorous Kelly and her uniformed staff appeared soon after dawn on Saturday morning to prepare for the wedding and we didn't have to feel shame on Madewood's behalf.

Kelly's team had concocted an enviable menu for the wedding guests, sophisticated yet still pure southern Louisiana, using the cornucopia of local fresh foods. The set-up was lavish; the luncheon centrepiece was a seafood buffet with a *pirogue* (a traditional Cajun fishing boat) filled with freshly shucked oysters on the half shell, and jumbo boiled shrimp with Louisiana seasonings. Later, what the menu somewhat modestly referred to as 'hors d'oeuvres by candlelight' included wild game jambalaya, chicken roulade with champagne cream sauce, bayou seafood, penne Affredeaux (we think it meant Alfredo), smoked duck and *andouille* gumbo, and eggplant and crawfish casserole.

During the reception Eve was approached by the brother-in-law of the bride, a young man with an accent as British as ours. He was one of the senior stylists at John Frieda, Eve's hairdresser in London, married to a Southern Louisiana girl and visiting his in-laws for this special family occasion. Once again we thanked the Providence that brought Ron's stubborn streak and sense of order to the fore and made us spring-clean that damn kitchen before they arrived. We'd have hated him to see us sweat!

A local family choir of gospel singers could be engaged to provide entertainment for special parties. A talented and lusty group to be sure, but you never knew how many would turn up. It depended on the day of the week and the inclination of the extended family members – of whom there were forty on a good day.

One Friday evening they were hired to perform for an overseas company's dinner in the ballroom. Only three singers turned up, large young women wearing alarmingly short, tight skirts and apprehensive expressions. They had impressive lungs; good voices, great harmonies and they did their best. The predominantly Belgian audience was appreciative, if a trifle bewildered, and they applauded as politely as they had listened.

Two days later, on Sunday, the choir swelled to twenty-eight. Straight from church they came, in royal blue satin choir robes and clearly in the mood for singing. The audience on this occasion fortunately outnumbered them, a luncheon party of forty-two, also from Europe.

The gospel singers made, if you will, an exceeding joyful noise, and we were carried away right along with the audience, feet tapping, hands clapping, joining in whenever we thought we could get away with it. The house resounded with gospel songs, hymns and spirituals.

Mid-way through the performance we were called to check in some new arrivals. When we got back to the family porch, one of the female choristers was laid out on a bench, being fanned by a couple of older women. The sick girl was unconscious for several minutes. We headed for the phone to call 911 for the paramedics but just then she came round, gently moaning, to a chorus of: 'You OK, honey. We got you. You doin' good. Praise the Lord.'

Hallelujah indeed. We stood back and wondered at the power of the gospel, assuming the young woman had been overcome with the emotion of the performance. Then we learned from one of the women tending her that she was four months pregnant and had eaten nothing since the night before. It was now 2.30pm, the temperature in the eighties, and the young woman had been singing her heart out first in church and now here, for nigh on three hours. A glass of orange juice and a bowl of gumbo with some cornbread, and she left for home with a song in her heart.

Secretary's Day is a big deal in America, as is Mother's, Father's and Grandfather's, and for all we know Second Cousins Once Removed Day. In beautiful downtown Thibodaux, Labadieville, Napoleonville, Donaldsonville and the other small towns within striking distance of Madewood, this day was a cause for celebration. Forty scions of business and industry – mainly members of the Rotary and the Lions Clubs and the Chamber of Commerce – had been induced to treat their secretaries. Now they arrived, the ladies with corsage pinned carefully on frock or on wrist, for the special luncheon (gumbo, salad, crawfish etouffée, bread pudding. What did we expect?) in the white-carpeted ballroom.

We had learned by now that Americans are early birds, especially at mealtimes. Arriving at 11.30 for a lunch that starts at mid-day is not unusual. What *is* unusual hereabouts is for luncheon to begin any later than mid-day. People in this hot and humid region often begin their office day at 8am. National Secretaries Day fell on a beautiful March morning, and the guests were enjoying the grounds in the spring sunshine, taking a conducted tour of the house if they hadn't visited before. The secretaries (all the bosses were men) wore crisp summer dresses, linen or cotton suits, neat short skirts with pretty blouses, and more than a few wore hats. They ranged from early twenties to late sixties. The bosses were no-nonsense Southern gentlemen, bluff and benevolent in lightweight business suits or sports jackets. This wouldn't be a long drawn-out affair: these were the movers and shakers of Assumption and Ascension and St. James Parishes. They had real estate agencies, law practices, stores and assorted businesses to attend to. They would not want to be seen to be playing *too* hard.

No drinks had been ordered either before or with the meal. As was customary, iced tea would be served along with ice water or home-made (packet) lemonade. This was a practice so alien to us that we stationed ourselves outside the ballroom ready to (a) greet the guests as they arrived and (b) ask if they would like to purchase a cool 'beverage' to sip as they enjoyed the garden or chatted before lunch. More than a few took up the offer, and we had two members of staff ready with silver trays to serve the drinks while we collected cash or opened a tab.

While the meal was served we went round the tables. 'Sir, would you care to purchase a carafe or a glass of wine? We also have beer and soft drinks, if you prefer.' Asked with a direct gaze and a smile at both host and guest, this pretty basic technique encouraged more than half of those present to buy drinks. What Southern gentleman after all wants to look cheap in front of his secretary? Those who disapproved of alcohol (or of paying for it) gazed solemnly back at us and said with Southern charm and often without referring to their secretary: 'Thank you, I don't believe we care for any beverages at this time. Just more iced tea, ma'am, if you please.'

Still, our revenue for drinks that day was well over $100. And that was $100 over budget.

It should have been obvious that every party that came to Madewood should be encouraged to purchase additional beverages, and we did our best to teach the staff to use a little sales psychology. Problem was, they had been used to doing certain things in certain ways, and budging them from their comfort zones was an uphill task. What would motivate them to change? Why should they care about an additional one or two hundred dollars of revenue? They were content with the wages they earned for the work they did. They had little interest in working harder – or smarter.

This would be one of the challenges confronting the new manager. We could arm him with the theory, the techniques, and the possibilities. Suggest ways he might help the staff understand the need to generate additional revenue. He, however, would be the one left behind to put them into practice.

We followed our dictum of sell, sell and upsell with every party booked in for coffee mornings, luncheons, afternoon teas, receptions or dinners, and attempted to draw the staff along with us. At the time of booking we encouraged hosts or organizers to order drinks suited to the menu. If the party had been booked before we arrived, we stationed ourselves in a strategic position as a welcoming committee of two. A quiet word with the host ensured we had his or her blessing to approach guests and offer drinks, then we circulated with silver trays of frosted glasses of sparkling white wine, red wine, and one or two soft drinks in glasses bulging with ice, American-style. Always we'd preface the offer with: 'Would you care to purchase a glass of wine or a soft drink ?' to make quite certain the guest knew it was not included with the meal. And added: 'That will be \$3 please – may I come back for that in just a moment?' (We were getting used to Louisiana polite-speak) This gave them time to rummage for change. We carried small notebooks and back at the drinks table scribbled a note of who owed what. We could only hope once more that the staff would learn by example.

On a Sunday morning we welcomed a party of senior sales personnel with partners on an incentive trip with a leading British insurance company. They were spending a long weekend in New Orleans, and a day or two visiting the bayou country. Exciting that they had booked lunch at Madewood, because this was one of the companies in which Ron's pension is invested! We made a special effort to sell drinks and the bar bills were impressive. We set out on tables in two rooms, attractive displays of our book, certain that these fellow-countrymen would know Claridge's and the other hotels. And we made quite sure they were aware that their company was responsible for our pension. Surely they would be in the right frame of mind to be major purchasers. They were certainly interested. Most of them leafed through the book, asked lots of questions about it and about Claridge's and about Madewood. And bought not one single copy.

Quite unlike another special party that arrived soon after 7am on a rare morning when we slept beyond sunrise. We were awakened by the sound of car tyres scrunching along the gravel drive in front of our cottage. We knew a party of schoolteachers was expected on their annual creative writing course, but not until 10am. A quick call to Janet revealed that they 'always arrived early' and the Charlet House function room was all ready for them.

Eve walked over to welcome the leaders of the seminar who had come to set up. Delightful women who in Southern fashion soon became her new best friends. There would be thirty-five ladies in all, high school teachers of English literature from around southern Louisiana. They met at Madewood every year to discuss creative writing – how to do it, how to teach it, how to enthuse their students about it. There would be informal discussions, comparing experiences, reading from each other's work, and generally 'sharing'. Then they would wander off individually for an hour or two to soak up the atmosphere of the house and the grounds to 'let this wonderful place speak to us, spend some quality time alone with our thoughts'. Inspired by their surroundings, each would then prepare a piece of creative writing, and they'd return to Charlet House to read their jottings aloud over afternoon tea.

When the group leader learned that Eve had written a book, she appeared excited – thrilled even – to have a published author in their midst! Would Miss Eve, they wondered, spare a little time to talk to the group about her work and did she by chance have any books to sell?

As luck would have it ... Eve was just as thrilled to be asked. She expected a little time to prepare but no, the ladies wanted her to speak right now, or at least a.s.a.p. And that is how the visiting female Jones found herself at 8.30 one sunny March morning, talking without notes for forty minutes to thirty-five smiling, encouraging ladies. There were questions galore. Chicken soup for the soul indeed for any writer! During coffee break, at a trestle table Ron had laid up with white tablecloths and a display of our books, the ladies purchased a heart-warming forty-five copies.

We weren't quite that forward in promoting our books on more formal occasions. Thibodaux and the surrounding bayou country was the centre of a massive oil and gas safety symposium. A party of sixty oil company and fire-fighting executives booked their last-night dinner at Madewood. We stood outside in the early evening sunlight to welcome a cheerful group as they started arriving in mini-buses and cars at six o'clock for dinner at 7.30. We were becoming accustomed to Louisiana-time early arrivals.

It was a balmy evening, the end of a successful and important week for them. Guests milled about in the grounds or congregated by the back porch to *kibitz* and exchange addresses. Here again, no aperitifs or dinner wines had been ordered and the price quoted was all-inclusive for the meal, iced tea and coffee. The visitors expressed an interest in the history of the house and we volunteered to have them taken around in groups to look at the rooms and the grounds. First, though, we asked the organiser's permission to offer beverages for sale. 'Oh sure', said the lady in charge. 'But they don't have to purchase them. The company will pick up the tab. Anything they want.'

Hard to believe a sales opportunity like this had been overlooked. These were hard-working, tough people and we suspected they could be hard drinking too. That evening we sold more booze than at any time in the history of Madewood. Whiskey and vodka, cocktails and highballs, wine or beer with dinner – to every table. The drinks bill came to several hundred dollars and Janet had a bad evening, worried sick about presenting a bill so much higher than quoted. The organiser didn't turn a hair.

'Are you sure this includes the drinks?' she said. 'This whole bill, honey, is less than our bar bills at most venues!'

Now will you believe us, we asked Keith and Millie when we next got together, when we tell you Madewood is the biggest bargain in the US – and it has to stop!

We suggested the opportunity to sell drinks shouldn't be limited to large parties. Several days a week during the tourist season a New Orleans company, Tours by Isabelle, sent a mini-bus or two that disgorged parties of visitors for a tour and light lunch (gumbo, salad, cornbread, bread pudding...). This was always a jolly party, anything from eight to twenty people seated around the table. We were soon selling a few beers, cans of Coke or fruit sodas. Even wine. A silver champagne cooler crammed with iced drinks was placed on the sideboard. Ice buckets held frosted carafes of white wine. The sight of this on a hot day was enough to remind visitors there was more to life than iced tea. And the well-tried principle of *pour encourager les autres* also applied. As guests saw others enjoying an iced Coke or a chilled Chardonnay, they often followed suit.

The staff, though, would get discouraged if more than two or three people in a row said no to the invitation to purchase drinks, and tended to lose interest. We urged them to persevere: just ten dollars-worth of additional revenue at one luncheon three times a week, we argued, became nearly four hundred dollars over a three-month period. And *that* was enough to pay wages for eighty hours when business was slack and work scarce.

6

The Cat's Tale

Madewood's finest feline played our heartstrings as though they were made from purest catgut. We loved her. She tolerated us. Sheba was a she-line devil in the guise of an English blue. This communication was addressed to her fellow-felines at our friend Mary Bailey's home in London.

Bella, Pedro and Pola
Mary Bailey's House
London SW18
UK

Hi Guys,
    How y'all doin' there in cold, stormy London? You don't know me, but I've heard a lot about you-all. Your 'owner' (so-called, but we know better, right?) Mary is mentioned so-o-o often here as an authority on looking after cats, their wishes and desires and their long-term health and happiness. And oh boy – do my new (and strictly temporary) owners need some guidance.
    But I forget my manners. Purrmit me to introduce myself. I'm Sheba. Once a Queen, but now alas no more. They got me fixed. No doubt they got you, too, but it doesn't stop us being friends, non?
    Not to be immodest, I am by any standards an exceptionally good-looking cat, kind of a velvety dove-grey with white socks and an ultra-soft white fur belly. Age ... well, who knows? I'm not old but I'm no kitten, you might say. I am highly vocal – more than any Siamese I've ever met – and I think that's what got the Joneses hooked so fast. I talked to them, you see, right from the beginning. Every morning when they came to the Big House from their cottage in the grounds at 7am (can you believe it,

the female Jones coming to work at that hour? I heard him say 'my wife doesn't do mornings', but boy – she does here!) Anyway, every morning I'd greet them halfway across the lawn, yelling for nourishment. Me, that is, not the Joneses. You can imagine, it wasn't too tough to convince 'em I was starving, hadn't been fed for eons, sadly neglected etc. etc. – same old same old, huh? They fell for it, of course. How were they to know Janet in the office was feeding me at 6.45 and Clem, the housekeeper, again at 9.30? Not to mention Michael, the weekend manager, who would fill my dish in the evenings when he got here. Is there no limit to the gullibility of the giant bipeds?

They rumbled me in the end, of course, but it took a while. And they still can't resist a bit of the old chat, which I deal out in spades now I know what it does for them.

I have a different "yowl" and "mi-a-ow" and "naow" and "oooh" and "gallll", what you might call a symphony of expressions for every occasion. I do, I must confess, miss a little intelligent conversation now and again – you know the kind, where you exchange banter then discuss affairs of state, the currency situation, monarchy versus republicanism, your personal stance on globalisation and all that. Pity all they can manage in the way of response is "Hooz a bootiful iggle pussikins then?" and garbage like that. Mind you, I do answer when I'm spoken to, even though their conversation is limited. Being of royal lineage automatically confers the nicest manners. Noblesse oblige and all that.

Anyway, where was I? Oh yes. After several weeks the Joneses were still unsure about my feeding arrangements. You see, my avoirdupois was understandably increasing by the week. In fact, if I weren't in mint condition, to put it as politely as I know how, they'd have thought I was pregnant. Pregnant! As if! When the only male in the vicinity is that feral ginger tom who lives under the house and exists purely (and not so purely at that) to keep the rodents at bay. What kind of a diet is that?

No, the weight problem is much simpler. If I play my cards right I get a handful of Kitty Kaboodles three times a day and wolf it down in unqueenly fashion, then each time I feel like a snack, set up the yowling and mewling routine. Have you ever had to exist on a diet of Kitty Kaboodles? Mary no doubt feeds you Real Food. Fresh food. Fishy things and chicken-y dishes and delicacies of offal and lightly steamed titbits. Oh, it moistens my whiskers just to think of it. Nothing of the kind, alas, for this Royal Highness. I dined on real food only for the one week

I was on antibiotics. What – I didn't share the antibiotics story?
It began when the female Jones noticed (bless!) that I was dribbling and sucking more than cats usually do. In fact every time I permitted her a few moments' cosying up, her lap was soaked (tee-hee!). Also, when I opened my mouth to yawn (they not being the most stimulating company) she thought my bottom front teeth might be missing and my gums looked somewhat inflamed. Well they would, wouldn't they? How would her gums be on a diet of dried Kitty Kaboodles? She won a few brownie points, though, because that weekend she asked a good friend of a good friend who is a veterinarian to come all the way down from New Orleans, nearly seventy miles away, to take a look.

And was that a drama fit for a queen!

Is there nothing the giant ones won't resort to? Talk about indignity. And in the middle of a sunny Saturday afternoon with a porch full of visitors. First the male Jones – who is the one I have to confess I somewhat adore – picked me up and held me in his arms. I don't often allow that, but you have to keep 'em sweet and he is cute. Turns out he never cared for cats, or so he said when he first arrived and tried to sidestep me. We soon got him over that, as you can imagine, and now I stuck my head beneath his armpit, which is my favourite place to be. Then Dr. Mike, the vet, without so much as a by-your-leave crept up behind me with this cage, and grabbed me by the scruff of the neck. Imagine! I can tell you I screamed blue murder. And I mean screamed. Spat. Hissed. Clawed.

From here on it gets worse. He hefted me and the cage and this great leather medical bag into the Red Room bathroom and attempted to commit surgery on me. I wasn't having it, of course. He wasn't going to get within a foot of Yours Truly without me getting a damn good bite and scratch in first. No doubt he bears the scars to this day. He had the last laugh, though. He had this needle. Two feet long I swear (and I did, trust me, I did). He used it to jab me in the rump and I was out cold for the next six hours. What an experience. While I was 'under', as they call it, he discovered I had gingivitis (so the female Jones was right, I must grudgingly admit) and while he was at it he gave my teeth a good clean.

When the FJ came in to check on me I was swinging my head from side to side in the cage, wild-eyed, shivering, almost out of control. She was beside herself but Dr. Mike said not to worry, I was 'only' hallucinating. Quite natural after the medication he'd given me. He said it had a street value of mega-bucks and junkies were always sneaking into his surgery to ask for it – they'd kill for the stuff apparently, it's that good. Well they're welcome to it is all I can say. Dr. Mike told the Joneses to leave me on the screen porch in the cage until (their) bedtime, and then let me rest quietly overnight to get used to real life again. I tell you fellow-feline-friends, when they did let me out I was staggering drunk for twenty-four hours. Next morning I could hardly walk, my poor legs kept giving way. Talk about hung over! Man, that was some bad trip. And you know what hurt the most? They laughed! Every last one of 'em except the female Jones who was nearly as upset as I was.

I wasn't gonna let them have it all their own way, though. Coming out of the bends I pooped in the cage, which they call a 'cat basket' (they do love their euphemisms, the giant ones). There were seven family and friends on the screen porch at the time. They didn't stay long I can tell you. Female Jones called Dr. Mike and he, bless his heart, turned the cage on end so I couldn't escape and cleaned up. Said he was used to it, but I noticed he lit a cigarette while he did it and called for another vodka martini right after, even though it was only 11am.

I was on antibiotics for a week, but the upside is that they had to crush them in half a can of tuna and that, let me tell you, after a diet of Kitty Kaboodles, was a rare treat – like caviar for the general.

Let me tell you about Dr. Mike while I'm about it. He's thirty-eight, tall, slim, blonde, gorgeous (so they tell me) and just the nicest person. He's coming back this afternoon so I'm about to make myself scarce just in case.

She-who-must-be-obeyed (that's-all-she-knows) wants another consultation with Dr. Mike because she's a bit concerned about the fact that I don't play. She doesn't know, when I jump out on them with claws extended, or when I sink my sharp teeth into them while I'm allowing a bit of a cuddle, whether I'm playing with them or attacking. They really are too stoopid to live, but you have to laugh.

As if all that weren't enough, fur-ther insults were to follow: the next Sunday afternoon they had the nerve to bring another cat here. Somebody thought I should have a friend. Did they ask me if I needed a friend? 'Bobby' (good name for a male who'd been fixed) was a rescued cat, jet black, about two years old. He was a bit low-slung and long in the body, green-eyed and absolutely insane with fright. Stupid humans let him out of his cage on the screen porch with half a dozen people around.

He took one look and froze. I took one look, opened my eyes as wide and threatening as I know how, and hissed. Threatened him with another 'fixing'. I'll teach 'em to mess with a feline who can trace her family line back to ancient Egypt. You had to feel sorry for him. He scat behind the huge cypress closet on the porch and hasn't been seen since.

They left food and water for him, and the second night there was pee oozing from under the press but that was the last. Clearly he's gone off (no, I don't mean he died there, we'd have smelled him, I mean run off). Female Jones is sure she spotted him the other morning at a sugar-cane worker's cottage half a mile away. Let's hope so. Not that I care, good riddance and all that, but they were worried sick.

Talking of pooping, which I was a while ago, remember? The other day I contrived to get myself locked into the Big House overnight. Normally they don't like me sleeping there and I make it my business not to let them know where I do sleep, but this time they thought they had outsmarted me. It was the day after they were all convinced they smelled a dead rat under the floorboards of the ballroom and maybe they had the ludicrous idea I might do something about it. Anyway, there was I, shut in tight as a Scotty-dog's sporran, with nowhere to go, if you get my drift, and, well, what was a gal to do? I made it as far as the dining room, crawled in behind the CD player close to the skirting board (and a floor-mounted air vent, mind. I am not totally without delicacy) and let fly. What a pile it was, too. It never fails to impress that one small-ish female cat can let loose such a heap of ... well anyway. When they came in next morning they went wild! The Joneses panicked because in barely an hour the first guests would be down for breakfast and the smell was truly appalling. They got even more cross because the three ladies on duty said yes; they had smelled 'somethin' real bad' too. It just hadn't occurred to them to look for what it might be. Of course I blamed it on the ginger tom. Told them he'd snuck in during the night and don't look at me like that. Laugh? I nearly repeated the misdemeanor.

If I have a fault – and I'm admitting nothing, you understand – I guess it's that I should be more active in the hunting department. There are twenty acres of grounds after all, but since the Joneses came here who needs it? Three square meals a day and half a can of tuna now and again says the extensive rodent and bird population is quite safe. Just now and again to keep my skills honed I'll dismember a mockingbird. They do ask for it, hopping and jabbering around me in circles and teasing and driving me insane. Just because they have fledglings in the tree under which I happen to be sitting sphinx-like.

Occasionally I'll have a frog. They come in all shapes and sizes here, from miniature translucent green ones barely an inch long to the bigger brown ones, which are more of a challenge the way they hop and dive out of reach. The little ones hide behind shutters and pipework or splat themselves against the windowpanes, and they're really hard to get at. Mostly it's so hot and humid I just give up and go lie down. We have a few snakes, too, but we have this arrangement that I don't bother them and they don't bother me. I can look quite menacing when it suits me, but what can I tell you – life's too short.

When I adopt my Queen of Sheba position, resting regally on the royal haunches, it means the Joneses or any passing guests attracted to my sable-like soft fur (and though I do say it myself, beautiful amber eyes) may stroke me a little. Not too much, mind. I let them know when to stop. I've only been a part-time indoor cat, you see, since Whitney died three months ago. I didn't mention Whitney? The black-and-white house-cat? Ah...he died in mysterious circumstances. Appeared to have 'fallen' off the roof and broken his spine. But hey – don't look at me.

I still have my wild outdoor-cat moments. Take last night. See, they don't like me pee-ing in the herb garden they planted, which strikes me as truly asinine since they put catmint in it. How typical of humans is that? Anyway, trying for once not to upset them, I peed in a giant plant-pot on the porch. And you've guessed it, they didn't like that either. So then I snuck into the kitchen, which is strictly verboten, *and managed to get halfway up the stairs to the bedrooms before they caught me by the scruff of the neck and put me out. Un-dig-ni-fied. It behooves me to understand why they no longer like me indoors overnight but you can't blame a gal for trying.*

I heard somebody say, 'If you can't beat 'em, join 'em', so a couple of weeks ago I took pity on the visiting Brits and moved into their really rather cute little cottage with them. I don't stay every night. Oh no. I don't want them getting ideas about owning *me. But every other night or so I'll go sleep on their settee or under their bed. They don't let me on the bed – yet – but gimme time. I usually try about three o'clock in the morning, very, very quietly, but she-who-must-be-obeyed always wakes up and shoos me off. I know for a fact he would let me.*

I'd like to think we'd get to meet one day, friends, but you know how it is. 'Dry bread to a crust' is how the male Jones puts it. It is good to communicate, though. Must rush – well, more of a haughty uptail saunter really – to check on the wildlife situation. They said to say to Mary 'au revoir and see you soon'. They're both worried sick about who'll look after me when they're gone. Too dim to realise there'll always be another set of 'Joneses' for the Queen of Sheba... They're going to miss me so much when they leave I almost feel sorry for them.

With most royal regards,

Sheba, the Queen of the Queen of the Bayou

7

The Car's Tale

For our first few weeks at Madewood we were without wheels. We planned to rent a vehicle, but as things turned out, hardly had time to think about venturing 'off property' as Americans say. There was so much we needed to focus on – the revenue, the occupancy, maintenance of the house and the grounds, staff training, marketing – just for starters. We were 'on' from seven in the morning until after dinner, lucky if we managed an hour or two to put our feet up in the afternoon. But it was our choice and a willing one. It felt good to be back in harness, even if Ron sometimes craved a *real* harness to help him cope with the daily lugging of suitcases up and down stairs.

Driving around to explore the attractions of southern Louisiana was a bonus we had looked forward to, but there was nothing that couldn't be delayed. There were other historic properties in the area that we should visit and compare: Nottoway, designed by the same architect as Madewood, now a hotel and conference venue; Oak Alley, a living museum with beautiful grounds and tours by costumed guides; Destrehan and The Cottage; Laura, with its unique archives (and putative 'home' of Br'er Rabbit); and Parlange, inhabited by the eighth generation of the same family and still a working plantation. All were on our list of must-sees. Eve longed to take 'the Cajun Man's Swamp Tour' which sounded too good to miss, especially after we got the hand-written directions and map.

'*When you leave the small town of Labadieville, go one mile after the St. Philomena Catholic Church (which is on your right). When you get to Hwy 398 which is after a Sports Bar/Conoco Service Station – turn right go about 20 miles. When you are near highway 90, 398 connects with 662. Stay to your left and make a left onto Hwy 90 EAST. When you get to Gibson, go right. On Hwy 90 EAST DO NOT TAKE HWY 20 TO*

SCHRIVER! Cajun Man Swamp Tour will be 10 miles from Gibson on the right side of Hwy 90. Look for his billboard on Antil Road. Plan to arrive 15 minutes before Boat Departs!'

After the tour we could stay overnight at *Audrey's Little Cajun Mansion*, a.k.a. Chez Maudry. Audrey and Maudry were identical septuagenarian twins, and we had phoned once or twice to book for guests. Whichever twin answered the phone, the other would be either on the extension or shouting in the background. It seemed the sisters were always in the midst of a major row. Whatever you said to one, the other would shout in disagreement, interrupt or contradict in the most fearsome manner. Then they'd break off to continue their argument. You'd be left dangling on the other end of the phone, too enthralled to hang up. Eventually one twin would apologise for the other and deal with your booking. Madewood guests who stayed with them brought back similar tales and loved every minute and, they said, had some great fresh-caught seafood Cajun style.

A pleasure postponed.

Millie and Keith were consumed by guilt that they'd invited us to consult and we'd stayed to toil. We couldn't convince them it was a labour of love, a novelty to get back to the basics of hospitality and a privilege to play a small part in bringing this historic property back to the starring role it deserved. And get paid for it!

Once a week, Janet or one of the staff would drive Eve into Napoleonville, two miles along the bayou, for her regular visit to Miss Dee the hairdresser. The salon was called *Visable Changes* (sic) and Dee the original Steel Magnolia with china blue eyes, candyfloss hair, and fuelled on real southern charm. The beauty salon ('twas ever thus) was the hub of local intelligence. Eve was introduced to *le tout Napoleonville*, and Dee kept her up to date on happenings great and small. At weekends Miss Dee exchanged blue jeans and frilly blouse for Scarlett O'Hara crinoline, applied the blusher and practised the pout, to step into her other persona as a docent or costumed guide at Oak Alley plantation house. There, at the end of the tour (this one we *did* manage before the end of our sojourn) she would sell the finest mint juleps in the south. The secret, she told us, is to use proper sugar syrup, not just add sugar as most folks do. If only...if only we could persuade the staff at Madewood to take such an interest and to soft-sell even half so effectively.

Ron's excursions were limited to those when Joe, the Marshalls friend, drove him to 'Gator Stop, the filling station-cum-café-cum-mini-market. There they'd pick up the addictively delicious shrimp Po'Boys, small soft loaves stuffed and overflowing with deep-fried shrimp, salad and mayo. Fries on the side. Health food it was not, but after decades of 'fine dining' and weeks of Madewood menus, it was a lunchtime treat, devoured picnic style on the screened porch.

Now and again for a change of scene we'd accompany Janet on one of her mammoth grocery shops.

Whether from bitter experience or just a natural tendency to look on the down side – for that way lay fewer disappointments – she seemed to anticipate the worst. Suppliers' bills had not always been paid on time, not from any sinister motive but because the Marshalls' involvement in other jobs often meant longer-than-intended absences from the property. Keeping up with office routines such as bill paying and cheque signing was a weakness in the set-up. As a result, one or two suppliers now and again withdrew monthly credit terms. Janet got it into her head that it would be safer to shop for the inn herself on a cash basis. The discount market was in Thibodaux, a supermarket the size of a small city. We helped wrestle nineteen bags of groceries into the back of her station wagon. (Driving back, we discovered the local Thibodaux Players had just finished a run of *Blithe Spirit*. How we'd have loved to hear the lazy, liquid accents of Southern Louisiana tackle the vowels of Noel Coward!)

Keith's unintentional game of fast and loose with suppliers was brought home to us when a local lady renowned for preparation and freezing of scrumptious seafood dishes called to tell Janet she had several pints of crawfish etouffée which a client had ordered then cancelled. She was happy to offer the lot to Madewood for seven dollars a pint. It sounded like a bargain to us, and Janet called Keith for the go-ahead. Wait, cautioned Keith: the price will come down. Sure enough, a few days later the lady rang again offering it for two dollars less. Again Keith said no. 'Wait two days,' he counselled, 'then offer her three dollars.' We were not surprised when the supplier refused. A week later, she called back – and agreed to Keith's price. The etouffée, by the way, was delicious!

Despite seldom leaving the property, we never became stir-crazy at Madewood; there was always so much to keep us on our toes. We were in no hurry to rent a car. It seemed daft to have it sitting idle most of the time. The solution came from Darrell Chase, Millie and Keith's great friend. By this time Darrell, who had been their travel agent, was seriously ill, unable to drive but utterly indomitable. In a gesture as generous and spontaneous as the man himself, he had a friend drive him the seventy miles from New Orleans to Madewood in *Brunhilde*, Darrell's treasured 1975 canary yellow VW Beetle convertible. The car was ours, he said, for as long as we needed it.

For Eve especially, it was love at first sight, just as it had been with Darrell himself when Millie introduced him to us in London. As often happens with love at first sight, rose-coloured spectacles obscured the loved one's faults. Darrell had few. Brunhilde, alas, had many. The (left-hand) driver's seat was stuck in one position, incapable of being raised or lowered, moved backward or forward. Ron's long legs made it difficult for him to drive. Eve's short legs meant her feet didn't reach the pedals.

The passenger safety belt was *hors de combat*. There was no wing mirror on the driver's side. No petrol gauge. No odometer. The radio was silent. The silencer was absent. The doors didn't lock. The window didn't open and the sidelights demanded brute force. The folding roof, once open, was difficult to close again in case of rain. Brunhilde in other words, was gorgeous to look at, divine to listen to, and virtually impossible to drive.

After Darrell's return to New Orleans the Beetle squatted untouched in the car park for days, until the Cavalry arrived in the form of our friends and weekend guests Jim and Pat Chandler from Texas. Pat is more than Eve's friend; they call each other 'soul sister'. Her husband Jim, former rodeo rider and Vietnam Purple Heart recipient, is the handiest of men. In no time flat (well, he gave up half a day of his holiday to do it) he scoured the local Ace Hardware for materials and fashioned a trio of wooden blocks that he fixed over Brunhilde's gas, clutch and brake pedals.

Eve practised on the quiet roads around the cane fields until she was reasonably certain she could drive the two-and-a-half miles to Napoleonville *(a)* without fear of certain death and *(b)* with sufficient competence not to attract the attention of Assumption Parish's finest. The noise from the engine was sweet – loud, to be sure, but sweet – and so long as Ron rode shotgun and told her when something behind looked like overtaking (no driver's wing mirror, remember?) we did just fine.

Eve drove, looking in the driver mirror for as long as she could. Ron, about-turned in the passenger seat, warned her 'Coming up behind you. Fifty yards... twenty ...*overtaking NOW...*'

We even made the thirty-five mile round trip to Thibodaux, which we considered a major breakthrough as well as a major misdemeanour. Clem and the staff said they always heaved a communal sigh of relief when they heard Brunhilde's noisy engine signalling our safe return.

One quiet afternoon before Eve's weekly appointment with Miss Dee, we stopped off in Napoleonville to fill Brunhilde's petrol tank. We couldn't tell if it was empty but neither could we take a chance of running out of gas on the highway. At the kerbside filling station in what passed as the town centre we parked by the pump and prepared to self-serve. Ron pointed the nozzle where he expected the tank to be. Nothing. He looked around one side of the car, then the other. Nothing. Eve clambered out and *she* looked all around. Nothing. A tall old man in bibbed dungarees over an impressive corporation, baseball cap on his head, matchstick wedged between his teeth, ambled out of the office. Without moving the matchstick or cracking a smile he murmured:

'He'p you?'

'Ahh...we're fine. I think. Thank you,' Ron answered suavely in Hugh-Grant-speak. Well, would *you* admit in a strange land to a strange man that you didn't know how to find your petrol tank?

'Just a small problem...won't be a tick.' In unspoken agreement, we looked around the car again, this time as though searching for the source of a bad smell. She lifted the bonnet. He opened the boot. (Bad enough these were back to front anyway in a VW, which we'd forgotten.) Still no hole. We had no choice. Dignity thrown to the winds, the former director of one of the world's grandest hotels confessed to the surly, burly senior that we couldn't find our petrol tank. 'Not our car, you see,' he excused. 'Borrowed.'

'Yep,' said the old-timer. 'Foreign automobiles...' (did he really mean 'foreigners', we wondered) and shook his head. Did nothing else. Just shook his head. His buddy, slightly younger at around ninety-seven, same bib overalls, battered felt stetson the only difference in their wardrobe, joined the first. Shifted his matchstick-toothpick. Shook his head. Added, 'Yeah. Foreign automobiles...tsk-tsk.'

At that point Ron pointed knowingly to a cap inside the boot and said, 'Aha! There it *is*, little sucker,' (just to prove how fluent he was becoming in Louisiana *patois*), and began to unscrew it with a confident smile. The two old-timers shook their heads in unison.

'Carburettor,' one muttered.

Eve began to believe wholeheartedly in the methane gas or chickenshit theory of propulsion.

Eventually, of course, we found the 'gas' tank. Exactly where it should have been, hidden under a canary-yellow cover that just had to be flipped open.

We and Brunhilde slunk off to find Miss Dee. Eve had been driven there a half dozen times, but finding the salon – a single-storey wooden structure with double windows, sandwiched between two houses – proved beyond us that day. We drove up and down and around the street where we believed it to be, several times (Napoleonville is a very small town) before admitting we once again needed help. The first passer-by we asked pointed it out – just a car's length from where we were stopped for the third time.

Eve emerged as usual within the hour, hair set and spritzed, looking as though a fall would fracture it. It would be fine in an hour or two by the time the humidity did its work and the 'set' dropped, she assured. Still enjoying the unaccustomed freedom of driving Brunhilde we stopped at the bakery to pick up some fresh bread. The notice on the door said, 'Gone out. Back at 3.30.' It was now 3.45 and the aroma of baking bread was tantalising, so we waited in the car for ten minutes before giving up when there was no sign of life behind the bakery doors. We hoped the bread wouldn't burn.

Backing into the side street to turn the car around, Eve gasped and said: 'Please. *Please!* Tell me it's raining.' Ron looked up at the cloudless azure sky, sun beating down through Brunhilde's open top. 'Oh God,' she moaned. 'Of all the pigeons in all the world, this one had to dump on *my hairdo...*'

If you've never tried to remove pigeon-poop from a hairdo that's been firmly sprayed – no, *concreted* – into place, then you can't even imagine what a challenge it is. Eve shrieked 'A tissue, dammit, *a tissue...*' and didn't seem to appreciate being told 'Bless you! But it's too late – the pigeon will be miles away by now.'

Relinquishing Brunhilde at the end of our stay was as hard as saying farewell to Madewood. We knew Darrell would be unable to drive her again. The best he could hope for was to sell his beloved Beetle to a collector. Nobody, however, could face the task of finding a new owner. Brunhilde sat at Madewood for several months, used occasionally by the family or visiting friends. When Darrell died, two close friends Jim and Lee Meehan bought Brunhilde. They lovingly restored the car to almost mint condition before transporting it to their new home in the California wine country of Napa Valley.

Millie took half of Darrell's ashes to Paris and scattered them in the River Seine (and a few, clandestinely, at The Ritz. How he'd have loved that!). The remainder was strewn around the live oak tree planted in his memory at Madewood where his friends gather each year for a celebration of his life. Giant vodka martinis, Darrell's favourite tipple, are consumed *in memoriam* and a wealth of tales told.

The lovely Brunhilde wasn't our only run-in with the Valkyries at Madewood. One afternoon we stepped outside when we heard the crunch of tyres on gravel that signalled the arrival of new guests. There, struggling to extricate majestic hindquarters from a modest four-door saloon were four big and boisterous lady tourists all the way from Germany. Red-faced and cheerful after a long, hot drive they were clearly happy to be with us. Hardly a word of English between them. Eve's German is pretty basic, but with a spot of arm-waving and a lot of goodwill on both sides, we got them up to the three rooms they were to occupy and left them to cool down with the promise of cool baths and pitchers of iced water.

Eve was in the office barely an hour later when the ladies emerged, less cheerful this time. The lead Valkyrie, bosom heaving, was practically snorting fire. The others ranged behind her in a formation worthy of the best Wagnerian staging.

'Ve vant leave,' quoth the leader. 'Please. Ve may leave but no Bill?' The chorus nodded in unison, arms crossed over gargantuan busts. Eve was dismayed. The quartet had seemed so happy a short while ago. It took some brave attempts at Anglo-German but eventually the message got across. The ladies were unhappy because they had expected en suite bathrooms. They had *private* bathrooms, but on Madewood's upper floor at that time (they are all en suite now) this could mean a bathroom that was private to the room, but not attached to it. Usually it involved walking out of the bedroom and next door to the ablutions. And no, we did not – yet – provide bathrobes.

71

Clearly embarrassed at *being* dissatisfied and reluctant to upset us, nevertheless the ladies signalled their intention to seek accommodation elsewhere. 'Ve vould like leave', they said again. 'But no Bill.' Eve was by now wondering who this Bill might be and why they were so keen to leave him behind when it struck her they didn't want to *pay*.

'Of course,' she replied. 'Naturally you shall leave if you are not happy. But please – let us try to help you find other accommodation. We want you to enjoy your stay in Louisiana.' She invited the ladies to take seats on the porch, had iced tea or coffee brought out to them, and sought out Ron to see if he had any better ideas. Of course he did!

Why don't we, he asked after consulting the occupancy sheet for the day, switch the bookings around? There is one booking for a couple who were promised a specific room, the others we've allocated ourselves. And it's three separate couples, nobody travelling together. Give me five minutes with the pair who might be disappointed not to get the room they requested, and I'll do my best to talk them round. This way we can put the three couples into the main house and suggest the Valkyries (for that was how we had begun to think of them) take over three *en suite* rooms in Charlet House.

Brilliant! Ron beamed his most irresistible (to ladies) smile and approached the leader with his suggestion. 'I'd like to show you some beautiful rooms I think you will like over there,' he said pointing to the annexe 'in Charlet House. They all have en suite bathrooms and you will have the house to yourself, with your own private balcony as well as that pretty garden outside to relax in and enjoy this beautiful sunshine.

'Let me show it to you. If you don't like it, then of course you will leave and we will help you. Why, you will even have the room Brad Pitt visited!' That may have been the clincher.

The ladies said '*Ja!*' 'Bill' was forgotten and we helped them settle into their new quarters.

Later that perfect spring afternoon Eve noticed Gladys, our septuagenarian part-timer, leaning out of the back kitchen window where she habitually perched on a stool to do the ironing. Surrounding her, three of the assistants clearly in a state of excitement. We couldn't tell whether they were laughing or indignant, but something was taking their minds off their work.

'Mr. Ron, Miss Eve. Y'all come see this,' cried one.

We hurried to the window, couldn't see what the fuss was about. 'Over there!' came the stage whisper, as they pointed to Charlet House. We still couldn't see anything. Just then a car pulled into the side entrance. As it passed the lawn alongside Charlet House the driver tooted his horn gleefully. Two of the ladies at the window guffawed. Two of the older ones tsk-tsked and shook their heads in disapproval. We went across to investigate as another car pulled in. This time we were close enough to witness the cause of the hilarity. There, in the middle of Catholic and Baptist-strict Assumption Parish, were eight quivering, monumental naked breasts, in full view of arriving guests and deliverymen as their owners, sunbathing naked as jaybirds on Charlet House lawn, gave cheerful waves of welcome to Madewood.

8

The Consultants' Tale

We tried to look at Madewood with three sets of eyes: first, with those of a first-time guest; then with the affectionate eyes of the family; lastly, as consultants. When we collated the comments from guests we noticed that the few who described the property as 'a little tired', 'in need of manicuring' or even 'some spit and polish', were those who stayed two or more nights. A stay of less than twenty-four hours means first impressions rule. People don't have time to notice what lies behind those first impressions, invariably made within minutes of arrival. After twenty-four hours they begin to pay closer attention to their surroundings, and that's when they're likely to notice shortcomings.

The features of Madewood that worked well and delighted guests deserved to be preserved. In fact if we could have bottled them, we'd have made a bigger fortune than Paul Newman's salad dressings. There were things that worked without help from us. Others that *should* be improved. Others still that *could* be improved, but at the expense of Madewood's charm and individuality.

Pointing out what is wrong is easy. More difficult is to come up with workable and affordable solutions. Madewood is a home first, an inn second. That is what produces its inimitable blend of elegance and homeliness. We had to take account of shortcomings that might be overlooked because of that. At the same time, not to let its 'home' status be an excuse for lack of care and attention.

Essential maintenance and repairs were overdue, outdoors as well as inside. However well intentioned we were about keeping costs down and doing as much as possible without serious outlay, we felt funds must be made available soon just to keep pace with the essentials. The figures made depressing reading. For the current year revenue was only $27,000 more than expenditure. Occupancy was just below forty-five percent for the year (not as dire as it sounds, given Louisiana's climate; the heat and humidity of the summer months keep visitors away.) From March to May and again in October, occupancy percentages were more respectable. Still, we considered fifty-five percent a reasonable goal for the following year, and a target of sixty-five percent thereafter.

The challenges confronting the business were:

* Too few overnight guests.
* Too few local or special-party guests to optimise the potential of food and beverage resources.
* Too few repeat guests.
* Too few guests staying more than one night.

Those could be improved with some basic marketing and promotion. Two- or even three-night stays could work well; there were other attractions in the area to divert visitors, and Madewood itself warranted more than a single night. We felt sure that more guests could be persuaded to return, especially those who lived within a few hundred miles. Americans think nothing of driving six to eight hours for even an overnight stay.

Banquet and meeting facilities were under-used. Madewood's exotic setting for weddings – the ceremony, the reception, the photographs and the honeymoon – should have had brides beating a path to the door.

Marketing and promotion were areas that could be tackled, initially at least, without too much expense. A little networking goes a long way, and we believed Keith, Michael and Joe (not Millie, since it would be a conflict of interest with her job at the Times) would make excellent ambassadors for the property. We envisaged more frequent talks to local business organisations and clubs – Rotary, Round Table, Lions, professional women's clubs. Individual businesses and targeted professions like banks, law or medicine could be approached in person, or through specialist publications, or with regular mailings to the target audience.

Christmas or birthday cards to previous guests would remind them how much they enjoyed Madewood and encourage them to return. In-house tour guides should view all day visitors as potential overnight guests, describe the accommodation package in detail and make sure they left with brochure and tariff.

The owners and the manager should never leave home without a stack of business cards and a few brochures. They needed to view every meeting, lunch, dinner or party as a sales opportunity.

A 'wedding pack' should be sent to every couple whose engagement was announced in local newspapers. With a target, we suggested, of two weddings a week during the season. This was potentially lucrative business for Madewood, but weddings needed careful costing. Up till now, for example, couples could use the grounds for photo sessions at a giveaway price. No more Mr. Nice Guy, we cautioned Keith. From now on, let's see a little more Mr. Tough!

Why not invite hotel concierges, tour companies and ground handlers, owners of limousine services from New Orleans and Baton Rouge for lunch or dinner to encourage them to send guests to the Queen of the Bayou?

Special promotions could be run during slack periods. For example a two- or three-night package aimed at new as well as previous guests. Or targeted special offers with complimentary champagne on the first night, fresh fruit and chocolates or flowers the second. A more creative approach when things were quiet, such as bed-and-breakfast for guests who did not want dinner. The owners argued that this would affect the house party atmosphere, a large part of the USP the 'unique selling proposition' of Madewood.

On the other hand, we suggested, flexibility should be uppermost in their approach to new business. On the Fats Waller principle of 'find out what they want and how they want it, *and give it to 'em just that way!'* The expression 'I'm sorry, we don't do private lunches' or 'No, we can't serve dinner outside on the lawn' and 'we don't do bed and breakfast' (even at short notice with empty rooms?) need not be part of the Madewood vocabulary.

Janet, who was responsible for most of the reservations taken by telephone, created a fine impression of Madewood on the phone with her husky drawl and elegant southern manners. However, if some of the other staff took those calls, the impression was less inviting. There needed to be a higher conversion rate from enquiry to booking; more efforts to convert one-night bookings to two or three nights; and to offer an alternative if the dates requested were not available. We suggested some 'visioning', describing the Madewood experience in detail *before* mentioning price (even though it was such a bargain. We wanted it to sound irresistible!) We made sure we did it ourselves, too. When the caller asked the price, the answer wouldn't be 'A hundred and eighty-five dollars per room plus taxes, sir.' Rather: 'you will be invited to meet your fellow guests over complimentary wine and cheese in the library before sitting down to a four-course dinner by candlelight. Coffee and brandy is served after dinner in the parlor.

'In the morning we bring coffee to your room, and a full plantation house breakfast is served in the dining room at eight. Then our guides will take you on tour of the house.

'Our rate for that is $185 for two people.'

Keith had done just that, after all, when he 'sold' the first Madewood package all those years ago. Let the customers see, we thought, just what kind of wonderful deal Madewood was still.

Later, the Marshalls would introduce their own website. But for now, they were included in a joint Internet listing with other B&B properties. When we checked this, we found it listed Madewood as having 'a dry ski slope on site'. 'Yes ma'am,' one of the assistants commented. 'Right over Highway 308 and into that ol' Bayou Lafourche!'

However important it was to improve business, there were the other equally pressing needs of the property itself to consider. We drew up a schedule of tasks according to priority.

a) Immediate.

b) Six-months.

c) Twelve-month target.

d) Three-year target.

e) Five-year target.

f) For future consideration.

(Rather than include a three-month category, we reasoned – no doubt a trifle cynically, but we had some experience of Madewood by this time – that a) and b) would sweep up anything between tomorrow and three months.)

Many of the recommendations required zero or minimal expenditure, so both staff and owners could see the property flourish as a result of their efforts rather than from cash injections. Service to guests, for instance, could be upgraded right away by some simple expedients.

- Fitting bell pads in the driveway to alert staff of new arrivals. Every guest could then be assured of a personal welcome. As it was, too many had to wait around until a member of staff noticed them.

- A daily arrivals list with room allocations given to all staff on duty. This would enable them to use guests' names, know where they'd come from, and encourage them to show an interest.
- Always introducing guests to another member of staff identifying each by name.
- Having a 'never say no' policy. Whatever a guest asks for, either try to arrange it or offer to find somebody who can help. *Want* to say yes!
- Always offering a bowl of soup and a salad to late arrivals who miss dinner.
- Always suggesting an alternative if accommodation is not available for the date requested. People *can* sometimes be persuaded to change their plans.
- Practise the six-foot-rule: never pass within a few feet of anybody – staff, guest, supplier or other visitor, without acknowledging them.
- When you see a guest sitting, standing or strolling, always at least ask – with a smile –'Is there anything I can do for you?'
- Morning coffee served in guest bedrooms in pots instead of cups so it can be kept warm.
- Dinner plates and breakfast main course plates warmed.
- Beverages displayed and offered for sale.

Administration needed tightening up, too, along with control of costs. We encouraged the Marshalls to consider a joint purchasing arrangement with other inns. Purchasing ad hoc at Wal-Mart had worked well enough, but the more successful the business became, the less time there would be for trips to the store, and the more money could be saved by bulk buying.

There was a need for systems to be put in place: stricter recording of income and outgoings, a follow-up system for settling suppliers' accounts, and another for provisional reservations and enquiries. A simple method of extracting and collating data to help with tracking potential repeat guests. Careful progress chasing of parties; food and beverage costing brought up to date (some annual lunch or dinner parties were still paying the same rate after several years). And the one that Ron found most frustrating – every letter, phone call, fax or e-mail regarding a wedding or special party to be followed up and recorded. Including detailed menus, room set-up, arrival times, and meal service, number of guests, deposit and final payment arrangements. Absolutely no detail left to chance. Sounds obvious? It wasn't being done.

We disagreed with Keith that he needed a computerised reservations system with so few rooms, but we did recommend something less sexy but more necessary – a good quality programme for accounting and financial control including payroll, and for food and beverage control.

No more free drinks except at wine and cheese! A small wine list should be introduced. A charge made for brandy or after-dinner liqueurs. The pour controlled using measures. *Every* party should be offered beverages other than complimentary tea, and encouraged to order wines to complement the food. A small, perhaps second-hand, ice-making machine could make a saving over the fifty dollars a week spent on bags of ice from the supermarket during busy periods. Suppliers should be asked to tender for wines and food and provisions.

The old kitchen at Madewood was an asset ripe for exploitation. It was in somewhat half-hearted use, exhibiting a few nineteenth-century kitchen implements, some paintings by local artists and a small stock of postcards and gift items. One of the tour guides was eager to be in charge of converting the kitchen into a businesslike gift shop and museum, and to have the coveted title of 'manager' of the shop. Certainly, with local crafts, recipe books, histories of the area and some good cookware, it could be a profitable enterprise in the making. There were stunning colour prints of Madewood that would make beautiful greetings or correspondence cards. The cook's recipes could be inexpensively bound in-house into a Madewood Cookbook (though as things stood it might qualify for the league of the world's shortest books...)

'Nobody,' we reasoned 'should be able to leave the property without at least one souvenir and one gift.'

When we suggested it would be a good start to clean the place up, get rid of unwanted junk and apply a bit of polish to the copper pans and antique household tools, the putative gift shop manager never mentioned it again.

Michael, when he took up his post full time, would oversee the introduction of job descriptions for the staff and a system for checking hours worked, against payroll. We helped him design a simple staff handbook; it was only fair to both employers and employees that they should know where they stood in matters of responsibility, discipline, hiring and firing. We hoped he would soon come to grips with staff rostering, so the optimum staff to cope with the number of overnight guests or an event, actually clocked on. It should not take more than four staff to serve a no-choice dinner for forty, but somehow there always seemed to be more. We agreed with the owners, too, that two assistants should be trained to take over from the head housekeeper and the cook, as the need arose.

In any work situation it's important to remember that an individual's hundred percent may only be your sixty percent. In evaluating the contribution and assessing the potential of staff, we could accept that for the most part they did their work competently, and without undue complaint. They were flexible in their approach to the hours they worked and the work they did, and it would have been asking too much to expect more. Yes, they might show more initiative in seeing what needed to be done – and doing it. Yes, they might have been more sales and PR aware. Yes, they might be more outgoing and show more interest in the guests. However, we would be content with a few smiles, a 'How are y'all today?', 'Did y'all sleep well?' or, in our dreams, 'Is there something more we can do for you?'

It's easy to fall into the trap of assuming what motivates *you* also motivates others. We cautioned Millie and Keith against expecting too much involvement in Madewood from part-time, sometimes short-stay assistants. They saw their work as just that – a job. They may have liked the job and they may have liked the house, but it would be unreasonable to expect them to care for it in the same way as the Marshalls or the retainers who had spent much of their lives working for the family.

Learn not to underestimate money as a motivator, we cautioned. Yvette, who was trained to be number two in the household, is a talented plain cook. Her home-fried chicken with jambalaya or rice dressing was terrific. We reckoned it would be a great addition to the menu, with a new soup and Janet's pineapple upside-down cake for dessert. Yvette's response was 'I don' know, Miss Eve. It's a lot of extra work. I don't need that right now.' However, when Eve joked about patenting the recipe and making money, she warmed to the idea. Which illustrates a long-held theory: if you want staff to respond in a positive way to *any* suggestion, first you have to ask yourself 'What's in it for her/him/them?' Staff on low wages, no benefits and all-too-flexible working hours need more than appreciation to spur them into doing things 'over and above'.

For the new manager we urged a fair and watertight contract of employment, a detailed job description and a complete list of his responsibilities, from purchasing to staff management. In addition, a schedule of priorities, a cash float and cheque-signing authority up to a specified amount. Our 'welcome aboard gift' was a bound book called *Michael's Management Manual*

In return, the Marshalls should have Michael provide them with his own schedule of priorities and ideas for the property, with short- and long-term plans, goals and targets. These should be practical and achievable: 'Occupancy to be increased from x to y within twelve months', 'Staff costs to be reduced by careful scheduling by ten percent within three months' or 'Cost of cleaning materials to be reduced by z percent by effective purchasing and regular stocktaking.' There should be targets for his personal development as well as for Madewood.

Keith had also asked us to help him clarify the owners' responsibilities, which we defined as being:

i. To keep up to date with Madewood's finances, maintenance, occupancy levels, future plans, staff affairs, general marketing and product development.

ii. To retain control while delegating to the resident manager responsibility for day-to-day running of the property.

iii. To establish a list of priorities for major repairs, maintenance and upkeep.

iv. To plan for short and long-term development of the additional properties on site.

v. To maintain regular weekly contact with the manager.

vi. To have at all times a general picture of the state of the property, its finances and its direction.

We urged Keith, in whatever plans he might make, to think of IRS. Not the Internal Revenue Service, (equivalent of our own Inland Revenue) but Increased Revenue Sourcing. For example, how much revenue might the Charlet House function suite generate over the next five years compared with an initial capital outlay (i.e. loan) to convert the space into two or three additional guest suites. If in addition they decided to construct another two suites in the unused Marquette House, revenue would increase substantially but … they would also need to plan for additional dining space and staff. Those were the things that would need to be discussed and planned formally from time to time after we left.

A Madewood Housekeeping Manual would be a useful tool for staff, especially trainers and newcomers. We were keen to encourage the general assistants to look, see and take the initiative to put right or at least report whatever might be wrong, when they cleaned bedrooms and public rooms. People outside the hospitality business don't realise how much detail goes into preparing a guest room to the highest standard. A house like Madewood and its guests *deserve* the highest standard. We didn't want to scare the staff by giving them too detailed a brief for every day, but this comprehensive room inspection guide should become routine to the person with overall responsibility, and it could be broken down into daily, weekly and monthly inspections:

- ✓ What is the first impression this room makes? Imagine you are a guest newly arrived. Does it appear inviting? Well kept? Or does it look dull, dreary or neglected? What would *you* think if you had never seen it before and were paying nearly $200 a night to sleep in it?

- ✓ Do the doors open and close easily and *quietly*? Door locks and keys, where applicable, should be tested. *

- ✓ Switch on all the lights. Do they work? Any bulbs dead? Are the shades clean, undamaged?

- ✓ Open and close the drapes. Do they move easily? Are they spotlessly clean? Thick enough to keep out the light?

- ✓ Test the air conditioning control. Does it work? Is it easy for guests to locate and to operate?

- ✓ Are beds neatly made? Bedspreads and comforters straight, clean, undamaged? Are the mattresses clean and in good condition? The valances clean and neat?

- ✓ Look at furniture, at curtains, carpets, equipment, ornaments. Are any of them shabby, worn, soiled or neglected? If they are, how could you make an *immediate* improvement?

- ✓ Cast an eye over the top of furniture and tables for stains or need of repolishing or varnishing.

- ✓ Are doilies or runners spotless? Are they really necessary? If so, then they should be cotton, linen or lace, not man-made fibre or paper.

✓ See that pictures and mirrors are hanging straight and at the correct level (pictures at eye level, mirrors to reflect head and shoulders.) Are they dusted and polished?

✓ Look at cards, notices, telephone directories, magazines, books, and information packs. Are they fresh and up to date, not dog-eared? Remove out-of-date or unauthorised material

✓ Check the desk for stationery and envelopes, blotters, pens or pencils, laundry lists and postcards. Is there a reasonable quantity of each? Ensure they are clean and fresh and replace if not.

✓ In the bathroom test all taps, sink plugs and flush levers or chains. Are they and all the bathroom fixtures clean and polished? Look at mirrors, towel rails and any exposed pipework. Be aware of how much more a guest can see while sitting in the bath – or on the lavatory!

✓ Check telephones, * ensure earpiece and mouthpiece are clean.

✓ Check TV* and radio-alarm clock. Make sure they are in working order and *cancel any alarm call* that may have been set by a previous guest.

✓ Open doors and drawers of armoires, closets, chests, dressing tables. Check shelves and drawers are clean, drawers lined with fresh white paper or lining paper. Could a guest put down a laundered white shirt and be sure it will stay clean? Do drawers slide open easily? Any handles need replacing or tightening?

✓ Is there an adequate supply of the right type of coat hangers (padded plus wooden skirt/trouser clips)? Discard any wire or plastic hangers left behind by guests.

✓ Is this room really clean, dust-free? Or has it been given 'a lick and a promise'?

✓ Check carpet and rugs, under the beds, behind and under radiators.

✓ Look at skirting boards, waste-bins, ashtrays. Mouldings and high-level woodwork – have they been dusted? (In earlier times a housekeeper would have checked by running white-gloved fingers over them.)

✓ If there's pot pourri in the room, is it fresh, clean and still aromatic? Is the container clean?

✓ Are the flowers still fresh *and the water clean* and topped up?

✓ Finger-marks removed from doors and handles? Is everything in order *behind* the doors?

✓ Check for loose fixtures, tiles, floorboards, air vents

✓ If you were a guest, would you be impressed or disappointed in the property because of *this* room?

✓ LOOK AGAIN AT THE FIRST POINT BEFORE YOU LEAVE THE ROOM!

*At Madewood rooms in the main house were intentionally lock, telephone and television-free.

In addition, a schedule of routine and minor maintenance was produced. As well as getting everything down on paper, this would allow tasks to be ticked off as they were completed, giving a sense of achievement to those involved. Some could be accomplished immediately – tidying and stapling stray electric wiring under tables and furniture; cleaning insides of cupboards in public rooms; replacing malfunctioning lights and electrical equipment; spot-cleaning carpets. Oh – and making safe every fragile antique chair in the house to ensure it wouldn't tip its occupant on to the floor.

Same for the grounds, gardens and outside of the property. There were plenty of jobs to be done that would show immediate benefits: sprucing up the outside washrooms was a priority – a deep clean, a lick of whitewash and a few flowers, with fresh hand towels, inexpensive mirrors and a bowl or two of pot pourri. Repainting wicker porch furniture didn't take much longer or cost much more – that was because Ron did it! Replacing the pebbles on the walkway between the main house and Charlet House with pea gravel (easier on the feet) could be scheduled for later.

Looking back on our 'Michael's List' for just one weekend visit, we realise how tough an assignment it must have been for someone new to the hospitality business, on what should have been his weekend off from the day job, and with the former director of Claridge's looking over his shoulder. We could have been kinder, but Michael rose to the challenge and we salute him for it. This is the list, chores broken down into ** please do now (or at least, this weekend!) and * please do if possible this weekend (he could always delegate...):

CHARLET HOUSE

• Repair bathroom curtain.**

• Inspect, tidy, clean and reorganise laundry room.*

- Remove junk from hall and under settle seat.*
- Clean outside porch lantern.*
- Clean and try to repair party suite restroom ventilator.**(Inspect *daily*.)
- Cut dead wood from banana palms, both sides of entrance.*
- Cut back creeper and tidy back balcony behind curtained window of room three* (guests *always* look behind a closed curtain.)
- Remove lavatory pan, basin and TV stored in 'Brad Pitt' wardrobe*(room one.)
- Clean and reorganise attic, consider use for storage.

OUTSIDE RESTROOMS
- Start *daily* inspection, cleaning and emptying waste bins.**
- Lock adjacent store and post sign to keep people out.*
- Affix 'ladies' and 'gents' signs to cubicle doors.*

MAIN HOUSE
- Repair legs of parlor settee or at least tidy up broken wood and *make safe*.*
- Experiment with spot-cleaning ballroom carpet.
- Sort out and tidy bookcase in library.*
- Investigate leak from base of lavatory in downstairs bedroom and repair with sealant if possible.**
- Tack up mirror trim in nursery bedroom and repair curtain rings.**

Trouper that he was, Michael hardly blanched when Ron handed over his list on a Thursday or Friday evening.

While we were there we could participate to the fullest, working alongside Keith and Millie, Michael and the staff to bring about as many improvements as possible. Soon, however, we would be gone. We could only hope those who remained would continue to 'polish the diamond' with vigour and enthusiasm.

We all had a bumpy ride that spring, and we don't think any of us will ever forget it. Over dinner on our last night in Louisiana Millie and Keith presented us with a framed engraved certificate that read:

Awarded this ninth day of May
in the Year of our Lord
one thousand nine hundred
and ninety-eight.

To their **most observant
personalities** (M.O.P.S)
Jones and Jones
a.k.a. Dad and Eve.

The all purpose
**DOCTORATE
MADEWOODIENSIS**
For services above
and beyond the
call of duty and the wild.

Presented with deep
affection and gratitude
from Millie, Keith, Naomi
and the remaining staff.

And after our departure? Michael remained as manager for nearly two years. His replacement, still doing a wonderful job at the time of writing, is Christine Gaudet, a chic Parisienne, hotel trained and experienced. She moved with her husband and daughter into 'our' cottage and under her guidance Madewood prospers and shines – even the silver! The Marshalls appointed a full-time groundsman and a full-time handyman.

It costs $259 plus 8.5% tax for the Madewood experience in 2004. Their splendid website promotes special rates for extended stays in January and February and in July and August. There are food, art, lifestyle and getaway weekend packages. Features in the most prestigious travel magazines such as Travel & Leisure and Conde Nast Traveller sing Madewood's praises.

Christine's love of cuisine and of cooking has resulted in a range of splendid new dishes – still with a local flavour. There is a small, carefully selected wine list. When we visited in 2001 we felt we had come home. And we were proud of the small contribution our input had made.

Just to make sure we keep a sense of proportion, though, three weeks after we left in that memorable spring of '98, we phoned from London to speak to the Marshalls. 'Jones?' said a voice we swear was familiar. 'Nobody that name here. Y'all must have the wrong number...'

9

The Congregation's Tale

If we thought we were ready to say our final farewells to the South, the South had other ideas. We felt reasonably familiar by now with the American way of life. The American way of death was a new experience. The American way with weddings was another. Before taking our leave, we'd experience both.

Millie Ball Marshall's mother died during our stay at Madewood. We had been expecting this sad news, and she passed away peacefully in the early hours of the morning surrounded by her family in her New Orleans home. We shared our good friends' sense of loss.

In Napoleonville, we took stock of our situation. Bookings at Madewood were at their heaviest at the approach of southern Louisiana's most temperate season. Without Millie and Keith and with Michael's managerial help only two days a week, we would have our work cut out to keep pace with the day-to-day running of the inn.

We were without a car that would take us safely more than a few miles. The question of our attending Mrs. Ball's funeral was tricky. We were devoted to her: having met her first as a guest at Claridge's, she soon became our friend. But it has always been difficult to persuade Eve to attend a funeral. She is sentimental by nature, more soft hearted than people believe, and because of the unusual number of bereavements she suffered when still a child, finds it hard not to sob her way through what is always an emotional ordeal, even if the deceased is someone she knew only slightly.

At the same time, if she feels her presence will be of any comfort to the bereaved, she will be there. On this occasion, given our circumstances at Madewood, we felt it unlikely our presence would be required. New Orleans is a two-hour drive away on a weekday morning. We were unfamiliar with funeral protocol in the US, and we wondered if in any case our attendance might be an intrusion into a family affair.

However, Millie did very much want us to be at her mother's funeral service. A friend arranged to collect us from Madewood and drive us back. We are truly thankful we didn't miss the most memorable send-off we ever witnessed.

This was a four-part funeral, and we learned that the New Orleans way of death is as different from our own sombre and formal affairs as the New Orleans way of life. To begin with, there is the wake, usually the day before the burial or cremation. Family and friends pay their respects to the deceased, who often is laid out as if asleep in an open casket in the chapel of rest. This has been described as 'a cocktail party without drinks where the guest of honour is not really there'. Millie's family chose not to follow the tradition, choosing instead a closed casket. We, too, were thankful to be spared the viewing, although many of our US friends find it odd that we don't share this custom.

The funeral service was held at the Presbyterian Church on St. Charles Avenue, in the Uptown area of the city. In the adjoining hall hundreds of wreaths and bouquets were displayed around the room together with photographs and mementoes of the deceased, including one that stood out oddly for the funeral of an 87-year-old woman. That was an autographed photo of basketball superstar Michael Jordan. Mildred had loved watching the sport, and he was her favourite player. The family received mourners before the service and exchanged brief memories of Mildred.

The church was packed with over two hundred friends and admirers. Darrell Chase, Millie's best pal and now our friend as well, set the un-mournful tone of the occasion. Darrell who himself would be dead of AIDS within the year, had been fond of Mildred. Knowing how she would have chuckled with the rest of us, he couldn't resist asking new arrivals: 'Bride's side or Groom's?' Millie read – or rather did not read – a fifteen-minute eulogy that not only paid loving tribute to the mother she adored, but had the congregation almost literally rolling in the aisles with laughter. Anyone who knew Mildred knew she would have opted for a farewell party over a mournful send-off.

Millie recalled her mother's foibles as well as her many admirable qualities, the fun family holidays, the occasions when that same family emerged red-faced after one of Mildred's straight-from-the-hip conversational gambits. She reminded us of the evening in Claridge's elegant Foyer when Mildred spied the late septuagenarian Senator John Tower enjoying a cocktail on his own. 'Why hello there, Senator,'

Mildred beamed. 'It's *so* good to see you. I'm with my friend Gladys Jurgens. Won't you join us?'

The Senator politely declined. 'Of course I knew his family,' Mildred told us. When a few minutes later she saw the Senator's guest was a be-jewelled blonde *d'un certain age*, she pursed her lips and added in a stage whisper, 'I wonder what his Mama would have thought of *that*'.

Millie's tribute to her mother could not have been more moving had it been the sermon of a practiced cleric. Afterwards she declared she couldn't remember a thing she said, but there cannot have been anyone in that congregation who will not remember it always. She had every last one of us laughing and crying in turn. Mildred would have loved it.

After the service we rose to leave, but this was New Orleans and we should have known to expect the unexpected right to the last. Unknown to the rest of the congregation, Millie's sister Betty had requested a piper. There was an uncanny pause in the instant before the sound of the bagpipes playing Amazing Grace resonated through the church. A kilted female piper stood in the doorway, ready to escort the coffin to the cemetery some miles away for the interment.

Had Al Jolson been around, he might have used his famous catchphrase: 'you ain't heard nothin' yet!'

As we joined the procession of cars on to the main road towards Metairie, a police motorcycle escort appeared to lead the way, bring up the rear, and stop the traffic to let us pass.

Because of the water table in New Orleans cemeteries like Metairie are above ground. They are virtual 'cities of the dead', streets of tombs and mausoleums and well-tended parks. Some well-off senior citizens have been known to throw 'tomb parties' after purchasing a plot, eager to make the most of it by enjoying a celebration of their lives in advance of their demise. Friends may arrange to share a duplex tomb with a view, and split the expense.

As our funeral procession arrived at the cemetery we followed the smaller crowd of people who couldn't possibly be called 'mourners' for the final act of thanksgiving for the life of Mildred Ball. This was her true farewell, attended by the family's closest friends. Clusters of pink and white balloons tied with ribbon streamers were festooned around the family tomb. Millie asked each of us to take hold of a ribbon and release a balloon to 'help mother's spirit soar to Heaven.' Everyone applauded after they let go of their balloon and Mildred's casket was slid into the tomb shared with her late husband Harold.

The sight of dozens of balloons, many of them released by prominent and dignified New Orleaneans, rising to the sky on a breeze that might have been sent to assist on an otherwise wind-less day, would be cherished as one of life's special moments.

Back in Mildred's elegant apartment in the Garden District, surrounded by the antique furniture, glassware and porcelain she had collected over a long lifetime, everybody tucked into platters of fried chicken, corn-bread, baked ham, pates, home-baked cakes and cookies, cream-laden pastries and cheesecakes – truly a celebration feast prepared by her family and friends and by the carers who had tended her during her final weeks of life.

We anticipated tears and a sad farewell to a much-loved lady. What we got was a marvelous, memorable party. What a way to go!

If we smiled our way through Mildred Ball's happy send-off, we would shed our share of tears later that same month. At a wedding.

The bridegroom was the son of Eve's 'soul sister' Pat Chandler. Eve had loved Seth since he was a small boy, and now he was to marry his beautiful Christi in the small Texas town of Katy.

This was our first experience of an American wedding. Correction: a *Texas* wedding. As with the funeral the week before, we were unprepared for the differences between 'ours' and 'theirs'.

We should have known things would be different in Texas. We love it. A friend born and bred in Texas describes it as 'the buckle of the Bible belt'. In many counties it's as hard to find a bottle of wine to purchase as a gun. On our first visit in the 1970s we saw a car sticker that read 'happiness is a warm gun.' (We never saw it again.) One we liked much better and sounds more like the Texans we know, promoted the Fort Worth Symphony with, 'fill the Hall, y'all!'

For a state that has produced more than its share of US Presidents and firmly believes it's the best at everything, you sometimes still get the feeling it's Texas against the world. Pat's husband Jim Chandler, Vietnam vet, cowboy and all-round good guy, greets fellow Americans by asking 'Which state y'all from?' Whatever *other* state they say, Jim retorts, 'Ah'm real sorry. We're from Texas…'

Jim and Pat built a beautiful home way out in the country an hour or so from Dallas. Green pastures and countryside all around. Theirs was a tranquil lifestyle, with dogs and horses and a few longhorn cattle. A couple of years later, with no warning, a rash of trailer homes broke out on every side of them. Hundreds of homes, without proper sanitation or utilities. There were no zoning regulations in place. Developers could build what they liked.

So our friends' pretty home, its value sorely reduced, sits like a freckle in the midst of an outbreak of chicken pox. Their three dogs and a cat have been savaged and put down after attacks by semi-wild domestic animals. Break-ins are rife. For the first time in a decade, they're installing a property-wide burglar alarm system.

Still, there is much about Texas to love, and it's not just the most irresistible accent in the United States, or the fabulous art collections in Dallas and Houston, or the most hospitable people in the world. We love their dance halls with names like The Crystal Chandelier, and honky-tonks like the Trail Dust and Billy-Bob's. We like dancin' the Cotton-Eye Joe to a group of fiddle-players. And we get a real kick out of watching Dallas's senior socialites visiting places like that, too, drinking beer straight from the long-neck and dressed to the nines in 'casual' designer buckskin. Years ago, before he became a wine writer, Stephen Brook wrote the book Eve always wanted to write about Texas. It's called *Honky Tonk Gelato*. It's a good read.

After the culture shock of Madewood, we were ready for a change of scene – and a culture shock of a different kind. First we spent a few days relaxing with Jim and Pat at their house in what was still at that time the countryside. After our busy weeks at Madewood it was good to chill out, commune with the horses, do a little sketching, and help out with day-to-day chores. Ron could be spotted, sketchbook or hosepipe in hand, the picture of contentment as he sketched the Dutch barns or watered the garden and the flowers that lined the driveway.

It was a piece of good fortune for us that the end of our stay at Madewood coincided with Seth and Christi's marriage, though we had already missed the long run-up to the big day. Arrangements for the wedding had begun long ago, first with the official photographs of bride and groom (in the US this usually means as soon as the wedding gown is purchased. An incentive, according to Eve who knows about these things, for the bride not to gain weight before the wedding.) We missed the engagement shower and engagement dinner, the wedding showers – recipe shower, linen shower, and kitchen shower; and lest the groom felt left out, the bachelor weekend camp and the tool shower *(sic.)*.

But we did get to Katy, Texas, in time for the wedding rehearsal dinner, an American tradition quite alien to us, but just as important as the wedding itself. We had been told to expect a dinner hosted by the groom's father, now remarried, for out of town visitors. We visualised a dozen or so 'invitees'.

Attendance at the wedding rehearsal itself was mandatory. Once again, we anticipated a handful of folk in the wedding party and a swift stroll down the aisle to work out positioning for the day. Instead, we were treated to seven bridesmaids and seven groomsmen, plus flower girl, plus ring-bearer following the bride and groom in stately procession through the Katy First Baptist Church to take up their positions before the clergyman, a relative of the bride. On the morrow there would be five ushers, too.

The rehearsal was followed by conferences with the 'wedding co-coordinator' (at that time virtually unheard of in the UK), the sound technician, the video cameraman and half a dozen nervous parents.

We were ready for a dry martini or a glass of wine, and it seemed an endless drive to the smart Willow Fork Country Club, where the rehearsal dinner was under way. A dozen couples? Do the math for yourself: just the bridal party, with partners plus immediate family made it close to fifty. Add to that, out-of-state relatives, friends and visiting firemen and there might have been eighty people gathered for the Mexican buffet. There was beer on tap for the men (women *could* drink it too, but few of them did. There was always iced tea...) We were flattered to be seated at the table of the bride's parents, mostly busy with the formal duties of the evening, and a couple from the other end of Texas who enjoyed telling us about their daughter whom they hoped would herself find a nice husband one day soon because 'she loves home life right after she loves the Lord.' Providing the entertainment on Eve's right was the rock musician brother of the bridegroom, George, in his usual ebullient spirits.

All seven pretty bridesmaids spoke for a few minutes. All seven handsome groomsmen spoke next. All fourteen, with just one or two exceptions, broke down in tears and ended with the words, on a sob and a hiccup 'Christi (or Seth) we love you.' One poor guy, a childhood friend of the bride's, couldn't even get past the 'Christi, Seth, ladies and gentlemen' part. His voice cracked and he had to sit down and let somebody else have a go.

The bride's father was next, a former local politician, father of five, and sibling of nine. He spoke for fifteen minutes and told of his own far-from-idyllic childhood and the importance of family to him as a result (he and the bride's mother were divorced a few months after the wedding). When he related the tragedy of his father's death, he cried, his children cried, we all cried.

Eve wishes she'd had the *chutzpah* to get up on her hind legs (she is not normally reluctant to do so) and speak for five minutes 'without hesitation, repetition, deviation or tears' about how she fell in love with the bridegroom when he was barely eight years old. After so many speeches reminding Seth how lucky he was to be marrying his beautiful Christi, she wanted to remind the bride just what a fortunate young lady she was to land such a handsome, caring and singularly spectacular human being as William Seth Terry III!

Instead the groom's father, lawyer and country town judge (Pat's ex-husband), rounded off the speeches with a ten-minute stint of his own – this time with less sentiment and some humour. Not that it mattered. By now the Country Club was awash with tears. The long drive back to the Ramada Inn was a riot of laughs in comparison.

The wedding itself was beautiful – just a bit of an anti-climax after the importance accorded to the rehearsal dinner, and with few speeches left to speak. The bride's brother-in-law, a minister of the Church of Christ, conducted the simple, very personal ceremony. The bride looked glorious in creamy silk, blonde hair, porcelain skin, delphinium blue eyes red-rimmed with tears that fell nearly as copiously as her father's. He was so choked up it took several moments to get out the 'Yes' in response to the question 'Do you give this bride...?'

The bridegroom was handsome as all get out in formal tail suit. And the multiple attendants did them proud. You couldn't help thinking of *Seven Brides for Seven Brothers*.

After the ceremony we were driven another long way to the reception lunch and dance at the Knights of St. Columbus Hall (nothing like inter-denominational bonding). There we all got down to the serious business of eating, drinking and boot-scootin' for the remainder of the afternoon. Even dolled up in our wedding finery, the country and western music selected by the DJ just made y'all want to git on up there and do it! The Cotton-Eye Joe, line dances, country waltzes – even the Chicken Dance (no, no, oh no, not the *chicken* dance)! There was a generous buffet and lots of wine. Not, we hasten to add, the reason Eve came a cropper on the dance floor, the combination of high heels and snug skirt proving less than a match for the chicken dance. Oh – and only a few, blessedly *happy* speeches.

Still the celebrations weren't over. That evening, twenty of us including all the parents and step-parents of the newlyweds took ourselves off to a boisterous dinner at Joe's Crab Shack.

This had been not only one of the most interesting and unusual but one of the longest wedding parties we'd experienced. Wouldn't have missed it for the world.

Except that poor Ron almost did. He was unable to do much damage to food or drink or dance floor, having been rendered 'armless. His left arm, held out stiffly in front of him, was barely containable in the sleeve of his jacket.

We had spent the morning in the emergency room of a local clinic after the arm swelled alarmingly, great red weals resisting every effort of treatment with patent anti-histamine remedies. The Lurch-like New Zealand doctor on duty had Ron bend over while he injected three different 'shots' and sent him off with a potent selection of creams and a course of antibiotics.

A small brown spider had bitten Ron while he (Ron, not the spider) wielded the hosepipe over the Chandler garden. He remembered the creature crawling up his arm, but as he was being stung by a wasp on his *other* arm at the same moment, he flicked it off and thought no more about it. The wasp sting, after Madewood, was nothing compared to the allergic infection from the spider. There was little actual pain or unwellness, just the discomfort of a balloon-like red arm that frightened the horses and the flower girls.

'It's an ill wind', he murmured at one stage. 'At least the antibiotics will keep me off alcohol for a week or two.' (Pity, as it turned out, since we were upgraded on the flight home and it was hell to say no to real champagne!)

For Seth and Christi the wedding had the happiest of outcomes: 'the heir' William Seth Terry IV (Will) was born almost three years to the day after that memorable occasion. And as we write, the family awaits the arrival of 'the spare' or in this case, quite possibly a pair of spares.

Our most memorable trip to the US had completed the circle of hatch, match and dispatch.

10

Lagniappe

Every State in the Union believes it is blessed in being different from every other. Elsewhere this may seem trite. In Louisiana the differences flaunt themselves. They assail the senses. Whether you're in a city like New Orleans or a small town in the Atchafalaya Basin, the looks and the sounds, the textures and the smells and the tastes of the food border on the exotic. And if you lack a taste for the exotic, don't even *ask* about Mardi Gras!

The people are different, too, emerging as they do from the 'cultural gumbo' that is Louisiana – Creoles and Cajuns, the Spanish who left an important legacy of governance and architecture; African-Americans and descendants of the British, the Irish and the Germans. The music of Louisiana, Cajun and Zydeco and New Orleans jazz, are constant reminders of its multi-cultural beginnings.

Every curious traveler owes it a visit. You will probably return. And when you do, the plantation houses that remain will open their doors and their arms to welcome you just as they did 150 years ago for the traveler making his 200-mile river journey slowly along the Mississippi from New Orleans to Baton Rouge and beyond.

Mostly it was the Creole French who established plantations along the Mississippi. They found rich, alluvial soil and a near-tropical climate. Anything would grow – tobacco, indigo, cotton, sweet potatoes, rice – and the crop that would make them rich, sugar cane. Two thirds of all the millionaires in the United States lived between Natchez, Mississippi, and New Orleans.

The planters built spectacular homes along the Great River Road beside the Mississippi. The river *was* the road, and the only means of reaching the plantations. The homes provided an escape from the humidity and disease of the New Orleans summer. The social season in the city began after the sugar cane was harvested, when the French Quarter glowed from the light of a million candles and the diamonds of the wives and mistresses of the rich. There were balls, opera, theatre and parties. Come summer, the revelers abandoned the city for travel to New York or Europe, and returned to the comparative coolness and healthier climate up-river.

In 1812 the *New Orleans* was the first of many paddle steamers to travel along 'the big river' for sixty years until the railroad came, carrying passengers, mail, cargo and of course slaves. The journey from Baton Rouge to New Orleans is nearly a hundred miles by road, almost double that by river, so passengers had plenty of time to gaze on one magnificent plantation house after another. They might have envied the opulent lifestyle of the owners of the mansions and their thousand-acre plantations, each one kept profitable by the labour of hundreds of slaves.

Yet in less than a century all but a few of the 350 plantations houses would be gone.

In the War Between the States – the Civil War – Louisiana fought as a Confederate State. In just two years from 1862 twenty major battles were fought for control of New Orleans, the most important city in the South and America's second largest port.

Many of the plantation houses were burned down, damaged and looted, or abandoned after the war by destitute owners and left to fall into ruins. Only a handful survive in southern Louisiana, but the good news is – several are open to the public.

The earliest planters' houses were relatively modest. They even called them 'cottages', built in French Colonial or West Indies style. Louisiana's climate demanded thick walls for insulation, high ceilings, large doors and windows for air circulation, and wide galleries or verandas for shade. The houses were often raised off the ground to protect them from floods and to catch the breezes – when there were any. They were built of *boussillage entre poteaux* (plaster between posts). *Bousillage* is made from mud mixed with Spanish moss and deer or horse hair then layered between posts of cypress, a wood in plentiful supply in that part of the world and resistant to everything from damp to termites.

A perfect example of these earlier houses is the **Laura** plantation house, about an hour northwest of New Orleans on the west bank of the river. Women ran Laura for eighty-four years, all of them descendants of the original owner. Whether or not this is the reason we couldn't possibly comment but ... it also has the most complete set of archives, over 10,000 pages of family and business records. The owners also claim it as the 'home' of Brer Rabbit, a hero of the children's books of Joel Chandler Harris based on plantation tales of the South.

As the planters became increasingly affluent and their acreage expanded, their homes became more elaborate; neo-classical Georgian, Victorian, Italianate. Most prestigious of all was Greek Revival style. Some of the relatively simple French Colonial 'cottages' were built over, added to or extended. Walls of *bousillage* were covered with plaster, slender columns replaced by stout pillars.

The grandest houses in the Greek Revival style were built by the new Anglo-American class of planters, who arrived after the Creole French and tended not to mingle too much with them.

The owners of the plantation houses were legendary hosts. There were no inns or places to stay along the river, and it was a point of pride that visitors were always made welcome. Besides, their arrival was an opportunity to catch up on news from the city and gossip from the other plantations. This flair for hospitality may have helped save a few of the houses, when their owners entertained both Union and Confederate generals during the Civil War, or when a Union officer recognized a plantation home where in more peaceful times he had been a guest.

Typical of these, and the oldest surviving home in the area is **Destrehan**, on the east bank of the river about forty-five minutes drive from New Orleans. It was built in 1787 in French Colonial style by Charles Pacquet, a 'free man of colour'. In other words, a slave who had earned or purchased his freedom. The original contract between Pacquet and the plantation owner Robert Antoine Robin de Longy still exists.

Charles (Pacquet) carpenter, woodworker and mason, obligates himself to construct a home of sixty feet in length by thirty-five feet in width for the sums and price mentioned hereafter ... one brute Negro, a cow and her calf, 50 quarts of rice in chaff, 50 quarts of corn in husks, and $100. Three years to build.

Destrehan's most illustrious visitor was the duc d'Orleans, later king of France and the great-great grandson of Louis XIV who gave his name to Louisiana. The story is that the silver used during the duke's visit was thrown into the Mississippi so that lesser hands would never touch it.

A more frequent guest was the pirate Jean Lafitte. For generations local people believed there was gold hidden in the walls of Destrehan, and would confide that on dark and stormy nights a ghostly pirate sometimes appears and points a finger at the fireplace.

In 1838 the house was bought and remodeled by Jean Destrehan in the Greek Revival style that was becoming de rigeur throughout the South. Original wooden colonettes were replaced with great white pillars, and walls of *boussillage entre poteaux* lathed and plastered.

During the Civil War Destrehan, the house that was built by a free man of colour, was turned into a Freedman's Bureau Colony to accommodate newly freed slaves. It was returned to the Destrehan family in 1866 and they remained in it until 1910.

Another house to visit is **The Cottage**, in St. Francisville, north of Baton Rouge. This is an unpretentious, rambling house that dates from 1795 when it was built as a country retreat. State Legislature Judge Thomas Butler enlarged it sixteen years later. Under his stewardship it grew to a twenty-room home with the unusual feature of four upstairs bedrooms with their own private sitting rooms. On the ground floor there are still remnants of the original wallpaper, imported from England and decorated with fourteen-carat gold leaf.

The Cottage was so famous for its hospitality that one contemporary report read *'The Cottage walls must have been made of elastic, since they never failed to stretch to admit a guest.'* So seriously did the owners take their responsibilities as hosts that when General Andrew 'Stonewall' Jackson stopped off with his entourage after the Battle of Chalmette, every last one of them was found a place to sleep – and the hosts slept in the pantry.

In more peaceful times, the family coach would meet visitors as they disembarked from the steamer. On arrival the ladies might be taken to the company room to remove bonnets and pelisses (coats). They might steal a glance in the *psyche* (mirror) to check whether their hair required a touch of pomatum after the ravages of the journey. Then into the parlor to sip cordial or maraschino or curacao with a little fruit cake while they got down to the serious business of gossip.

The men, *naturellement*, had more important things to do. First, no doubt, an inspection of the crops and a discussion of business, then into the book room or the taproom where the mint juleps waited on a silver tray.

The wealth of the planters allowed them to provide the most lavish meals, served with imported French wines to accompany each course, often on Sevres or Limoges porcelain and, of course, with the finest silverware and crystal. To trap the plague of flying insects at mealtimes, there were upturned glass domes resting on deep saucers. These had spaces around the rim, while inside was a channel filled with sugar syrup. The insects would find their way into the pool of syrup and die, if not happy, then at least not hungry. Hardly an attractive addition to the dinner table, but necessary in the humidity of the swampy countryside. And of course there were plenty of servants to replace the dishes as the corpses accumulated.

Indoor serving-men would operate a cooling system by waving rope-driven fans over the dinner table, and after dinner the house party might continue with music, recitations, card games or even a ball.

A house we're fond of for its eccentricity and its history is **San Francisco**, not far from Destrehan on the east bank of the river. No connection with the state of California, or with the San Franciscan order of monks.

It was built in the 'steamboat Gothic' style in 1856 for Edmond Marmillion, who wanted the effect of a ship's deck and salons, and a belvedere like a crow's nest. Heavy square brick columns support the lower floors, and graceful Corinthian columns bear the weight of the huge attic and entablature. The lower floor was built of brick because of the danger of flooding, and the upper ones of cypress.

Money was no object to Monsieur Marmillion, and he commissioned the finest rosewood furniture, frescoed ceilings and painted friezes by Dominique Canova, cousin of Napoleon's favourite sculptor.

The project cost him his entire fortune, leaving Marmillion without a penny. *Sans frusquin* was slang for 'without a penny' or 'my last red cent' and San Francisco derives from that. M. Marmillion died just a year after his mansion was completed.

The largest remaining Greek Revival Style mansion in the region is **Nottoway**, built in 1859 to the design of Henry Howard, the architect of Madewood. His client John Hampden Randolph owned a plantation of seven thousand acres and a workforce of several hundred slaves. He told Howard 'build me the finest house on the River Road' and named it after his family home in Nottoway County, Virginia. The mansion is in Whitecastle, on the river's west bank, north of Donaldsonville and south of Baton Rouge.

Nottoway was ahead of its time; inside there was running water and indoor bathrooms on each floor. Fireplaces burned gas manufactured on the estate.

Of its sixty-four rooms, the grandest is the oval white ballroom, with Corinthian columns and archways, twin crystal chandeliers and hand-carved marble fireplaces at each end. Even the maple-wood floor is white. The ballroom wasn't just a luxury: the Randolphs had three sons – and eight daughters. Grand balls were held to introduce eligible young men, and seven of the daughters had their weddings in the white ballroom.

The hospitality of the house may have saved it from destruction in the War, when a Union gunboat officer ordered a cease-fire as soon as he recognized the mansion at which he had once been a guest.

These days Nottoway, owned by an Australian physician, flourishes as an inn, conference center, banqueting and concert venue, all of which have enabled the house to be restored and lived in once again.

Houmas House, an hour from New Orleans on the river's east bank, takes its name from the Houma Indians who occupied the land around it. It stood at the centre of a 10,000-acre sugar plantation when it was built in 1840. In more recent times the house was the location of the film 'Hush Hush Sweet Charlotte'.

In 1857 Houmas House was acquired by John Burnside, an Irish bachelor who became one of the most successful planters in the South, with 20,000 acres and a two-million-dollar fortune. He transformed the house to its present Greek Revival style, with Doric columns on three sides supporting recessed galleries and a hipped roof.

On each side of the house are two independent rounded structures, not unlike the *pigeonnieres* found in other houses. But these are *garconnieres* and any birds that visited were not of the feathered variety. These were bachelor quarters built to house the young males of the family when the sap started rising and they were considered old enough to be instructed in the facts of life – usually around twelve years old. Fathers, older brothers or uncles would introduce the boys to the ways of the world – smoking, drinking, and (who knows) perhaps even wild, wild women?

The *garconniere* might also have served the purpose of keeping the rough boys away from the innocent daughters of the house so they would not become tainted or learn things a lady should not know.

The owners of the mansions got up to all sorts of contrivances to save their homes during what many Southerners still refer to as 'the recent unpleasantness between the States'. Some householders gave elaborate dinner parties for the invading Union soldiers. John Burnside saved Houmas House by claiming immunity as a British subject.

In the twentieth century the house was acquired by a New Orleans dentist, and in this one, a wealthy new owner completely refurbished both house and gardens. Houmas House was re-opened to the public in 2003.

Few of the plantation houses are still privately owned, let alone inhabited by the same family. An exception is **Parlange**, in False River, opposite San Francisco. Built in 1759 by the Marquis Vincent de Ternant with a grant from the French Crown, the pretty raised Creole house is open to the public by appointment. Parlange remains the family home of Mr. and Mrs. Charles Parlange, the eighth generation of the family to live there. At weekends the house is overflowing with children, grandchildren and great-grandchildren of the overwhelmingly charming octogenarian 'Miss' Lucy Parlange, every inch the Southern matriarch.

This is still a working plantation, with cattle and horses, corn, soybeans and of course, sugar cane, though nothing like the size of the spread in the mid-1800s when it had ten thousand acres and two hundred slaves.

Our favourite Parlange story concerns the daughter of an earlier scion of the family. Virginie was a great beauty who married a French banker and went to live in Paris. In 1883 John Singer Sargent painted her portrait and scandalized *le tout Paris* when it was hung in the Paris Salon. In fact, he was forced to withdraw it, for he portrayed her as a wanton aristocrat in a revealing low-cut black gown with one strap fallen off the shoulder, looking as though she had just experienced a most satisfactory session of *l'amour*. Her family was so outraged the painter fled Paris. But not before he had painted the strap back on to her comely shoulder!

The portrait was eventually bought by the Metropolitan Museum of Art in New York. The artist begged them not to reveal the sitter's name, and they gave it the title *Madame X*. It was voted one of the fifty favourite paintings in the Met. And of course, a copy has pride of place in the drawing room at Parlange.

L'Hermitage dates back to 1812 and is an early combination of the French Colonial style and Greek Revival elements, extensively renovated in the mid-nineteenth century. It was commissioned by Marius Pons Bringier as a wedding present for his son Michel Doradou Bringier when he married the fourteen-year-old niece of the Bishop of New Orleans.

Michel had served with the revered General Andrew Jackson, and named the house The Hermitage after Jackson's home in Nashville, Tennessee. This being Louisiana, it soon became *l'Hermitage*.

Like many others, it was confiscated by the Union Army, but after the war Michel's son Louis Bringier was able to repair it and get the plantation up and running again with the help of the former slaves of the family, now called 'free persons of colour'.

For sheer drama, there is nothing to beat the approach to **Oak Alley**. It was built on the banks of the Mississippi in 1839, on the site where twenty-eight magnificent oak trees were planted by a French pioneer 150 years before. The owner was Jacques Telesphore Roman III, brother of the governor of Louisiana. While he was content to run his plantation, hunt and fish, his wife Josephine demanded a house that would do justice to the avenue of oaks.

Twenty-eight Doric columns echoed the number of trees, as did the double row of twenty-eight slave cabins. The veranda extends twelve feet out from the walls, which keeps the house in shade most of the day. Tall windows and doors face each other for cross-ventilation, and the ceilings are twelve feet high. Interior walls are brick and sixteen inches thick. Oak Alley is an unusually cool and elegant house, deceptively simple with four rooms on each floor leading off a central hallway. This was typical of many French planters' houses, designed to make the most of any breezes during the stifling summers. On top is a belvedere from which M. Roman could survey his land and the Mississippi River just outside his gates.

The Roman family's fortunes sank without trace during the Civil War. The house was undamaged but the family was forced to leave. It's a 'museum house' now, and the grounds, while nothing like the extent of the thousand acres of the last century, are ablaze with magnolias and azaleas in spring. Cottages accommodate overnight guests, and the plantation's sugar-cane fields extend into the distance.

Used as the location for several movies, Oak Alley is the most atmospheric of houses. It is somehow harder to scoff at the legends and ghost stories they tell here. Sightings range from the ubiquitous lady in black seen strolling in the garden by many visitors, to the candlestick that inexplicably flew across a room in full view of thirty-five visitors from a Gray Line bus tour. The most odd concerns a photograph taken by visitors in the pre-digital camera era. When the photographs were developed, one showed an image that does not correspond to its reflection in the mirror behind it. The image on the photograph shows a young girl with long hair gazing through the French windows. What is actually reflected in the mirror is a headless dressmaker's dummy on display in the room.

The photograph is on view. Go – and draw your own conclusions. The ghosts of the Old South have their own tales to tell.

Information and further reading:

The plantation houses above each have their own websites

State of Louisiana Office of Tourism
www.crt.state.la.us

'Plantation Homes of Louisiana and the Natchez Area'
David King Gleason, *Louisiana State University Press 1982*

'Louisiana's Plantation Homes, The Grace and the Grandeur'
Dick Dietrich and Joseph Arrigo, *Voyageur Press 1991*

'A Return to Splendor'
Paul & Lee Malone, *Pelican Publishing 1986*

'Ghosts Along the Mississippi'
Clarence John Laughlin, *Bonanza Books 1961*

Part Two

'The Captain's Sober. We Sail at Midnight...' *

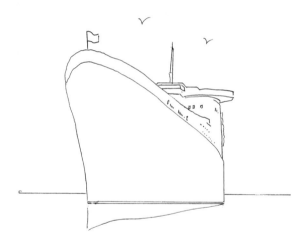

*Line from a 1930's movie screened on board ship.

11

Have Tales, Will Travel

If only we had a pound – or a dollar – for every time one of our friends in the US travel business told us:

'You know what? You two have had such great experiences, you should lecture on cruise ships.'

We always gave the same response. 'We'd like that. How do we go about it?' It's like telling somebody 'you ought to write a book' or 'you should be on the stage'. Sounds good – it's just not that easy to put into practice.

Mostly they didn't know either. Then, the year before Ron retired as director of Claridge's in London, one of Florida's top travel agents Stewart Fabrega gave the response we hoped for. 'I'll talk to somebody at Cunard.' Stewart got back to us with the name of the New York agent who booked the guest speakers on Cunard ships. He, in turn, provided the name of the UK agency. We invited the late, lovely Dianne Coles to lunch and the three of us talked non-stop. She passed our details to her star assistant Philip Gosling, who booked the speakers for several cruise lines. The rest, as they say, is history. These days, there are few agents; we'd just go straight to the cruise lines and ask for the name of the executive who books their guest lecturers.

Ron would have it that we got into lecturing on cruise ships because, when he retired from what he calls the day job, he was 'a rotten golfer, had no hobbies, and had acquired a very expensive habit.' Fortunately, the 'very expensive habit' joined him in the new venture.

That first summer of our new direction coincided with the maiden season of P&O's Oriana, and we were 'launched' on a new career. It just might be the best job in the world.

Our first cruise as guest speakers took us to the Norwegian Fjords and Iceland. Like several others we would do over the years for P&O,

this one had a food and wine theme. It was master-minded by the group's corporate chef, Mike Monahan, and we worked as a team with television chef Tessa Bramley, owner of the Old Vicarage restaurant near Sheffield. Ron based his slide presentation *Revelations From a Life in Grand Hotels* on our first book. He added a second talk, *Entertaining Royally*, on banqueting and special parties, describing it as 'a romp across the tabletops of time'.

In the early years he also spoke about the *Grand Hotels of Europe* and *Great Hotels of the World*. We made it clear these were purely personal selections based on a lifetime's experience as manager and guest. Alas, audiences became so indignant when their own favourite hotels were left out, we decided to take the diplomatic line and abandon those presentations. We were amazed at how unforgiving our fellow-travellers could be if they preferred Venice's Danieli or Gritti Palace while we chose the Cipriani, or considered the Dolder Grander than the Beau Rivage, the Mandarin Oriental in Hong Kong more worthy than the Peninsula.

Eve, the 'wino' of the family since she went back to school for a year to get her Diploma in wine studies, provided tastings and wine talks for the 1,500 gourmandising passengers, and some additional training for the ship's wine stewards. People always eat and drink abundantly on board ship, but on the wine and food theme cruises it was multiplied five-fold. When passengers weren't eating and drinking their way through the regulation five meals a day (breakfast, lunch, afternoon tea, dinner and midnight buffet) they were listening to talks about food, watching cooking demonstrations, or lining up for wine tastings. How any of us found time to go ashore remains a mystery. Eve was reminded of her first interview with Robert Carrier, the celebrity chef and food writer, thirty years before, when she asked him what it was about food and wine that excited him so much.

'That's easy,' he said. 'Tell me another hobby I can indulge three times a day after I'm seventy!'

That first cruise, the ship was full of Robert Carriers, most of them qualifying for the 'after seventy' with years to spare.

Our previous experience of cruising was restricted to a few elegant transatlantic crossings in the 1980s on QE2. Our first surprise a decade later was to catch sight of our fellow passengers at the cruise terminal in Southampton. Instead of the affluent middle-aged professionals in designer casual wear, we joined long lines of seniors with tight perms and polyester trews, a veritable sea of anoraks. We were too quick to judge; as audiences, they were stars. Attentive, numerous, appreciative and eager to ask questions. We learned a valuable lesson: it's not always the most expensive cruise ships that provide the most rewarding experiences for speakers.

In our first year or two of cruising, we experienced the whole range of ships, from Silversea to the bargain cruises of the Airtours company on Carousel. Once we had shown ourselves to be reliable, inventive and popular with the passengers, we were 'on the list' of regular speakers. Some lines even have speakers graded by a selection of passengers; if the 'score' falls below an A rating, that's the end of cruising as guest lecturers on that ship. Glad to report, we passed.

Our 'unique selling proposition' is that we can provide two for the price of one. Custom and practice is that a speaker may bring a companion to share his or her cabin and full board. With both of us 'performing', we should have been entitled to bring two companions and occupy two cabins or staterooms. As it was, the ships were happy to save a cabin for paying passengers, and we were happy to be allocated a higher cabin grade. We are also quite content not to get paid, because lecturing on liners is a fabulous way to 'work your passage' and see the world.

The style of life on board varies as much as the passenger profile. On Silversea ships, a couple of hundred passengers paid a rack rate of a thousand dollars a day in return for everything their hearts desired. Dom Perignon in a silver ice bucket awaited in our balcony suite. When we finished it, our stewardess replaced it, unasked, with another. Dinner was a la carte, whenever guests wanted it and with or without table companions. A selection of wines were offered to complement the dishes, along with aperitifs, digestifs and cigars for those who wanted them. All gratuities were included, too, and a stern note issued to the effect that crew members accepting tips could be sacked (though none did refuse).

It was hard to spend money on that ship, and with only one exception that we were aware of, nobody took advantage. People who pay that much for the cruise experience are used to the best food, wines and cigars at home, and don't need to 'fill their boots' when they have the chance. A great contrast to the 'I've paid for it, so I'll 'ave it' approach you find on cruises where costs have been pared to the minimum. On one of those, we heard a woman shriek to her friends, 'I 'ad *eight* lobsters from buffet.' Perhaps she was on the seafood diet – if you see food, you eat it.

With experience we learned that on larger ships with a capacity of around fifteen hundred, if presentations attract five to ten per cent it's counted a success. Some of Eve's talks on the super-liners like Oriana, Arcadia and Aurora drew four hundred – but those included wine tastings. Folks will always turn out for that, come hail, rain or Mediterranean sunshine. On board the Saga Rose, *Revelations from a Life in Grand Hotels* was so popular with the audience of British seniors that it was standing-room only, with people sitting on the steps of the stage and perched on chairs brought into the aisles.

That was an exception. You also learn not to expect too much. On our first cruise, Ron was flattered to find forty people sitting quietly in the theatre twenty minutes before his presentation was due to begin. Good start, he thought. Then he realised most of them were there to make sure they got good seats for the bingo that followed his talk.

We learned to haggle in the cruise director's office as soon as we stepped on board, for the prime spots and the best venues. Mid-morning is good. 11.30am not so good; the captain's message from the bridge is at noon, broadcast all over the ship on the PA system, right in the middle of your talk. Nor do you want to be on at 12.15pm, since half the potential audience will be at lunch. The other slot to be avoided is the 2.30pm after-lunch 'graveyard session' when the same half of the same audience may be napping noisily throughout the talk. Snores and snuffles can reverberate through a quiet auditorium as can the small moans of protest that signal a wife digging her spouse in the ribs to wake him up. Far from feeling insulted, this always gives us the giggles – difficult if the talk is a remotely serious one.

On larger ships we sometimes had the impression there were more lecturers than passengers. On Royal Viking Sun, crossing the South Atlantic from Mombasa to Rio, the cruise director took us aside. 'Ron, Eve, I'm really sorry about this. Head Office has sent me so many "enrichment lecturers", I don't know what to do with them. Would you mind not doing anything for the first week? After that we have six days at sea and you'll be speaking on alternate days. Just relax this week and enjoy the cruise. Is that all right?'

We put up with it on the basis that it's a dirty job but somebody has to do it...

On average we're expected to do four presentations a week between us. They last for forty-five minutes to an hour, including time for questions. We realised that if we wanted to cruise for longer than a week or two, we had to build up our portfolio of presentations, and we can now offer more than twenty. Ron's staples remain hospitality-oriented. People are interested in this theme and, very important to authors, it also provides the opportunity for book signings.

As cruise lines were forced to cut costs, tutored wine tastings were less in demand – by the company if not by the passengers. Many ships encourage their own wine stewards to conduct the tastings. A good ploy but … Eve had provided occasional wine training for the stewards on P&O ships, and while they were a wonderful bunch of young people, most of them were Indian or Philippino. They did not drink wine, either for religious reasons or because it was not part of their culture. Also, there was often a difficulty in communication. Their command of English was excellent (especially compared with our command of *their* languages), but not quite excellent enough to lead several hundred passengers through the complexities and the aroma and flavour nuances of eight wines.

Cunard was among the companies to come up with the sensible solution of inviting wine suppliers from the relevant ports of call in South Africa, Australia, California or Europe. The producers or retailers take their wines on board with them. Tastings are promotional exercises for the suppliers and the ships don't have to pay for the wines.

Eve still gives wine talks and tastings when asked, but enlarged her portfolio to include a series of talks about the Victorians and Edwardians (woe betide anybody brave enough to ask if she remembers). There's one on *The Dollar Duchesses* who swapped their US greenbacks for blue blood by marrying British dukes; *Rough Manners and the Midas Touch* traces the history of the transatlantic Astor dynasty. *Those Above and Them Below* tells of the two families under one roof in the Victorian country house, and *Hanky Panky in the English Country House* reveals some of the goings-on at the Victorian house party.

People 'shoreside' appear surprised at the amount of work that goes into these talks. Putting together a presentation takes time, application and some financial outlay. Audiences are used to the highest standard of lecturers, and don't fail to let performers and cruise directors know if they are not up to scratch. Preparation is everything. You start with an idea or something catches your imagination – a story about Nancy Astor, say, a scene from a television programme, even a chance remark. Your own talk must be different from any you saw, heard or read before, and it can take months of research, reading your way through a dozen or more books, interviewing, obtaining permissions and having up to forty slides made to accompany each presentation. These have to be top quality, especially when your talks are also broadcast on one of the ship's television channels, to every cabin, for twenty-four hours.

If you are not a natural speaker and you care about how you come across, you can spend hours rehearsing and polishing; in front of a mirror, into a tape recorder, before someone else. Every day for a week before your 'spot' you read and re-read your script so that when you're on stage you know your material well enough not to need more than brief notes.

It goes without saying that you have to enjoy performing. It helps to be a bit of a show-off, and accept the inevitable stage fright that goes along with it. The best advice we were given came from two sources. Dorothy Sarnoff, a longtime friend who coached a US President and several Vice-Presidents in public presentation, wrote a book called 'Never Be Nervous Again'. One of her techniques for getting to grips with your audience is this.

'Before you begin, look around at them, let your eyes travel over them at *their* eye level or just above. Smile. Take a few seconds to say to yourself, "I'm glad I'm here. I'm glad *you're* here. I care about you. I know that I know!"' Sounds simple, but it works, the tiny delay causes a frisson of expectancy among the audience, and it puts you in the right frame of mind. After that, Dorothy reminded us, 'Make sure you sound *conversational*. Always remember to speak *to* or with your audience, never talk *at* them. Start with a catchy opening, end with a *socko* finish!'

Another shipboard lecturer in a presentation on public speaking said: 'flatter your audience. Speak slowly. Pause regularly to concentrate people's attention; stop speaking, let them wait for the next word.' And one other piece of advice we've always adhered to; dress slightly better than your audience. If they're in shorts, you're not. If they are jacket and tieless, you wear a tie (female speakers, a jacket, trouser suit or dress). And if they're in cocktail clothes, you might be in black tie or evening dress.

We never take for granted the adrenalin rush that comes when the cruise director introduces one of us with a build-up worthy of a vaudeville headliner. You step up to the microphone, the lights dim, and you're on stage with a sea of expectant faces looking up at you and emanating 'OK – so *entertain* me' with every breath. But then again, there's nothing like that moment at the end when it's all over, the lights go up, and the applause indicates that you've done a good job. After that, you 'belong' to the passengers, and they are likely to stop for a few words or a shared experience around the pool, in the bar, or at mealtimes. They may even queue to buy your books! It's how you make friends and influence people – to swell the ranks at your subsequent talks.

We like the idea of doing joint presentations, and developed *A Little of What You Fancy*, an audio-visual history of the music hall. We were able to do this when our friend Michael Brooks, a Grammy-winning record producer in New York, sent us a CD set featuring re-digitalised original recordings of music hall stars like Marie Lloyd, Nellie Wallace, Billy Bennett and George Robey. Some of the recordings are over a hundred years old, yet the quality of the sound reproduction is sharp enough to identify every word. When audiences give in to the temptation to sing along, we know we're on the right track.

The chronicle of our Louisiana Spring, featured in Part I of this book, resulted in an illustrated tour of the plantation houses of Southern Louisiana that we call *Belles of the Bayou*.

Our third book *Gastromania!* was published as a result of a gourmet quiz we devised as an 'added extra' at short notice. It's a trivia-type quiz with the questions based on eating, drinking and entertaining – subjects close to most cruisers' hearts. They love quizzes and team games, too, so this has been a winner and we're sometimes asked to do two different sessions. It's a light-hearted forty-five minutes but can become quite heated and even more fun when French passengers are present. They always think they know more about food and drink than people from any other country, and argue the most trivial points fiercely, though usually with good humour. We bump up the enthusiasm with 'spot prizes' as well as awards for the winners.

After every session of *Gastromania!* somebody would ask if we had published it in book form. 'No,' we admitted, 'we haven't, but we'd like to.'

The couple who shared our taste for vodka martinis in the Princess Grill Bar of QE2 called our bluff.

'We'll publish it,' they said, with almost alarming confidence. A few months later *Gastromania!*, published by Smith-Holliman in the United States, appeared on both sides of the Atlantic. And we made two grand friends in Glenn and Barb Holliman from Newport, Pennsylvania.

On some ships speakers are be invited to take part in the after-dinner show, when sunglasses may be needed to protect your eyes from the glare of a million sequins (and that's just from the female passengers' gowns. Add a bevy of showgirls in scanty sparkled costumes and who needs lights?) Most nights the professional on-board theatre group stages a musical show, alternating with a 'headline' entertainer who might be a household name – or not. We have endured comics who ranged from bad to worse. A few had original material, though most repeat the same old gags, on every ship, on every cruise. We learned to expect jokes about ship's lavatories, jokes about the age of the passengers, jokes about the captain's announcements from the bridge. Singers use much the same repertoire, too. Many of the performers go from ship to ship throughout the winter, singing the same songs from the same shows, tear-jerking ballads belted out at top volume *and* close to the microphone *and* amplified. We often wondered why these performers or the cruise directors or the people who book the acts don't compare notes to avoid so much repetition. Many regular cruise passengers travel on several ships during the course of a year and they, too, must get tired of the same-old same-old.

We've also listened to concert pianists of rare talent, 'multi-instrumentalists', sopranos and three other tenors. Watched conjurers, dancers and puppeteers. We've heard Gerry (without the Pacemakers) and Wayne Fontana and the Mindbenders (yes, they're still around and they are *fabulous!*) And the Oxford Chamber Orchestra, who staged a 'QE2 Proms' so magnificently we had them hired for several years for Marlborough College Summer School while we were on the faculty.

On one ship we were asked to introduce Oscar-winning 'stars' in a lavish tribute to the performers, music and dance from fifty years of the Academy Awards. On another, Eve played with Lionel Blair (he should pardon the expression) in the game show 'Give us a Clue'. And she joined the panel on Saga Rose for a session of 'Call My Bluff'. We were happy they didn't need us for another old game show called 'Mr. and Mrs.' on board Carousel, but no doubt would have joined in if required. Enter into the spirit, we always say, or stay at home.

Ron often thinks of Gypsy Rose Lee in this context. She was the legendary stripper whom he met when she stayed at in the Midland Hotel in Manchester. Gypsy, the film based on her life has a song 'You've Gotta Have a Gimmick'. If you have, and you can talk about it 'without hesitation, deviation or repetition', then guest speaking on cruise ships is a great way to spend part of the year. Always provided, of course, you are a good sailor. We've been lucky that our sea legs have not let us down – yet. But even Admiral Lord Nelson got seasick, and *mal de mer* can strike at any time, even after years of painless sailing, so we take nothing for granted.

We know a retired headmaster, who donated his specialist marine stamp collection to QE2 and is now invited to give lectures on it. Retired geography teachers, historians and anthropologists act as destination speakers, introducing passengers to the ports they will visit. Artists teach passengers how to paint; bridge teachers keep the fanatics indoors in all weather. Retired military men share wartime experiences. Nutritionists speak about ageing gracefully, and television personalities and best-selling authors share the secrets of their success. Chefs cook. Ministers preach. Old movie stars reminisce. There's room for everybody with a tale to tell.

12

Going All the Way

After five years as guest speakers on cruise ships, we decided we liked it so much we would fulfil a lifelong ambition and take a three-month, ninety-day, 42,000-mile world cruise. Would this, we wondered, satisfy our wanderlust? Whet our appetite for more? Or put us off cruising for good?

Even in 2000 there weren't many ships that sailed around the world. We'd have loved QE2 but the prices, for the standard of accommodation we wanted, were beyond our reach. Saga Rose was fine for a short 'working' cruise, but didn't appeal for the long haul. Oriana it was, then, despite her passenger capacity of 1,900. We had been on board as guest speakers and we knew that for a twelve-week voyage a vessel of 69,000 tonnes (about the same weight as we put on at the dessert buffet) would be comfortable in long-haul situations and stable in rough weather. She is spacious enough to allow you to be as anonymous or as sociable as you like, and her skilful design included lots of quiet areas.

Oriana's Millennium World Cruise Itinerary
Southampton January 5th
Madeira
Barbados
St. Lucia
Bonaire
Panama Canal
Acapulco
San Francisco
Honolulu
Lahaina (Maui)
Fiji

Auckland
Sydney
Fremantle
Bali
Hong Kong
Bangkok
Singapore
Phuket
Sri Lanka
Seychelles
Durban
Cape Town
Namibia
Cape Verde
Tenerife
Southampton April 5th

Only one of us could be described as having curmudgeonly tendencies (we'll let you guess...) but our 'worldy' would test the limits of our good nature. On a venture of this kind and at this expense – something just short of £20,000 including what we thought was a generous forty percent discount – there's a real danger of anticipation being better than realisation.

Come January 5th 2000, we prepared to take a three-month leave of absence from real life. No bills. No politics. No meals to cook. No decisions to make. Cocooned in a floating community of 1,700 passengers, just two hundred short of capacity, and eight hundred crew, a complex ten storeys high with its own theatre, cinema, entertainment lounge and casino. With launderettes, cocktail bars and pub, restaurants and cafes, its own shopping mall – even a hospital.

At Southampton, we joined the first of many long lines we would encounter over the next few months. A glance at our fellow travellers made us feel like striplings. The ship's comedian, himself no more spring chicken than we were, reckoned if we'd cruised into Athens the Parthenon would have come out to look at *us*. But then, how many people who are not retired can take three months off for a world cruise?

We christened it the booze, schmooze and snooze cruise.

Regular world cruisers – and there are plenty – can be hard to take.

Like permanent residents in a hotel, they consider the ship, the facilities, even the crew to be their personal domain. The opening conversational gambit is always the same. Even when Eve was twenty, she didn't get asked half as many times: 'Are you going all the way?' Followed by: 'Have you done it before?' Then: 'Which ships?' (to provide an opening for a rundown of *their* favourites.) If we do it again we'll have t-shirts printed with, 'Yes. Many times. On lots of ships.' Or maybe just for devilment: 'No. We're world cruise virgins.'

Our first days at sea we sailed through the chilly English Channel and across the Bay of Biscay (or the Bay of Biscuits, as one new cruiser called it), that least favourite stretch of the stormy Atlantic between the west coast of France and the north of Spain. Newcomers all, we were constantly side-stepping fellow passengers in the narrow corridors, identified by letters of the alphabet from the top, A deck, down to F or G. Everybody's trying to sneak a glimpse into other cabins to see if they're bigger or better than their own. You know they're going back to their cabins (as you are to yours) to pore over the brochure and find how much money they could have saved by sharing a four-berth inside cabin on Uganda deck (a.k.a. Squid Row). Worse – much worse – is when they start telling you about the sixty percent discount they haggled out of their (un-named) travel agent while neophytes fume over their miserable thirty percent reduction.

Many of the 350 passengers taking the whole cruise were regular 'worldies'. They did this *every year*. We never discovered how they could afford it, hard though we tried. *We* certainly couldn't and these did not appear to be wealthy people. Our inquisitiveness verged on the impertinent. What did they do or had they done for a living? How was the stock market these days? We admitted to having an insurance policy mature, hoping it would elicit a return 'Oh! So did we.' But no. This one was a retired gas fitter. That one had been a warehouseman for thirty years. Another, a typist or a shop assistant. Nobody we spoke to gave any indication of where the £20,000 *a year* was to be found, short of admitting they lived very frugally nine months of the year in Croydon or Leicester or Swansea in order to feed this expensive habit. Later, we met one couple on the beach in Manly, New South Wales. They had disembarked to spend their usual six weeks in a rented apartment before returning to the UK on another cruise ship. Voices rising with glee they confided, 'We've just found a McDonald's where you can buy an ice cream for *five cents*!' Maybe that's the secret.

On long-haul cruises passengers have no excuse for neglecting their fitness regimes. In fact we couldn't have survived without the daily workout offered in Oriana's fitness centre to help counteract the effects of hot and cold running buffets from dawn to midnight. Two treadmills for a passenger complement of 1,700 meant that fitness enthusiasts were allotted a fifteen-minute time slot. Every morning there was a long line of assertive seniors, eagle eyes glued to the second hand of their watches, ready to threaten the outbreak of World War III if anybody over-ran their time by a minute. Oh, the arguments! The veiled threats! The plaintive cry of the one *on* the machine: 'But I only got on three minutes after my time' while the next in line wagged a stern finger. 'Doesn't matter. Time goes by the gym clock. Ten o'clock slot means 10.15 *off*.'

Never mind that there were half a dozen exercise bicycles, four cross-trainers, rowing machines and step machines unoccupied! The truth is that cruisers love to queue.

Nobody would *dream* of coming back later. Queue-jump for an instant to read a menu or see what's going on, and you risk death by a thousand 'tut's'. They'll form an orderly line for the gym, for lunch, the ladies' loos, the midnight buffet, the Captain's cocktail party – oh, they'll queue for an *hour* for the privilege of shaking that man's hand.

Cruisers also love to complain. The best ship is always the one they just got off. We actually heard somebody say: 'we never 'ad weather like this on t'Canberra...'

Oriana's captain was a whiskered seafarer with a legendary ability, according to the regulars, to seek out rough weather. He believed in keeping his passengers fully informed; even if it meant waking us up in the middle of the night to do so.

We had managed a rare early night, and when Eve woke to the sound of a distant alarm bell around 11.30pm she thought, if it concerns us, there'll be an in-cabin alarm or announcement.

There was. In fact there were four. Captain prefaced his announcement with 'There's nothing to worry about', which only brought to mind Corporal Jones in Dad's Army crying 'Don't panic, don't panic...' Nobody would have given it a second thought if the Captain hadn't kept waking us with updates. Apparently smoke was leaking from one of the garbage incinerators. We had to hear every detail of the ducting in and around and behind it.

Crew members were put on emergency standby (routine procedure) at their lifeboat stations on stairways and passages around the ship. One of our waiters had been performing as Cilla Black in 'Blind Date' in the crew bar. He was obliged to man his station in the Crow's Nest bar in full drag and make-up, allowed time only to change from stiletto heels into his own shoes. A mate carried off the red wig, but the sequined gown and fishnets stayed put.

At the second alarm Captain sounded a little breathless, his voice slightly more concerned. He repeated the previous announcement. You need to understand that the fire alarm squealers in the cabin of a cruise ship are louder and more disorienting than any others except those in American hotels. If there had been an emergency, trying to think, dress, make a decision on which way to turn, with your head literally bursting with the din, would be unimaginable. Sleep is impossible. Ron slept. A dig in the ribs to wake him so he could share the misery would have been futile. In seconds, Eve knew, he would slide happily back into the Land of Nod, din or no din.

After the last alarm, a happier-sounding Captain reassured us 'Everything is under control'

He appeared to relish, as cruise ship captains do, the PR side of the job. In fact, captains speaking without notes and without illustrations, about their job, have given the best lectures we've heard on any ships. Oriana's commander was no exception.

Resplendent in best blues or tropical whites, he would greet guests, up to six hundred at a time, to his 'welcome aboard' parties with a secret handshake learned from the Queen. Shake the punter's hand in the usual way while at the same time pressing them on into the room with your left hand on their arm. Difference is, when the Queen does it, you don't notice you're being moved along.

His guests received, the Captain would introduce his senior officers and tell jokes – often much better than the comedian – after which, those who had not sidestepped the fizzy wine and snagged a proper drink, would be out of luck. Drinks service would end and passengers eased out of the lounge and into their respective dining rooms.

One thing we could never understand is why, when the captains are so socially accomplished, the officers assembled to meet passengers, are so inept. On every ship, even QE2, with only occasional exceptions they stand around in cliques, agreeable fellows and ladies all if the passengers approach them and initiate conversation, but almost never willing to make the first move. The cruise line that trains the ships' officers in social skills and the art of conversation will get our business every time. We'll even provide the training!

Oriana's officers were mostly British, worked long hours with responsibility for the safety and security, health and well being of the 2,500 souls on board. They did enjoy the occasional opportunity to let their hair down. When the ship officially crossed the equator ('officially' that is, because it might cross back and forth several times during the course of a world cruise), almost everyone on board gathered on the pool deck for the traditional crossing the line ceremony, when the Captain asks permission from 'King Neptune' to proceed on our course. People do many silly things, including dressing up as Neptune and his followers and initiating 'pollywogs' crossing the Equator for the first time. On some ships this takes the form of making passengers kiss very large and very dead fish before jumping into the pool fully clothed. Our staff captain – the most senior officer after the captain – took on some of the passengers in a battle to see who could keep their balance riding the "greasy pole" erected in the outdoor swimming pool while bystanders chucked coloured goo. Far more fun on that crossing (at least Eve thought so) was the very 'cheeky' rendition of *The Full Monty* by five good-looking young officers in tropical whites.

Ron claimed he found a more interesting way to pass the time on those equator crossings watching the water in our bathroom basin changed from flowing clockwise down the plughole to counter-clockwise!

Monday February 7th was the day that never was. On Sunday the 6th our journal records 'There will be no tomorrow. Today will *not* be yesterday tomorrow for tomorrow never comes. At 10pm on February 6th we crossed the International Date Line; at midnight we put our clocks forward by twenty-four hours. So we will go to bed tonight, Sunday, and wake up on Tuesday morning. We're sorry for anybody who will miss their birthday "tomorrow" but at least they'll be able to knock a year off their age!'

Two parts of the ship were busy all the time: the casino and the launderette. In the casino, glassy-eyed matrons spent long, sunny days tugging handles, pushing buttons or feeding coins into the gaping maws of the slot machines. The launderette was a great place to form a queue for the dozen washer-dryers and meet other women. There seldom was a man in there, and if there was, then it was a good bet he was single. Eve almost developed an inferiority complex as she watched one lady press five pairs of her husband's trousers, and another iron a week's supply of cotton panties (people still iron underwear?)

Short cruises seldom have more than two or three days between ports of call, but ocean crossings can mean as many as six days at sea. It can't be too many for us. However exciting it is to visit new places, experience different ways of life, being at sea is what it's all about. There is no better inducement to exercise, even for sloths like us, than the deck of a ship in the early morning, before the heat of the sun renders you soporific. At day's end, on the other hand, watching the sun set over the ship's bow is more calming, we feel sure, than a pack of Prozac.

On sea days, you can be as active or as lazy as you choose. On deck there are traditional pastimes like quoits (the game where you throw rope rings over wooden pegs) and shuffleboard, plus cricket nets, golf chipping range and laser trap shooting.

Indoors there are classes – line dancing, watercolour painting, and the making of gift boxes. The ship's waiters demonstrate napkin folding, and the social hostess shows passengers fifty ways to tie a scarf. We've been offered cooking and ice carving demonstrations, blackjack lessons and theatre script reading.

That's in addition to the daily menu of 'enhancement lecturers' or 'enrichment speakers' ranging from the academic to the comic to the Joneses. On our world cruise there were American political commentators, experts on managing personal finance, a military historian, best-selling novelists, a 'life coach' to instruct us on improving our performance in every area imaginable, and a nutritionist hell-bent on prolonging our lives by ingesting an almost entirely wholegrain diet. Bridge fanatics (and aren't they all?) have their own resident experts and shut themselves away for days on end, come sunshine or exotic ports of call.

Choose to stay on board on shore days, on the other hand, and the ship is yours, the entertainment blessedly minimal. No queuing for the gym, no complaining about towels left 'illegally' to secure deckchairs, peace and quiet around the pool or the sun-deck or the library.

Passengers become protective of 'our' ship. When we learned that Oriana had a U.S. Port Health Inspection in San Francisco, we were as keyed-up as the restaurant and galley brigades who prepare and serve eight thousand good meals a day for passengers and crew. Not that there was anything to be nervous about. Oriana's immense galley was the cleanest Ron had seen in half a century of looking at hotel kitchens. However, if a ship doesn't make the eighty-five percent pass mark, it may be barred from American ports. Our ship made ninety-eight percent and in the dining room, we cheered.

We dined at a table for two. For the more gregarious, tables of six or eight are the norm; dinner companions change on each segment of the cruise as passengers disembark to be replaced by newcomers.

Our cabin on Oriana was, if you will, small but perfectly formed, and more than adequate. It was an outside cabin on C deck, just above the middle price range. Great thought had gone into the design and though wardrobe space was at a premium, it had fridge and television, a bath and a shower, and a large picture window instead of the small, high portholes in older ships. Unlike many passengers, we do spend time in our cabin so were not interested in paying less for an inside cabin, often with bunk beds, on a lower deck. We would find it hard to wake up not knowing if it was day or night, and not to be able to see the sky and the ocean.

After a decade at sea and writing travel features, Eve devised the first Jones Law of Packing. That is, *no matter how much you pack, you never have anything to wear*. Two or three formal nights each week demand dinner jackets for men and long or formal dresses for women. Other evenings are 'informal', meaning lounge suit and 'cocktail dresses'. On 'casual' nights men may be jacket- and tie-less. Then there are 'smart-casual' evenings, and we have never been quite sure what that means. Even Americans, who coined the phrase, give different explanations. And of course there are the 'theme nights' when you *could* dress up in Wild West gear or Carnival ruffles, Ascot hats or Japanese costume. The trouble with Oriana was that P&O encouraged cruisers to bring as much luggage as they wanted on a three-month cruise. Then provided wardrobe and drawer space for a week's worth of clothes.

One answer that works well for many women is to restrict the travel wardrobe to black and white. Whenever you long for colour it's easy to add a scarf, hair band, tropical sarong or chunky jewellery. Fabrics make all the difference; natural linens, cottons and silks always feel better than man-made fibres. Should black and white not work, then navy and cream or brown and tan might.

Eve's other travel fashion weapon may be the world's best-kept secret. Knits by St. John. We noticed the best-dressed American women wore a selection of the most sophisticated designer 'knitwear' (far too plebian a term to describe the clothes) that was always recognizable and highly covetable. They were out of our price range until we discovered *sales*. Every visit to the United States we make a beeline to the best stores and check out the sale rails. Last year's models maybe, but absolutely classic. The best thing? You can roll them up, crush them into a suitcase, forget to hang them up and those suckers *never* crease.

Had our sea legs let us down or our forays to the sales on two continents caused Ron to have palpitations, Oriana had two doctors, half a dozen nurses, a fourteen-bed infirmary, operating theatre, and emergency resuscitation room. Even its own mortuary, an essential piece of kit given the age and condition of many passengers. On an earlier cruise on another ship we lost three people – two passengers from heart attacks and a crew member who jumped. The widow of the first victim, who died unexpectedly right after we sailed from the port of origin, refused the Captain's offer to turn back. 'My husband,' she insisted, 'would have wanted me to continue the cruise without him.' Rumour had it the chef on that trip mounted a twenty-four-hour guard over his walk-in freezers...

Ships make great efforts to ensure passengers don't miss the important routines of home. The captain conducts a Sunday non-denominational church service in the theatre or the entertainment lounge. Larger ships have a Catholic priest, Protestant clergyman and a rabbi on board, and QE2 has a designated synagogue. There are regular meetings of Rotarians, Freemasons, and Alcoholics Anonymous. 'Friends of Lois and Bill W. 3pm' denotes your AA meeting.

A world cruise provides a portfolio of memories so full you could live off the afterglow for years. The best gift of all is time; time to listen to the sea in all its moods and time to learn to recognise the different nature of oceans. Time to linger over a partial eclipse of the moon; time to wait for the green flash that occasionally follows a perfect, cloudless sunset; time to count the stars with no city lights to obscure them.

There are few places more romantic than the deck of a ship at midnight (usually deserted, as fellow passengers queue for the midnight buffet). One of our guest lecturers was an astronomer. He had forty of us with our binoculars out on the top deck at midnight with all the ship's lights out (illegally, it should be said) as he gave a guided tour of the stars and the planets.

Transiting the Panama Canal was one of the twin peaks of our lifelong travel experiences. Ron's first transit was in a troopship half a century before, in a great deal less comfort.

'For me and my thousand shipmates it was the first fresh water wash – and I'd swear, our first fresh water *tea* – for six weeks!'

This time our steward brought tea at 5am, and by 5.30 we claimed a couple of deck chairs on the sun deck as we waited at anchor opposite Cristobal.

At 6.30 the sun made its first appearance on our port bow from behind a veil of clouds. Half an hour later it glared whitely down and by 8.30am we were already feeling the burn on our left sides. As our friend New York wit Alfred Steinel put it, 'Bagels at seven, locks at nine...'

Oriana joined a small queue of cargo and passenger ships as she prepared to exit the Atlantic Ocean on her way to the Pacific. It took most of the day to enter the canal and make our way through the locks that first raised our ship to the level of the man-made fresh water Lake Gatun, and then lowered it by eighty-five feet to meet the Pacific. The canal locks are 110 feet wide. Oriana is 105.5 feet wide. The transit is possible only with the help of the 'mules', little railway engines, one on each side, two at the back, two at the front, that pull the ship through.

During that long, hot day in January we couldn't help but reflect on the tens of thousands of lives lost during the building of this incredible feat of engineering. Lives lost to yellow fever, malaria, explosions and untold perils. They say that for every *sleeper* of the railway line a life was lost.

Cruise liners, depending on tonnage, pay the country of Panama up to $140,000 for each transit of the Canal. When you consider it saves a 7,872-mile trip around the base of South America the economics make sense.

Twenty-two miles across Gatun Lake and then the ship glides through the Gailard Cut, rain-forest on each side so close we were convinced we could reach out and touch the trees. The eerie sound of birdsong echoing high in the trees provided a musical background all the soporific afternoon. Two more sets of locks at Pedro Miguel and Miraflores, and our transit was complete. Almost without warning, Oriana 'descended' into the Pacific Ocean, and at 5pm passengers were cleared to go ashore at Balboa, Panama.

On the dockside local people had erected a virtual city of stalls selling crafts ranging from panama hats to flutes. All around was the stench of human waste. We were glad we didn't jump to conclusions when we spied a huge printed sign against what we thought was a wall: *No. 1 Slop Tank. No Smoking.*

Twelve days later a helicopter rained flower petals on to the deck as we sailed into Honolulu at daybreak. Musicians, grass-skirted dancers and a storyteller staged a two-hour show on the quayside. We had realized the previous year how natural graceful movements seem to be to many Hawaiians. We had been in the airport departure lounge on Maui, near a group of teenage girls saying good-bye to a friend going off to college. There were a few older women, too, the lightest of whom may have weighed two hundred pounds, clad in traditional muumuu. Without preamble they whipped out mandolins and performed Hawaiian farewell songs. For twenty minutes they played, swayed, sang, harmonized and held us spellbound. Nobody else in the lounge took much notice. Apparently it happens all the time.

Jack and Roxanne Shoemaker, whom we'd met on a previous cruise when Jack was the Episcopalian clergyman on board, met us on the quayside with leis. Ron's was crimson with a chevron pattern; Eve's a wedding lei of tuberoses with white satin ribbon. As he placed it around Eve's head Jack said, 'There! You're a vestal virgin now.'

Ron asked 'And what d'you call a vestal virgin's husband?'

'Lucky!' Jack quipped.

We four spent a wonderful day together, exploring Honolulu and its beaches, whale watching, marveling at the sunset over Diamond Head, dining *al fresco* on the terrace of the Waikama Beach Hotel. On our way back to the ship late that night, we stopped off in Chinatown to watch the lei-makers at work, ladies with deft fingers threading flowers on to long needles – fifteen minutes to make the simplest lei, three times longer to fashion exquisite wedding leis. The most expensive was less than fifteen dollars.

As we sailed away the next evening at dusk we followed the heartbreaking tradition (for we'd like to have kept them) of casting our leis into the wake of the ship. If they floated back towards the shore, we would return to Honolulu. They did. We did.

Oriana eased out of her berth and the Captain announced that we were 'surrounded' by whales. The ship would sail out very slowly so as not to scare them. Everybody hastened up to twelve deck: all around were single whales, pairs, and females with calves. They frisked, they blew, they leapt out of the water like Nuryevs of the deep. Sleek, glorious creatures just showing off, playing with the great white whale that was Oriana until the half-light sent them slowly on their way.

13

Sybarites at Sea

It struck us around the halfway point of the world cruise that we were thoroughly comfortable as sea-sybarites. The first time we returned from a long day's shore excursion sighing 'Ah! It's good to be home...' we knew we were hooked.

With an average of two or three days between ports of call, the likelihood of passengers going 'stir crazy' was minimal. In fact, the more days we spent at sea, given reasonable weather, the better we liked it. We loved our exotic ports of call, too, the 'faraway places with strange-sounding names' as the old song described them. And yet, some of the least exotic ports of call proved the most exciting.

We were treated to a fearsome traditional Maori welcome from the dock as we sailed into Auckland Harbour in New Zealand. Painted faces, spears, sticking-out tongues, the lot. We had to pinch ourselves to believe we were on the other side of the world – Down Under, the Antipodes, a 26-hour flight from home – with no pain, no strain, no jet-lag.

The city was en fete for the Americas Cup yacht race. The holiday atmosphere was infectious and we packed more sightseeing into one day than we managed most places in a week, from the Sky Tower to the Sea Aquarium, the Museum of Art and the Harbour Bridge. Built as a four-lane highway, the bridge proved too narrow for Auckland's commuter traffic. The Japanese designed an extension that was 'clipped on' to make six lanes. It's known as 'the Nippon clip-on'.

We passed on the half-day visit to a seabird colony of gannets. Ron said, 'All we have to do is watch the passengers at the Lido buffet.'

Sailing out at dusk we looked down from Oriana's top deck at the Americas Cup contenders surrounded by an adoring flotilla of the world's most expensive private yachts. We couldn't resist calling down, 'Hah! Call *that* a boat?'

Thank heavens we crossed the Tasman Sea before St. Valentine's Day dawned. Worse than anything the Bay of Biscay has thrown up (if you'll pardon the expression). We were fine, but sleep was impossible with the creaking of the ship, the crashing of waves against the hull, and the unrelenting rocking, rolling and pitching. We felt sorry that the 1,150 passengers disembarking in Sydney had such a stormy last day on Oriana.

Ron celebrated Valentine's Day by exhibiting six of his drawings in the ship's art exhibition.

Our first pulse-quickening view of Sydney Harbour and the Opera House was filtered through the veil of a torrential downpour. We didn't care; we just sat out on deck and got soaked. This was what we'd come for.

We jumped ship for a week so we could re-visit the city Ron fell in love with fifty years earlier, when he was stationed there for a year after war service in the Pacific. We kept our cabin and left everything on board, spent five days with our old friends Professor John and Verity Norman in Sydney. Ron and the Normans became friends in the early 1960s, when Ron was manager of the Royal Station Hotel in Hull. John, now an eminent professor of surgery, was a young Australian dentist with a ravishing blonde bride, and he was working in order to raise the money to study medicine in Leeds. John recalls, 'I used to hand over a cheque for my tuition fees every term to the secretary of the medical school bursar. One morning she told me, "you are the only student in your year paying fees!"

Exciting and dynamic as Sydney is now, Ron found the places he visited half a century before relatively unchanged, along with the warmth and friendliness of the people. Our longer Australian sojourns are recounted in chapters nineteen and twenty.

At the end of our few days we flew west to rejoin Oriana as she left Fremantle, on the opposite coast of Australia.

Six weeks to go and we were not in the least eager for our voyage to end. There had been changes on board since Sydney. Fifteen hundred new passengers for a start, a few of them homeward bound to Southampton, most taking a two- or three-week segment of the world cruise. In the restaurant our waiters John and Isidore had gone on leave to India, replaced by Jagdesh and Bosco. Other waiters on stations around us were Philippino. We said hello to Nazareth and Asuncion,

Resurrection and Piety. And at lunchtime next day, to Poly and Joly.

There were plenty of new and exotic experiences still to come: Hong Kong, which we expected to be teeming, chaotic and unfriendly. It *was* teeming, but had a vibrancy and energy that reminded us of New York. We did all the things visitors should do; had a couple of suits made, a few shirts. We'd have paid as much at home but ... the tailoring was superb and with two fittings the tailors finished the garments in less than forty-eight hours.

Hotel groupies, we made a dream visit in Hong Kong to one of the world's most exciting hotels, The Peninsula. The management kindly offered to collect us from the ship (a couple of hundred metres away) by vintage Rolls Royce, but we resisted. We were welcomed by the lovely Sian Griffiths, the hotel's long-term director of press and public affairs. But the first familiar face to greet us, before we'd got half way across the lobby, was a beaming Michael Wilson, the concierge son of a famous concierge father. Wilson *pere* had spent many years as head hall porter of London's Grosvenor House Hotel, a leading light in the brotherhood of the Golden Keys (the concierges professional body). We had known his son Michael as head hall porter at The Savoy in London, a sister hotel to Claridge's, before he moved to Hong Kong.

The Peninsula's restaurants are world class. Sian Griffiths reported great success with the addition of a 'chef's table' in the kitchen at Gaddi's, its premier restaurant, where diners could oversee the chefs as they prepared dinner. So successful, in fact, that similar arrangements were made in two other of the hotel's restaurants, Spring Moon and Felix.

Before they could congratulate themselves again, however, the restaurant critic of the Asian Wall Street Journal accused the chef's table of being too far from the action, too sterile, too polite. Even though the pre-lunch tour included the garbage recycling system! The critic wrote: 'everything seems so organised, everyone is so polite...that half the fun goes out of it.... The Chef's Table experience could benefit from a bag of spilled flour, the sound of crashing glass, and a dash of bad behaviour.'

Chef Philip Sedgwick's response is unprintable.

A Star Ferry took us across the Harbour to have a look at the elegant Mandarin Oriental Hotel. Another surprise greeting, from a young receptionist who had left Claridge's only a few weeks earlier.

Later that week, cruising in tropical sunshine sixty miles off the coast of Manila, the new captain's noon bridge announcement informed us: 'Expect rain and snow today.' Eh? 'And temperatures of around minus thirty-two degrees.' Long pause. '...In Siberia.'

We had heard Singapore described as 'Disneyland with the death penalty', and we were warned on board that it was an offence, punishable on the spot, not to flush the lavatory, to smoke in a taxi queue and to spit. Chewing gum was frowned upon to such an extent it was not even sold in Singapore. Yet in one day we counted three un-flushed loos in three five-star hotels. A man in a taxi line calmly smoked a cigarette. And a baggage-handler in the cruise centre spat on the floor. Quite a bit of gum-chewing, too. No sign of the flush police, the tobacco brigade or the spit patrol. Perhaps it's being mildly defiant that makes life interesting.

Ron and I discovered when we first met that there were half a dozen historic hotels we both longed to visit. Some, like Shepherd's in Cairo, no longer existed. Others we'd managed to see. We honeymooned at The Cipriani in Venice, stayed at The Ritz in Paris and enjoyed regular visits to Reid's on the island of Madeira. Now, thanks to this magical tour of the world, we could cross a few others off our list.

Tales of Raffles – bastion of colonialism, home of the Singapore Sling cocktail, the last tiger to be shot in Singapore potted under the billiards table, were manifold. It's hard to imagine it could live up to the legend. But we could *see* Somerset Maugham in the suite that bears his name. We ordered Singapore Slings, of course, in the Bar and Billiards Room, and learned that the tiger story is – sort of – true. Not the wild man-eater of the legend, shot by a brave resident, but a poor mangy creature that escaped from a circus and was shot, half-starved and cowering under the floor of the billiards room.

That night we took, to Ron's astonishment, a white-knuckle cable car ride suspended hundreds of feet over Singapore and the sea. Eve has no head for heights, and refuses every ride at the fairground, but the sight of those fairy-lit glass boxes moving in silent lines overhead, proved too hard to resist. She found it fine so long as she held on tight, didn't breathe, didn't move and didn't look!

While our fellow passengers spent long days on expensive shore excursions in air-conditioned coaches, we often opted for a glimpse of how local people go about their daily lives. One of Eve's favourite ways of doing this is to find a local hairdresser.

She has had her hair washed in Chinese 'Fairy Liquid', head bent over a tin sink with plastic buckets of water to rinse. Sat mortified in Kyoto while a gaggle of teenage girls with glossy black tresses giggled furiously behind their hands as their friend struggled to blow-dry wispy western hair. Growled with impatience while a pair of busty Caribbean islanders left her every few minutes to gape at their favourite soap opera on TV.

In a shopping mall in Manila, on the other hand, we both luxuriated in a unisex salon where they gave us first-class haircuts for the two of us, beard trims (just Ron) manicures and pedicures in double quick time, with great charm, for twenty dollars.

In Thailand three young women spent three hours over a shampoo, blow-dry and manicure. Eve decided life was too short to wait for a toenail paint job.

Instead, we treated ourselves to Thai massages at a 'salon' that was highly recommended. The passenger in front of us on the ship's shuttle bus explained how a painful back condition that had afflicted his wife for years, had been completely cured by the senior masseuse at this salon.

'Now the wife can bend her knee and pull her foot up to her bum' he said. Whatever turns you on, we thought. 'Don't go anywhere else,' this man warned. 'There are places you just don't want to know about. But this one's tops. We're off there ourselves this-after'.'

Following his directions we crossed the main road and took the second side turning. Litter clogged the gutters. Children played barefoot in the dust. Mangy dogs scratched and sniffed. There was no mistaking the salon, a double shop window with tattered net curtains, pungent aromas of incense from around the miniature shrine on which sat pieces of food and glasses of water.

We peeked inside, to be surrounded by half a dozen chattering females whose ages seemed to range from eighteen to eighty. They beckoned with hands, arms and smiles: 'you come. Ver-y nice massage. Ver-ry best Thai massage.' We made a swift appraisal of the premises, exchanged glances and reached the same conclusions, a) there was no way we were going to get out of there without *something* and b) there was no way we were going to permit more than a manicure in those surroundings. The ladies had other ideas. Still giggling, they made way for Madame. Clad in fetching cheongsam, she had a will of iron and the wrinkled, lived-in face of a chain smoker.

'You do manicure? Pedicure?' we asked naively. 'Sure, sure. Best manicure, best pedicure. Best massage. You need Thai massage. Our girls best in all Thailand.' We are deeply ashamed to admit we gave in. Madame called two of the younger women and led us up an uncarpeted, unlit staircase. A dusty landing gave on to a beamed attic room. On the floor a dozen mattresses lay in two dormitory-like rows, mostly uncovered, a couple with rumpled sheets. Around each, a makeshift curtain, only one of them half pulled around the fat, white torso of a grunting European. From the ripples in the fat we assumed a masseuse was working the other end.

'Come. Come' our two ladies signalled as Madame bowed and took her leave backwards, still beaming to reveal the gaps in brown-stained teeth. The girls indicated mattresses next to each other, three beds down from the fat man. 'You take off clothes now. You lie down.' At least we had the gumption to insist they put clean sheets over the mattresses. At least, we *think* they were clean sheets. We undressed as far as we were prepared to, and lay down. The masseuses did a creditable job, no different from a regular non-Thai massage, with no funny business. All in silence except for the last five minutes which were punctuated with chirrups of 'you like? Is good massage? I good girl? You very rich. You give big tip?'

Our sixty minutes up, we leapt to our feet, hastily dressed, over-tipped (well, the whole thing only cost fifteen US dollars) and belted down those stairs never, we vowed, to rely on the kindness of strangers when it came to recommending personal services.

We did repeat the experience in a five-star hotel in Bangkok two years later. A proper Thai massage this time. Trained operatives in flower-decked cubicles walked up and down our spine, bent every joint far beyond the limits intended by nature, and left us feeling newborn.

In Phuket (pronounced Pookette if you've always wondered) the ship anchored at 7.30am; it was already twenty-eight degrees (83F). When we summoned up enough energy, we joined the queue for the tender to go ashore. Just in time to see the poor sods who'd got up early and taken the first tender. They were drenched to the skin from a brief downpour that cooled the air substantially for us.

We rode a local air-conditioned (i.e. windowless) bus up into Phuket town, a bone-shaking journey of thirty-five minutes. The driver assured us it would take seven, but that was timetable-time and failed to allow for conversation-time. The bus stopped for passengers to shout to friends on the street, drivers to exchange news; it slowed down so the driver could light cigarettes and chat with the passengers. It was overpoweringly humid and dusty in the town with its hives of dry goods, spices, nuts and grain-stores. We took the bus back down to Patong Beach and enjoyed another half-hour 'tour' with polite local people. A heart-warming experience for two dollars, compared with the fifty dollars other passengers were paying for the half-day ship's tour.

Along the beach there were dozens of tempting restaurants to choose from. We settled on an inviting-looking, cool place with a patio and potted palm trees. It was called Tropica, and we had to take on trust the standard of kitchen hygiene, the food and the lavatories. We needn't have worried. The first person we saw as we were shown to our table was Alistair Dawson, the executive chef from Oriana, and his wife. They had spent their honeymoon in Phuket and often eaten at Tropica. Sound choice!

Two beautiful ladies bowed us out with smiles and *namaste*, the graceful gesture of palms touching one another in front of the heart signifying 'peace'. They urged us to return soon.

An hour later Eve discovered she was missing a fifty-dollar bill and realized we had given it to the waitress as a tip, in mistake for a Thai fifty-*baht* note (about two dollars)! No wonder the farewell was even warmer than the welcome.

Not every port was as friendly as Phuket. As we eased into our berth in Colombo, we were looking forward to a visit to Sri Lanka's famous elephants orphanage, a sanctuary for motherless calves, animals too old to work and others with nowhere to go. An announcement from the Bridge informed us that all shore leave was cancelled. There had been a terrorist bomb blast in the city centre the evening before, near where we planned to have lunch. We would re-fuel and sail right out again. Fine with us, we thought, let's *go*. First we had to re-fuel, and the late arrival of the fuel bunkers gave us a nervous seven-hour wait while a gunboat circled our ship like a curious grey sea-mammal.

We made up for that disappointment in South Africa, with a tour of the Cape vineyards and cellars, a visit to the colonial Mount Nelson Hotel, and time to spend with our friends Harold and Anthea Eedes and John Tovey in Cape Town. Next day we sailed into Walvis Bay, Namibia, to a welcoming committee of seals, dolphins and porpoises capering all around us.

In the afternoon, we splurged several hundred dollars on a three-hour flight over the Namib Desert in a five-seater plane. We expected the desert to be dun-coloured, flat and sandy. What we saw was a psychedelic panorama of hills and valleys and shifting sand, an art deco landscape of geometric shapes, sand dunes ranging in size from hummocks to small mountains, in rose-red and garnet, gold, black and purple. Green patches, too, where the sparse vegetation and trees grew in straight lines along dried-up riverbeds.

Our pilot, Karl, took the aircraft up to two thousand feet and we all felt like potatoes roasting around a joint of meat, even with the window flaps open. At four thousand feet it was bliss, with cool air instead of hot oozing through the vents. The desert staged a spectacular downpour of rain for us. 'We're lucky if this happens twice in a year,' Karl told us. In a few minutes we'd passed through the shower and looked down on herds of oryx, the large African antelopes, at old diamond mines, and as we approached the coast, a shipwreck from 1905.

Over the Atlantic, Karl dropped the plane to a hundred feet and coasted along miles of beach where colonies of basking seals turned the sand black.

He pointed out the salt flats, white then pink, mauve and purple and red, the colour coming from the same algae that makes flamingos pink. Plenty of those, too, flying in formation or settled on rocks, and flocks of pelicans, both white and brown. Back on the ground, the five of us looked at each other and Ron said: 'A thousand people don't know what they missed.'

On our way back to the docks we stopped off at a local liquor store, called a *drankwinkel*. The German proprietor, middle-aged, unshaven and sweating fumes that could have fuelled our plane, grudgingly accepted US dollars but overcharged. By the time we realized it we were half way to the ship. We went back, to be told he had 'charged a bit extra for my trouble'. Trouble? 'You pay in US dollars, I charge for my trouble making change.' Fair enough, we thought, but *double*? He reluctantly handed over a five-dollar bill.

We made it as far as the door this time before we realized that he should have returned fifteen dollars, not five. Again, he made us stand for ten minutes while he prolonged a conversation with a customer. Again we argued, still very politely, that he had made a mistake. With even worse grace he tossed another five-dollar bill on the counter. 'You take. You leave.'

The nearby beach town of Langstraand looked inviting – pastel-coloured villas, white beaches on one side, desert on the other. Nice for a holiday, we thought. Not too long a flight. Perhaps we'd be back. A few months later one of the Sunday newspapers printed an article warning would-be British holidaymakers that this was something of a last outpost of the German empire. On Hitler's birthday, it reported, shops, homes and businesses were apt to fly the swastika. No return visit, then.

We sailed out of Tenerife, one of the Canary islands that we knew well from beach holidays of years gone by, on the first Sunday in April lulled by a warm day and a glowing sunset. Captain warned of stormy weather ahead. That night the sea became deeply grumpy, lashing our ninth deck windows. Both pools were netted and spuming. Captain again: 'There is worse to come!' (This is a rehearsal?)

By next day, the Atlantic was extracting its penalty for all the wonderful weather we'd enjoyed for most of the voyage. The ocean bucked and reared and did its damndest to toss us off balance like a horse in a rodeo. The temperature dropped to fifteen degrees (58F). At noon captain tried to reassure us things should improve after we rounded Cape Finisterre, off the north-west coast of Spain. He confessed that for the first time in his life he was looking forward to the Bay of Biscay, notorious for its rough seas.

Mid-afternoon, gale force eleven and Oriana changed course slightly 'for navigational reasons'. We tried to concentrate on packing nine suitcases. The price of cruising is packing. Two would go straight to Oriana's sister-ship Arcadia, which we were to board in a week's time.

An announcement from the bridge warned passengers to expect late arrival back in Southampton – probably three or four hours, but maybe more. 'Do not be worried,' captain tried to sound reassuring. 'Oriana was built to deal with conditions like this. She is totally safe.' Now where did we hear *that* before…?

At 3.20pm the ocean had worked itself into a fury. It felt as though a tidal wave belted the ship. The din of shattering glass and china and crashing furniture was everywhere. All glasses and bottles smashed in the bars; the restaurant forfeited two hundred cups; the Conservatory suffered some damage and the occupants some minor injuries. The head waiter told us it was the first time he had felt afraid on a ship. The orchestra pit in the theatre was wrecked, chairs and music stands overturned and equipment smashed. The photographers' lab was trashed.

Passengers couldn't get into some cabins when wardrobe doors shook off their hinges and blocked the doors from inside. Glasses and television sets knocked over by the force of the wave spewed broken glass.

Ron was in the Pacific Lounge with the art class when the grand piano rolled across the room. It took four men to heft it upright.

Nobody was allowed on deck and at midnight the sea was still rockin' and rollin'. We were lost in admiration for the crew. They had worked all afternoon and evening, rest periods cancelled, to clear up, and by dinnertime everything appeared to be in its place. For passengers with an appetite for dinner, the dress code was changed from formal to casual. Apart from that, we were only personally affected by the cancellation of one of Eve's training sessions for the wine stewards.

Another day and the waves crested forty feet and splashed over deck twelve, but the wind was down to force nine and the temperature a chilly nine degrees (48F). The few ships we passed looked half-submerged in the troughs.

Oriana would be a day late returning from her world cruise. For passengers it was an inconvenience. For P&O, a disaster. These ships are used to a ten-hour turnaround – re-victualling, re-loading, re-fuelling, re-embarking a full load of passengers and sailing out the same afternoon. We had to spend an extra night on board. P&O had to feed and water us and put up more than a thousand passengers in hotels around Southampton until their travel arrangements could be changed.

The first week in April. Home after three months at sea. In Southampton it was snowing.

14

'Two Dozens of Mangos as a Token of Love'

Eighteen months after our Oriana world cruise we returned from a visit to the USA. Alf, one of our stalwart quartet of car park attendants at our London apartment complex, welcomed us home and said he was holding a package for us.

'It arrived last week, Mrs. Jones. I'm afraid it's – well not to put too fine a point on it ... a bit miffy.' Alf handed over a cardboard carton wrapped in brown paper and tied with string. It felt moist and it was indeed 'a bit miffy'. We took it upstairs to investigate and inside found a carefully hand-written note:

Two dozens of mangos as a token of love
From Jagdesh, your waiter on Oriana

Half were over-ripe beyond redemption. The others, we consumed on the spot. No fruit ever tasted sweeter.

We met Jagdesh when he and his colleague replaced our two original waiters at the halfway mark. Jagdesh was a smart young man whose luxuriant moustache made him appear older than his twenty-three years. He was already a top-flight waiter. His sense of anticipation was sharp, he genuinely cared for the welfare of his guests, and he had great natural charm.

We did what we could to encourage him to pursue his ambition to take a degree in business studies, and urged him to keep us in touch with his progress. We exchanged occasional e-mails, but never managed to be on the same ship again, even though he and we sailed many more times on P&O vessels.

Eve had long since forgotten she once confessed to Jagdesh that her favourite food was mango – especially the small ones fresh from the markets in India. The flavour and the aroma is nothing like the well-travelled, well-stored monsters sold in UK supermarkets. Jagdesh told her 'When I get home I am going to send you a fresh mango.'

We were touched by our gift of 'two dozens of mangos as a token of love'. Thank you once again, Jagdesh, wherever you are!

His colleague, Bosco, also from India, told us he was a painter:

'I paint psychedelic pictures,' he explained. 'Fluorescent, with special inks. I take them to a gallery in Bombay and when they sell one, I get a cut.'

Attempting a compliment, Eve said: 'Ah! The Salvador Dali of Bombay.'

'No,' said Bosco, looking puzzled, 'The Chengi Gallery.'

There were numerous non-sequiturs, we recalled, that week of the crew changes. At the demonstration of Indian cuisine next morning, the guest chef showed us how to make minced lamb and lentil cakes.

'If you find the mixture too coarse, put it into the blender to make it smooth enough to roll out. Then you can either form it into patties or make a balls of it...'

Our Philippina wine steward, Ferlita, told us she had once again filled in her day off with domestic routine. She was always cleaning and tidying her cabin or doing her laundry or ironing or mending. Not that she wasn't ambitious; she told Ron, 'One day I work for you, sir, in your own hotel.' We teased her that we were on a mission to find her a husband. 'Somebody who can buy you a hotel of your own, somebody very rich, very old and very frail.'

She smiled shyly. 'Oh no, sir, madam. I don't like the smell of the grave.' A wise young woman.

Travel carries with it the privilege of meeting the most special people in the most unexpected places. Some with whom you share your voyages; others who look after you; and those you meet fleetingly on visits to places of which you can say with reasonable certainty 'you may never pass this way again.'

Take the islanders of Yasawa I Rara in Fiji. Their home is a tiny slice of paradise, one of fifty Fijian islands and the most northerly of the Yasawas chain of islands. No shops, no cafes, just a few houses, mostly huts with reed thatch or tin roofs, a crescent of white sand and coconut palms. Goats leap over the rocks; chickens scratch in the dust. Barefoot children called 'Bula!' in greeting, and a few stallholders offered the usual t-shirts, sarongs and shells. But in a desultory manner, less interested in selling than in looking at us and wishing us 'Bula!' Most of the island's three hundred inhabitants, it appeared, had come out to greet us.

We were not allowed to take food ashore, not as much as an apple; or to picnic, or have a ship's barbecue as planned. The visit was permitted only if the ship promised to send a clean-up crew at the end of the day to pick up litter. A sad reflection on *our* so-called civilisation. The islanders could not have made us feel more welcome, though our port lecturer reminded us that at the turn of an earlier century they might have greeted our approach with: 'Great – here comes lunch'!

By our standards, the people of Yasawa I Rara are poor, but they don't see it that way. A young man who spoke good English explained 'we have everything we need right here. Growing or swimming or grazing.' He was eager for news of Arsenal, one of London's premier football clubs, and fetched his mother and half-a-dozen family members from their hut to introduce to us. Through him, they said what a pity it was that we did not visit the island when we were young, because then we would have been sure to come back.

'You visit when you are old,' he translated flatteringly, 'we will not see you again.'

Oriana paid its dues to the island by arranging a doctor's surgery on board. Thirteen islanders came for medical attention that otherwise might have involved more than a day's journey for them.

The most unassuming people often are the most extraordinary. Our cabin steward on our three-month world cruise was a happy-go-lucky, super-efficient father-of-two from Goa, in India. This man had more facets than a square-cut diamond. We discovered that he was the crew's Mr. Fixit, possessed of entrepreneurial skills that would be the envy of an MBA graduate.

He let slip that he was eager to go ashore for a few hours in Honolulu. 'I have many Valentine's bouquets to arrange.' Aha! And we thought he was a happily married man. He laughed and explained that this was business. He showed us photographs of his 'business', a double-fronted shop. On one side, his barber's saloon. On the other, his children's clothes and toys shop. In front, his florist's shop. His wife runs the business with a couple of relatives in Joseph's absence. On his three-month shore leaves, he takes over.

He had, he said, 'invested a large sum of money, about sixty dollars a day' to a florist from a major flower emporium to teach his wife and helpers to arrange flowers, make wreaths, bouquets and posies.

For St. Valentine's Day he had taken thirty-nine orders from crew members to send bouquets to their loved ones.

Joseph was not the only entrepreneur on board. There were opportunities a-plenty for making a little extra. Tailors who work as cabin stewards are in demand to do repairs and alterations for both crew and passengers. Those who worked as barbers at home have their work cut out – literally – keeping up with shearing the locks of the crew below decks.

Waiters working at a lower grade can enhance their wages when the restaurant brigades 'sell' a breakfast or afternoon tea duty. On QE2, even the top restaurant waiters take turn serving afternoon tea, the least popular meal service because it cuts down their already meagre rest period between luncheon and dinner. Afternoon tea duty 'sells' for forty dollars. Breakfast service sells for a little more at fifty dollars, which sounded expensive to us. Our Queens Grill waiter disagreed: 'Fifty bucks for a lie-in seems good value if you've been partying all night...'

We met our share of sea-monsters, too. Like the couple who occupied the table next to ours.

They were elderly and well born (as they frequently reminded us). Every evening there was a different complaint and another nugget of information designed to impress. They objected to the ships' photographers and expected the polite team of snappers who came around the dining room once or twice a week, to remember that they, out of a thousand passengers, did *not* want their photographs taken. *Ever.*

'Of course one can behave differently here,' Mrs. whispered after she asked Eve to snag some grapes from our waiter and pass them across to her table. 'One wouldn't dream of doing this with one's friends.' Ron, trying yet again to lighten the atmosphere, said: 'That reminds me of the Noel Coward lines *"some people's behaviour away from Belgravia..."'*

Mr. responded: 'He was just a ponce, y'know.'

He then asked Ron about the 'crest' on his striped shirt (this being a 'casual' night). 'Not a crest,' Ron explained. 'Just the logo of some ponce designer...'

Another pair shared their technique for making the most of captains' cocktail receptions. We must have commented on the fizzy wine served as 'champagne'. 'Aha,' they chirped. 'It *is* possible to get a proper drink. As many as you like. And with the price of this cruise – why not indeed?

'You must walk through the throng, ignore the glasses of wine and the measly gins and tonics on the waiters' trays, and make a beeline for the dispense bar at the back of the room. Station yourself there, and as soon as you see a waiter return to the bar for refills, ask him nicely for a gin and tonic or a whisky and soda. You hold on to that, and do exactly the same thing when the next waiter gets to the bar, only this time you ask for just a gin or a Scotch, tip that into your first glass, and give back the empty one. You've now got a decent-sized drink.'

By contrast, the lady who celebrated her hundredth birthday on board had no desire to impress or to take advantage. The ship arranged a spectacular breakfast buffet in the captain's lounge – exotic fruits and fresh-pressed juices, croissants, Danish pastries and of course champagne. One of the admirers clustered around the birthday girl asked: 'Have you got your breakfast,dear?'

'Nay luv,' she replied. 'I never eat breakfast. A bit of bread n' butter'll do me, same as always.'

There was another party for Stella that afternoon – a grand 'surprise' bash during her ballroom dance class. With full ceremony, the captain presented her with her telegram from the Queen!

On QE2 we 'ran into' a man we greatly admired. Jogging gently round the deck one morning (promenade deck – five times equals one mile), Ron tripped over the feet of this gentleman who was napping peacefully in a deckchair. We stopped to apologise and only then noticed the slogan on his t-shirt:

Seen it all, done it all, forgot most of it.

As is the wont of people on board ship, he was happy to share his story. He told us he was ninety-two years old, had been brought up in the ghettos of Philadelphia, a largely black area where he'd been ridiculed and bullied for being white.

'Now what rankled about that is that I wasn't white. I'm red. My background was Red Indian, or what you'd call Native American these days.'

Later in life, he became first a graphic designer, then a businessman, and finally was ordained as an Episcopalian clergyman.

Now he was enjoying an extended honeymoon with Bonnie, his bride. She was eighty-six. Her new husband told us more.

'Couple of years ago I was on this ship and became very sick with kidney problems. I was sharing a cabin with this lawyer I'd never met before. The ship's doctor said they had to put me ashore as soon as we got to Manila; they couldn't treat me on board. The lawyer told me I was probably going to die, and I'd best put my affairs in order.

'I told him they were, but what he meant was, if I died in the Philippines, I should leave instructions about what to do with my body.

'Fair enough, I thought, so I signed instructions to the effect they should ship my remains back care of the stewardess on whichever airline flew me back to the US.

'Well, as you can see, I didn't die. I spent five weeks in the hospital in Manila, and they took real good care of me. When I got home, I decided it wasn't a good idea to live on my own, so I moved into sheltered accommodation. That's where I met Bonnie.

'We were having breakfast one morning and I thought, "Why, she really seems to like me." One thing led to another, I proposed, and here we are!'

Don't get the idea that romance at sea is confined to the passengers. Officers and crew live in the confined space and the unusual atmosphere of a ship for months at a time. Sometimes the outcome is happy. Colin Parker, QE2's cruise director, became engaged to beautiful Chisa, the ship's Japanese social hostess. They 'retired' from shipboard life in 2002 to marry, and their daughter, Victoria, was born the following year.

On Royal Viking Sun, the 'headliner' Turkish pianist Naki Attaman fell head over heels for Judy, the assistant cruise director. They married and set up home in Ankara, Turkey.

Beverley Maclean, personal assistant to QE2's hotel manager, was engaged to Chief Engineer Will Robinson. Our Yorkshire assistant purser, Claire, had just married the ship's plumber. Her colleague was newly engaged to an engineering officer. Chief pursers marry pretty girls from the ship's shops; captains have tied the knot with entertainers; and bandleaders have married head housekeepers (known on ships as deck supervisors.)

We still get occasional telephone calls or e-mails from a wine steward or a waiter or a purser asking; 'Do you remember so-and-so? We've just got engaged.' Or in one case: 'I've got the job at Buckingham Palace!'

On shore excursions we often had guides who were hard to forget, like lovely, one-of-a-kind Kitty, who 'adopted' our group in Thailand.

The ship docked at Laem Chabang, which meant a two-hour coach trip into Bangkok for sightseeing. Kitty warned us with a smile: 'you must please remember me when you come back to bus. I no remember you. You all look same to me.'

She also warned us about shopping. 'You careful, please. You buy only *genu-wine* fakes. Not buy fake fakes.' She urged us to visit her good friend Nicky whose shop sold only 'genu-wine fakes'.

The 'shop' was a roadside stall piled high with Ralph Lauren shirts and Cartier watches, but no sign of the 'Louis Vuitton' bags Eve was looking for. Nicky grinned: 'you want? I get.' And handed us a sixteen-page illustrated catalogue! Eve chose two. Nicky – from where we know not – 'got'. She also managed to sell us four Polo shirts and a Cartier watch that we haggled from twenty down to eight dollars because we didn't really want it. It was just such fun doing business with Nicky. The watch was a beauty. What's more, it worked perfectly until the ship was out of sight of the harbour.

On the coach back to the ship, Kitty pointed out a new housing development, a terrace of brick maisonettes, not unlike the kind you find in the UK. 'These unusual here,' she remarked. 'Thai people not like. What happen when you go home late night, very drunk? How you know which house yours?'

She spoke for a few minutes about religion in Thailand. One passenger asked about Christian churches in Bangkok, another about freedom of worship. Then an American behind us asked: 'Do you have many Jews in Thailand?' Kitty paused and looked puzzled at the abrupt change of subject. Then she gathered her thoughts, beamed her big smile and replied. 'Oh yes. Sure. We have *many*. We have pineapple juice and orange juice and mango juice. Many kinds.'

For reasons we can't even guess, we seem to be attracted to the ship's clergy. We didn't always know they were clergy when the friendships developed. Royal Viking Sun sailed from New York one Christmas missing most of its passengers when a snowstorm closed the airports. We had just spent a weekend in New York at the fabulous Michelangelo hotel and a short cab ride to the docks got us on board before the roads were blocked.

Several hundred passengers – and the captain who should have taken command in New York – had to be put up in hotels and flown to join the ship in Miami a few days later. We enjoyed a tranquil cruise down to Florida on a half-empty ship. We began exchanging greetings, then conversations, and then jokes, with another couple who clearly were having as good a time as we were. He was a giant of an American, affable and confident, she a petite, effervescent South African. Only when our fellow passengers joined the ship in Miami and the captain got around to introducing the officers and clergy, did we learn that Norman Mendel was the ship's rabbi.

They were relative newlyweds. Heather had been divorced and left to bring up two small children on her own in South Africa. Her rabbi, an elderly man and a wise counsellor, said it was time to look around for a suitable husband. As it happened, he was also in search of a successor to take over on his retirement. He flew to New York to interview several applicants and when he returned, took Heather aside. 'Have I got a rabbi for *you*…?'

Norman and Heather were married and the family returned to live in Los Angeles, where Norman was president of the City of Hope charity, and in Carmel, where he was rabbi to a community. We stayed at their beautiful home in Carmel, and the Mendels drove us out to look at a church next door to a golf club. One side of the signpost pointed to the left and said: 'play'. The other pointed right and said: 'pray'!

Another year, as QE2 glided out of Honolulu, we noticed a couple smiling and tearful by turns, taking more photographs than anybody else, long after other passengers had joined the 'sailaway cocktail' scrum. Ron asked if they'd like him to photograph *them* with the island in the background. They said yes please. They had, they explained, lived in Honolulu for seventeen years, Jack as head of the largest secondary school in the US, and Roxanne as music teacher and flautist with the Honolulu Symphony. Their home was now in Oregon.

They were on board, as we were, to 'work', only instead of lecturing, Jack was the Episcopalian clergyman and would officiate at the Christmas and New Year services.

Again, an easy friendship developed. We visited them in Hawaii, where they spend a month each year, and they visited us in London when Jack had an exchange visit to a parish in Derbyshire.

QE2, despite its size, is a great place to make friends. We learned early on that the best place to work on your tan is the sun (or helicopter) deck. You pay a modest sum at the beginning of the cruise, and the comfortable loungers, with towels and cold drinks when it's hot, blankets and bouillon when it's not, are yours for the duration. Kindred spirits tend to gather there, too.

It was on the sun deck of QE2 that we met another rabbi and his wife. Lois was an outgoing New York publisher of educational books. Her quiet husband Leonard was an eminent cosmetic surgeon. We use the word *was* advisedly. For Leonard had retired at the age of fifty-nine, so he could study for the rabbinate at a New York Seminary. Three months after our meeting, he was ordained as a rabbi. A year later they visited us at our home in the Cotswolds, and we caught up with Leonard's groundbreaking work, following his ordination, in bio-medical ethics.

Making friends with the clergy reached its apogee on Oriana, when Eve fell for the ship's rabbi. The feeling was clearly mutual. Just as well he was eighty-six and she, a blissfully wedded woman.

We had noticed this bearded, frail man walking with the aid of a stick, enter the dining room for lunch. He was wearing shorts, Hawaiian print shirt, and a yarmulke. The waiters treated him with great deference and, as they always did with the old or infirm, took special care of him.

We talked to him on deck and found him to be somewhat deaf, but a man with a heavenly smile and a keen sense of humour. He sounded as if he were of European extraction, could be erudite and witty, but was tired by anything more than light conversation for more than a few minutes at a time. He kissed Eve's hand the first time they spoke, and thereafter every time they met or parted.

Rabbi Felix was a great ecumenicist, clearly genuine in his desire to invite non-Jews to share the Friday evening Shabbat service.

We attended promptly at six o'clock in the Iberia Room, where a lady waited with yarmulkes to hand out to the visitors. We wondered if we had let ourselves in for a long, incomprehensible service, but as we arrived an American passenger turned to his wife and whispered: 'The rabbi's on first sitting for dinner at 6.30 so this shouldn't take long.'

We were curious about his background. Somebody of his age must have lived through the beginnings of World War II. Sitting holding his hand on deck one sunny afternoon (he took it and wouldn't let go!) Eve probed gently and learned that the rabbi had been a teacher in Hamburg.

In 1939 he and his new bride were able to get out of the city. His parents did not. 'They died in hell,' is how he put it.

'I never had an inclination to the rabbinate', he went on, 'But we arrived in Manchester to find all the rabbis had been called up. The choice was, if you want to stay, you can be a rabbi or you can be a rabbi.' Sixty-one years on, he was still a rabbi!

Letters were exchanged, including one that Eve treasures, in still-beautiful handwriting 'Saluting the exquisitely and extraordinarily beloved Lady Eve and her current Prince Consort...' It concluded 'May you both reign in glory and brilliant harmony, you are most perfect creations of our good Lord'. After a year or so, there were no more letters. Rabbi Felix, may you know how much affection you inspired.

15

Half the Fun is Getting There...

How quickly you forget the pitfalls and pratfalls that travel with you. There were times when it seemed to take longer to get to the ship than to take the cruise.

On board Royal Viking Sun, then part of the Cunard fleet, en route from Mombasa, Kenya, to Rio de Janeiro, we recuperated from a doze of 'getting there'.

'There's nothing like a relaxing journey – and this was nothing like a relaxing journey,' Eve wrote to a friend.

'Farringdon Station, we thought, seemed like a good place to begin. Why bother with taxis to Victoria in the evening rush hour when we can catch a Gatwick Thameslink train in the City. Our friend Cliff Green dropped us in the jam-packed road outside the station to a farewell chorus of angry car horns. We were handicapped by four suitcases; two long sets of stairs; no lift; no escalator; no porter; and a million ill-tempered commuters.

'There were three empty seats in the carriage. I was forced to take the window seat, with just a mini-seat between me and the man munching garlic-and-tikka flavoured crisps washed down with a can of strong cider. Ron was opposite, one row behind. Two of our suitcases blocked the carriage doorway, the other two blocked the aisle. It worked. Until the next station when a fifteen-stone commuter reeking of cigarettes – clothes, hair, breath – sat in the mini-seat. He *overlapped* me.

'Gatwick seemed uncharacteristically quiet. Our friend at BA promised to do his best with our usual upgrade, and assured us "it's all in the computer". It was. So was everybody else's. Every seat in first and business class was taken. We gritted our teeth and prepared for the exotic sights, sounds and smells of convict class. The plane was packed. A night flight to Africa. Fifty per cent of our fellow travellers were infants who screamed and smelled of soiled diapers. The other fifty per cent were adults who had anticipated their long journey with a curry lunch. And forgotten to pack the deodorant.

'We won't talk about the "meal" or the heads. The movie might have been good, only I couldn't see the screen over the back of the seat in front. I did get to finish "First Wives Club" in one seven-hour sitting. Sleep? Don't be daft.

'Ten minutes early in Nairobi and, as Hildegard Knef sang, "From here on it gets worse…"

'In the collection of concrete sheds they're pleased to call the international airport, we were met by the nice lady from Abercrombie and Kent. There was, she informed us with a big smile, a three-hour wait for our connecting flight to Mombasa. She hands us our "welcome package", a much-used manila envelope containing an equally well-thumbed photocopy map of downtown Nairobi and four paper luggage labels in case we went on safari. Then she had a brilliant idea. She lead us in an unseemly dash (more of a saunter, really, but she assured us it was a Nairobi dash) over to another concrete hut where she managed to get us on a flight due to depart in fifteen minutes.

'"It's a Fokker," she said. She was right. A Fokker Friendship to be precise, and one *did* get awfully friendly on a plane so small and cramped they took away my spectacle case to put in the "hold". The Fokker taxi-ed, then we all sat and steamed moistly for forty-five minutes. No air conditioning. Ninety-five degrees. At last the pilot turns around to face us and says "Sorry, folks. I'm going to taxi back to investigate smoke coming into the cabin.

'You *do* that, we thought. Ron, who didn't share this until the next day, was at that exact moment reading the lead story in the Kenya Times. "A small passenger aircraft yesterday burst into flames eight minutes after take-off, killing eight people". It was flying (you guessed it), Nairobi to Mombasa.

'We sat and stewed some more in the terminal (good description) hut of Nairobi International. After forty minutes I could delay no longer. Despite refusing all liquids for half a day, I *had* to go to the ladies room.

'I will spare you details save that all lavatory seats and cistern lids had been removed, presumably (from the look of things) for ease of access.

'Coming out of the single operational cubicle as I was going in was a tall, elegant lady. As we washed our hands together under the trickle of cool water from the tap, I said: "I think you must be Moira Lister." We knew her reputation as a stage and movie actress. She played leading roles in films that included "The Yellow Rolls Royce", "Not Now Darling" and "The Deep Blue Sea" alongside Vivien Leigh. In conversation it emerged that Moira, actress and fellow guest speaker, and her daughter were going on to Royal Viking Sun that day (Thursday, the 14th) and expected to sail at six o'clock. No, we argued, she sails on the 15th. We spend one night in a hotel.

'We approached an evil-tempered man Ron guessed must be the ship's comedian. He confirmed that indeed he was, and *he* expected to sail that evening.

'I hauled out our contract. "Friday 15th" it said, clear as can be. But... mistakes can be made. What if we booked into the Serena Beach Hotel and the Sun sailed without us? Could Moira Lister and the comedian both be wrong? Could Philip, our agent, have got our contracts wrong? We tried to ring the UK. At Nairobi International airport you could only do this by a) making an appointment with the operator or b) taking a cab into town to find a post office with international telephone facilities.

'Just then they called our flight. Instead of flying direct to Mombasa, this Fokker would first touch down at Malinde. No, we hadn't heard of it either. Just a man with earmuffs and table tennis paddles, a shed, and pick-your-own luggage off a handcart. Another half-hour stew in 100 degrees (but for the solitary ceiling fan it would have been 105) while the plane *re-fuelled*. It had only been in the air for a half-hour. Moira Lister still looked cool and elegant, an exotic flower tucked behind her ear.

'Many hours later than scheduled we staggered off the plane into the brand-new airport at Mombasa. Streamlined, white walls, red roofs – one of the "happiest" airports we've seen. Just six months old, in a country desperate for tourist dollars but with a runway too short to accommodate jumbo jets. Pity.

'A&K turn up trumps again with a warm welcome, and when the luggage is off-loaded we had access to our Royal Viking Sun tickets. Moira Lister didn't *have* any tickets. They confirmed that we sailed on Friday the 15th. We learned that the ship docked that morning and most of the passengers had gone on a one-day safari. Thank you Cunard! Good of you to let us on board for the extra night. Not!

'Now we were glad they didn't. The Kenyan people we encountered were friendly and eager to please. Some air-conditioned taxis would have been pleasant, but that's a quibble. The humidity on the thirty-minute drive from the airport was stultifying. The Serena Beach Hotel is paradise for a lazy beach holiday; miles of white sand, hot, hot all-day sun, terrific service.

'All around, however, were reminders that this tourist paradise is in a Third World country. Wimp that I am, I refused to leave the hotel compound on foot day or night, surrounded as it was by mud-hut and tin shack villages occupied by the poorest of the poor. We are told that the pinnacle of ambition is to become a waiter or a porter in a hotel like ours. The staff worked so touchingly hard to make sure guests have a good time, and they are so proud of their jobs and their hotel. They sometimes got things wrong. So what? The smiles, the apologies, the attempts to put things right were so real, the mishaps seemed trivial.

'As we waited to check in, a couple turned around and after a moment's hesitation the man asked: 'Mr. Jones? Mrs. Jones? It's me. Shirish. Shirish Desai.' Shirish had been the accountant at the Athenaeum Hotel while Ron was general manager in the 1980s. He and his wife, Narissa, were holidaying at the Serena Beach. The fact that they had left London to live in Dallas some years before, made it an even more unexpected reunion.

'Finally aboard Royal Viking Sun, the Beatles song "Here Comes the Sun" is broadcast over the open decks as it is every time the Sun sails.

'My first presentation focused on Thanksgiving and which wines best complement the traditional turkey dinner. I told them turkey is a pretty accommodating bird – it'll fly with almost anything – but once you stuff it, dress it, garnish it, sauce it, and surround it with the profusion of flavours of cranberries, succotash, sweet potatoes et al, everything changes. Suggested a good upfront California cabernet or Chardonnay (red or white is fine with this meal); for the antipodean passengers a ripe and fruity Ozzie Shiraz; for the rich Brits, an aged claret, and for ourselves a *Clos Vougeot* wouldn't go amiss but hold the trimmings.

'After a stop in Durban, South Africa, we went ashore in Cape Town to escort a shore excursion to the Cape wine lands.

'Then the rare treat of six days at sea while we crossed the South Atlantic to Rio.

(Several days later)

'At noon today we were half-way into our ocean crossing when the captain announced an SOS from an oil tanker with a first mate who had been badly injured. They had no doctor on board. We did, plus a team of nurses and an operating theatre. Royal Viking Sun turned around and headed for the ship in distress. Captain expected to reach it around midnight.

'At 1am the sea was so rough our ship couldn't get closer than a mile and a half to the tanker. Two seaman volunteers (and dozens did volunteer) accompanied the doctor on a dangerous and heart-rending mission in a small lifeboat. They returned with the injured seaman and stretchered him on board with difficulty. You could hear the poor man's screams all over the decks. He had fallen eighteen feet off a ship's ladder, had a broken leg and severe burns.

'Our ship's doctor operated straight away, and by the time we enquired next morning, the patient was resting peacefully. We took him to Rio, and from there he was airlifted home. To Norway. The seaman was Norwegian and spoke no English. Our ship's doctor was Swedish and all the nurses were – Norwegian!

'Even after sailing twelve hours out of our way, the Sun docked in Rio only a fraction later than scheduled.'

A year later we were headed again to the Royal Viking Sun when another of those 'all's well that ends well' journeys threatened to put paid to our cruise. Eve wrote to our agent Philip Gosling.

'This cruise did not begin well. We had barely settled into the car taking us to Heathrow early in the morning (and you may have heard: I don't do mornings) when Ron, in that irritating way husbands have, asked "You do have the tickets darling?" Now, I am the woman who might have *invented* the expression "spectacles, testicles, wallet and watch" (except that I always seem to be missing something.) As an experienced traveller I do not appreciate being asked to double-check something as routine as tickets.

"Of course I have the tickets," I snapped.

'We felt happier when we were upgraded at Heathrow and crossed the Atlantic comfortably ensconced in Club World using Air Miles tickets. Our friends Jack and Mary Daniel, who ran a hotel in San Francisco, were at the airport to meet us and we went straight out to dinner. They dine at six, hangovers at 7.30.

'Pasta half way to my mouth I suddenly suffered one of those moments when your whole life flashes before your eyes. "I *don't* have the tickets." Hit me like the proverbial ton of bricks. If I had them, they would be in the black leather case I *always* keep tickets in. I knew they weren't there.

'Next day, a Saturday morning, we looked up the phone number of the docks, the port authority, Cunard in New York, Cunard in Miami, Cunard's representative in San Francisco (whose names and details were of course on the tickets.) Nothing. Zilch. Zero. Or as we were soon to learn in Mexico – *nada*. Those we did find were closed for the weekend.

'Nothing for it but to walk around San Francisco singing "Has anybody seen our ship?" We found it, not at Pier 39 or Pier 45, where it usually docks, but at Pier 31, a long way away. We would have asked somebody, except Ron recalled the old Liverpool joke where somebody says "Excuse me, where's the urinal?" and gets the reply "'Ow many funnels does it 'ave, wack?" Fortunately, Royal Viking Sun does stand out, and the hour's walk to Fisherman's Wharf via Union Street no doubt did us good.

'It had been a beautiful cool, sunny morning. Halfway along Fisherman's Wharf the skies opened and we were soaked in minutes. Ron found a stall that sold him a collapsible umbrella for me and a yellow polythene rain-cover for himself. He looked like a walking condom. I strode ahead to find somebody in authority, concerned they might think he was with me.

'A helpful pair of stevedores sent me to the Port Manager's Office. Nice Mr. Al Prat, for that was his name, ushered me about quarter of a mile to the RVS gangway. Nice Philippino security guy waved me, ticketless and with no proof of identity, on board. Easy as that. Colin Parker, our favourite cruise director was in his office. He issued a slip that said "welcome on board" or words to that effect.

'Moral No. 1: Speakers who leave their tickets behind pay the price.

'Moral No. 2: It's easier than you think in the late 1990s to walk on board a supposedly tight-security ship.

'Our presentations went down well, including Ron's three and my two new ones *The Night They Invented Champagne* and *Wine and Food Workshop*.

'Favourite Mexican port this trip was Puerto Vallarta, a resort that may draw us back. Only partly because it boasts *three* Sergio Bustamante galleries. We treated each other to some stunning jewellery and cufflinks for half the price it would cost in the U.S. So tempted by his wonderful sculptures, too – Salvador Dali meets Nikki de St. Phalle – but they're too big to carry home and *where* would we put them?

'Two grand days in breezy San Francisco before we flew home. Now it's back to "auld claes 'n parritch" and a three-foot stack of mail, cards, messages, faxes. Nobody to cook, serve or wash up.

'I wish we hadn't sacked the maid and the butler before we left...'

As we accepted more – and longer – invitations to fill guest lecture spots on a variety of ships, our 'turnarounds' became almost as efficient as the ships'.

We disembarked from Arcadia in Southampton one Saturday morning in July and returned to our apartment in the Barbican to change, open mail and re-pack. By 4pm we were welcomed aboard Silver Wind at Tower Pier, a ten-minute walk from home. She is probably the most beautiful of the fifteen ships we cruised on; spacious suites, exquisite food and mostly outstanding service.

The cruise would take us with a handful of other British and 150 American passengers, all around the British Isles, down the west coast to Cornwall, up to the Highlands and Islands, and home via Edinburgh.

The Americans enjoyed Eve's talk on the whiskies of Scotland and even more, the tasting afterwards.

We took in the best of British scenery as one perfect summer's day followed another, enjoyed the welcome of a maiden visit to Fowey, looked out at the Castle of Mey and thought fondly of the Queen Mother, whose home it had been, and trudged over the heather on the Isle of Skye for yet another whisky tasting in Dunvegan Castle. First-time visitors to our country couldn't believe they could read books on deck in broad daylight close to midnight. 'Is the weather always like this in summer?' they marvelled. We didn't feel even a twinge of guilt as we replied, 'But of course!'

The ship's doctor was a bantamweight Italian in his thirties. Every day at noon he appeared by the pool in fashionably abbreviated swim trunks. He made his regulation once-round-the-poolside strut before executing a perfect swallow dive into the water. A couple of swift laps were followed by another head-high circuit of the poolside, nodding and smiling to a bevy of simpering, taut-faced elderly ladies. They worshipped him. We began to suspect they took it in turns to get 'sick'. Usually in the night. You'd hear them at breakfast next day: 'I had real bad stomach cramps/nausea/faintness/pain. Piero came up and gave me a shot (usually in what they call 'the butt') and I feel just *fine*.' We'd have given anything to know what it was he 'shot'. Vitamin E? Some magic concoction of his own? It seemed to work for whatever ailed them.

We never got to try the 'shots' but we did get to enjoy his company when he invited us to join him for dinner. Positively preening in summer whites, he told us in halting but competent English that he was 'Italian second, *Tuscan* first.' He even issued a cordial invitation to visit. Eve asked if he was married. 'No,' he said, 'No wife. Not yet.' Fiancée then? 'Ah *si*. Several. I am *Tuscan*. Is normal, no?'

Piero stopped teasing when he was persuaded to talk about his career. He had been an Air Force doctor, and specialised in surgery under hypnosis. 'Only on volunteers,' he assured us. He had, he said, performed many operations on air force pilots, with a success rate that caused much surprise and fierce controversy. He hoped, after his sabbatical year as ship's doctor, to return to this work.

While *il Dottore* added interest and the Italian equivalent of *joie de vivre* to the cruise, the restaurant maitre d' ensured it didn't go to our heads. We got off to a bad start. We arrived on board to find an invitation in our suite; would Mr. and Mrs. Jones please join the chief engineer for dinner. After the captain's 'welcome aboard' cocktail reception, we presented ourselves at the dining room and told the maitre d' who stood unmoving behind his desk, of our invitation. 'The chief engineer doesn't usually dine before 8.30pm,' he told us. We said we'd come back. Regarding us with undisguised suspicion, he said. '*Who* did you say you were?' Ron told him again.

'I don't know you. Do you have your invitation?' No, we replied, why should that be necessary? Was there a problem?

With less charm and more coldness than we imagined *any* Italian capable of, he told us, 'you have made a mistake. I am not expecting you.' Ron told him we'd take a seat on the sofa outside the restaurant and leave him to sort it out. The cruise director, on his way into the dining room, caught sight of us and asked if we were waiting for someone or if he could help. We explained, as matter-of-factly as we knew how, and without complaint, what had happened and why we were waiting. He spoke with the maitre d' and returned with an apology.

'I am so sorry and very embarrassed. It seems the invitation was delivered to the wrong Mr. and Mrs. Jones. The couple dining with the chief engineer are regular cruisers and well known to the maitre d'. I'm afraid he hasn't dealt with it very well, and I can only hope you will overlook such a bad start to your cruise.'

Of course we did. Alas, the maitre d' did not. He refused to speak to us, seat us or acknowledge us for the entire two weeks at sea. Catching sight of us, he would turn his head aside and sniff, like a six-year-old in a huff. After a few days of this Eve tried to reason with him and suggested he let bygones be bygones and make a fresh start. His reply was an outraged squeak. 'Your husband accused me of not doing my job!' After Ron's half a century in the hospitality business and a reputation for diplomacy, we had no idea where *that* came from, but we refused to let it spoil our trip.

The captain and officers were Italian, most from Sicily. Handsome. Charming. Charismatic. At least, Eve thought so. Ron revised his opinion one morning as he posed the question 'How many sailors does it take to float a lifeboat?' In this case the answer was 'too many, too long, too bad!' We watched with a group of anxious passengers while a dozen men wrestled with the boat until it hit the water – and the impact broke a window. Lucky it was only a drill.

The George Cross island of Malta is a popular port of call. We grew fond of the island when we were visiting lecturers at the Institute of Tourism Studies. We arrived on this trip on Remembrance Sunday, one that would be engraved in our memories from unpromising beginning to perfect end.

We left the ship early, anticipating a romantic ride in a horse-drawn carriage to the cathedral for the special service. Half-way there, our driver was turned back by an ill-tempered policeman clearing the streets for parades of ex-servicemen, boy scouts, girl guides, cubs, brownies et al. The whole place looked deserted; we'd come early on purpose, but rules are rules.

By this time the driver was as angry as the policeman because he had to take a two-mile detour on the nearest thing Malta has to a motorway. The horse flattened his ears, frothed at the mouth and bolted. Eve was hysterical. Ours must have been the only horse and carriage in the world to maintain a steady forty miles an hour. The racket was deafening. Traffic to the right of us. Traffic to the left of us. Traffic in front and behind. Nobody seemed to find it *odd* that a horse and carriage, a cursing driver brandishing a whip and two passengers with hands covering their heads were careening along the motorway. They just found it a darn nuisance, leaned on their horns and barely swerved to avoid us.

The horse took the main roundabout at a gallop and slowed a little on the hill that led back up towards the old city and the church. We sat in a queue of traffic for twenty minutes, the poor horse still lathered and panting. Passengers too. The service was due to begin in five minutes. 'How far to walk?' we asked the driver. 'Just over there,' he said, pointing ahead. 'Two, three minutes.'

We climbed down on legs that still trembled and started walking. Ten minutes later we were still walking. We could see the church spire way in the distance. We jogged the last quarter mile, and arrived out of breath midway through the service, just as the congregation was about to stand for the two-minute silence. *This* is what we had come for and we gave thanks we had arrived in time – and alive.

That evening, as the ship sailed out of Valetta Harbour, the sun setting over our port bow, the captain held a service of Remembrance on the open deck. We all stood as the George Cross island receded into the distance, saying farewell with a hymn and a prayer at the end of a day we won't forget.

We try to make time to attend some form of worship while we are at sea. Mostly it's the non-denominational Sunday service, but it may just as easily be the Episcopalian or a Catholic Mass, or Friday-evening Shabbat service. For us, it is as much as anything else a time out for quiet contemplation and giving thanks.

On most ships the non-denominational Sunday service consists of forty-five minutes of readings, hymns and prayer, but now and again you may encounter what we christened a 'happy-clappy-Cappy' whose service can be more like a revivalist meeting. We arrived a few moments late for one of those and were obliged to take seats near the stage. Big mistake. An hour into the service, with boisterous singing, a tearful testimony from the ship's comic, and the captain clearly relishing every moment of his once-a-week chaplaincy, we found it impossible to edge our way out without possible offence to the captain. So we stayed, prayed and swayed to the bitter end.

16

Salute to the Queen

Our favourite ship? QE2, first, last and always! It is QE2, you'll notice, or Queen Elizabeth Two. *Not* QEII or Queen Elizabeth the Second. Touchy subject: while the ship was built with great pride on the Clyde, the Scots take exception to Her Majesty, who launched the vessel, being called Queen Elizabeth the Second because there never was a Queen Elizabeth the First of Scotland. QE2 it is, then.

She is a properly ship-shaped ship, one of the last. There are floating hotels, floating casinos, floating gin palaces and fun-liners. Most of them top-heavy, ugly vessels, wedge-shaped and looking out of place in all but the gaudiest ports. To watch the monster Seven Seas Voyager dominate the Grand Canal in Venice, overshadowing the waterfront and skyline of the most glorious of cities, is to understand that mass tourism and in particular mass cruise tourism, has gone too far. How can you compare those giants – and we include the new Queen Mary 2 – with the classic, seaworthy lines of QE2 and a few of the remaining smaller ships like *Saga Rose, Silver Wind* and the Seabourne vessels?

When QE2 sets out from New York for the three-month marathon world cruise, a new team of white-flannelled, navy-blazered 'gentlemen hosts' prepares for the onslaught of mature movers, the bickering of bridge partners and, judging by the occasional permanent pairings, the possibility of romance. It's a good gig for a mature man of outgoing nature who likes to dance and play bridge, enjoys the company of ladies and makes a presentable escort. In return he pays a nominal amount to an agent who arranges a berth.

QE2 is an expensive ship, and the regulars consider themselves members of the most exclusive club at sea. One lady from New York goes one better. She might be called the 'Queen Bea' because she *lives* on QE2. She is a feisty, well tailored octogenarian, and finds it less expensive than checking into luxury sheltered accommodation in New York. Her cabin is a modest inside one, on a lower deck, but it doesn't matter, because she doesn't spend much time in it. She is, she says, having the time of her life. Exotic ports of call. Bridge every day at sea. A troupe of distinguished gents to dance with if she wishes. Invitations to captain's and officers' receptions most evenings. And visits from her family who join her on board from time to time.

We overheard Beatrice complain one day to the purser's office – about what, we have no idea. We only know she concluded, straight-faced, with: 'No doubt about it. *This ship is going down...*'

Not that seniority is always a guarantee of dignified behaviour. Another regular cruiser could be seen around the pool most mornings, in full view of the cafe. She was South American and seventy, but clinging limpet-like to thirty-nine. She wore – almost – a string bikini, straps lowered to half-mast to reveal most of a pair of formidable southbound bosoms, and a thong that disappeared as though into an ageing walnut. The face was feline, the brow botoxed into unmoving submission, lips collagen-enlarged into such a trout-pout she was unable to close her mouth or smile. She spread herself on a lounger and sunbathed looking nuder than nude and ten times as rude.

An Australian at the next table gasped. 'Thank God I've finished my breakfast! Now I'm going ashore to buy a mirror like the one she uses...'

Yet for us, QE2 has always been full of special people – both passengers and crew. We were constantly meeting old friends from previous cruises, from other ships, and from unexpected places. We felt an instant kinship with a jolly lady who was introduced to us as 'Lady Marian'. She had a Deep South accent and we were intrigued. 'I used to say Maid Marian,' she explained, 'but I've lived too full a life. You should know, Ron, that I am a member of your club. I'm an OBE.'

'Really?' said Ron.

'Oh yeah,' she came back. 'Over Bloody Eighty'.

She is also, we discovered, the sister of one of our old friends in New Orleans, Col. Albert Wetzel. Marian is a widow and one evening confessed: 'my husband's been gone thirteen years now, and I take this cruise most years. Every morning I look up to Heaven and tell him: "Sorry darlin'. I miss you, but I *love* being independent. And by the way – thank you for the money.'

The special people all stand out for different reasons. It makes us ashamed to admit our hearts sank in the Queen's Grill, QE2's top restaurant, when our charming, fun and sophisticated neighbours Gerald Tarantino and Alfred Steinel disembarked in Honolulu. We were told their place would be taken by a family with two 'lively' young boys. The maitre d' said this with a perfectly straight face, but we knew him well enough to take this as a kind of warning that all might not be as tranquil as we'd become accustomed to.

That afternoon, as we stood in line for a cab to take us to the Royal Palm Hotel, a boy who overheard us arranging to share the taxi with a fellow passenger, looked us in the eye and remarked: 'I hope you guys are not booked into a suite at the Royal Palm. Lemme warn you – they are *small*.' He told us he'd stayed there overnight prior to boarding the ship and was not impressed. Another lad we assumed to be his brother contradicted him forcefully, and we jumped into a cab to get out of earshot of the bickering match that ensued.

You guessed it – that was the family. Into dinner they trooped, ebullient mother, elegant godmother, *the boy* and an older brother. We think it must have been about 8.30pm when we began to eat our words. And, man, they tasted *good*! The Shamel family are from North Carolina and they just might have been the world's most fun table companions.

Mother Malinda and godmother Janet had come along to supervise the schooling, on this world cruise, of fourteen-year-old Benjamin and Sam, then eleven. Ben was a delight, a young gentleman-in-the-making who wore his tuxedo with as much élan as he carried off the inevitable American teeth-braces. He developed in charm and wit as the voyage went on, and soon it was hard for us to keep up with him. Sam was, well, eleven. He showed remarkable patience and resilience in dressing up in smart suit, bow tie and waistcoat most nights when he would – naturally – rather have been playing pool or computer games with his friends.

Shore excursions were educational, homework done diligently every day with assignments and projects set for both boys. Malinda, Janet and their friend Warner worked hard setting projects and overseeing homework to compensate for the boys being taken out of school for the most exclusive 'home schooling' in the world! We missed them when we disembarked in Sydney.

On the same cruise were two Spanish sisters from Valladolid. When they came aboard in Southampton their English was limited. Every week they spoke a little more and a little better. Until, that is, the day after both of us had presentations in the theatre. These were relayed throughout the day on the ship's in-cabin television.

Teresa and Carmen caught up with us in the cruise terminal in Melbourne:

'Eve. Oh Eve. You look so *bad* on TV. We saw you. Is true. You are *ugly*.' They must have seen how taken aback we were, so not to play favourites, they turned to Ron. 'You, too, Ron. You both *so ugly*.' Unable to keep straight faces we gently explained that a more diplomatic way to express it would be 'the lighting did not flatter you. The TV did not do you justice.' At least, we hoped that's what they meant...

QE2, like Royal Viking Sun, had not only the best cruise director in Colin Parker, but also one of the world's great hotel managers, John Duffy. He is an affable Liverpudlian who oversees a staff of 830 and looks after up to 1,750 guests at a time. For four to six months he has few days off, endures long separations from his family, yet he has been in the job twenty-three years. He loves it – and it shows!

Ask John how he is and the answer is a full-beam grin and 'Never better, thanks' or 'Just wonderful. How are *you?*' We've never seen him look frazzled or tired, he always has time to stop for a brief chat along the several miles of corridors on twelve decks under his supervision. He has a down-to-earth good humour and a feet-on-the-ground approach to the haughty and the naughty who come into his orbit.

'There isn't another ship like the Queen. And there are no other guests like the Queen's guests! I've got to know so many of them over the years, and it's my job to make sure they don't want to go to any other ship.'

What makes this hotel manager's job so different is his captive audience. 'They are with you for five meals a day and up to four months at a time. You accommodate them and feed them, you entertain them and look after their health and well-being. And that's just the passengers. There's the crew to look after, too, some of them on the ship for seven months at a stretch.

'Every hotel or restaurant ashore has busy nights and quiet nights. Diners arrive separately, over two or three hours. We can have a thousand dinner guests entering our main restaurants within an hour.'

The most fortunate diners are looked after by maitre d' Andrew Nelder. If we owned a restaurant, Nelder would be the man to run it. Add

Denis Burchill and you'd have the dream team. The Queen's Grill may be the official top tomato of the ship's five formal and two informal restaurants, but the plush Princess Grill is first choice for foodies when Andrew and Denis are in charge.

Prodigious as Nelder's knowledge of food and wine is, we thought we had stumped him over the sexual mores of the plant *chicoreum intybus*. We were assured by a couple of Michelin three-star chefs at the height of the nouvelle cuisine revolution that the sweet radicchio is the female of the species, and the bitter-leaf version the male. We swallowed the story along with the radicchio.

Nelder took the view that 'the answer lies in the soil' and all depends on where the plant is grown. Plausible, but further research revealed that early or late picking accounts for flavour difference. As, of course, does the species of radicchio.

None of us have been able to confirm the male and female theory. Sooner or later one side or the other is going to have to give way, when the ship's charities, for which passengers and crew work hard to raise money during the world cruise, will benefit by fifty dollars.

Deepak, one of our favourite Princess Grill waiters, is a native of Nepal, the land of Kanchenjunga and Mount Everest. The proud son of a Ghurka soldier, he told us 'My Dad always hoped I would follow him into the Ghurkas, but I chose a three-year hotel management course instead. Now I'm working on QE2 I can tell him: "Yes, Dad, I kept my promise. I am serving the Queen..."'

On one of several Christmas Days on Cunarders we anchored off Grenada by accident.

No, QE2's captain didn't get lost. A heavy swell prevented our scheduled visit to Tobago, which was a pity since we had arranged to meet neighbours from London who were spending a holiday there. Instead, we made an unscheduled visit to Grenada, and we must say the islanders took it pretty well. How would *you* like two thousand uninvited guests dropping in for the day?

Taxi driver Finba McQueen took us on a three-hour tour. It might have taken two hours had he not stopped half a dozen times to pass the time of day with drivers going in the other direction. 'Everybody a friend on this island,' he explained. 'If they not friends, they family.'

With a population of 95,000 on 120 square miles, that's quite a family! The islanders are proud of their British heritage, and America-friendly, too. You still see graffiti proclaiming *'God Bless You America'* and *'Thank you God and Thank You USA'* referring to the 1983 Cuban invasion when US medical students were taken hostage. Things are different now. The new state-of-the-art hospital was built by – Cuba. Grenada achieved independence in 1973 and Finba was at pains to explain, 'We celebrate with a wonderful Carnival, but we hold it in August so as not to clash with Trinidad's in February.'

After Grenada we awoke to the juicy green hills of Dominica off our port bow. It was just cool enough in the early morning to walk sixteen laps of the deck before going ashore, Walkmans tuned in to a local radio talk show. It was New Year's Eve and most callers wanted to 'praise the Lord Jesus for a good year passing'. Our favourite though, was the man who looked forward to celebrating 'twenty-three years of marriage to my best friend.' They were expecting a child in March. 'Your first?' asked the female talk-show host.

'Oh, no-ooo.' said the caller with some pride. 'Just the first with my wife.'

When our ship reached the Philippines the Japanese fleet followed us into Manila harbour. We weren't sure it was the Rising Sun on the flag until we spied a group of elderly Japanese ladies on deck waving what appeared to be their underwear at the white-uniformed young sailors lined up like rows of skittles. Closer inspection revealed the ladies to be waving silk scarves.

Ron confessed to a feeling of déjà vu when one, then two, then more frigates glided alongside our ship. Last time he saw that many at one time, he was wearing a tin hat ready for business on the British battleship King George V. This, we were assured, was a friendly visit.

We returned to St. Helena 'the island the world forgot' for the second time in six months. Seven hundred miles from its nearest neighbour Ascension Island (also the nearest airport) and 1,300 from the west coast of Africa, St. Helena – the islanders pronounce it St. Hel-een-a not St. Hell-ena – is the most remote community in the world.

Napoleon lived out his exile there. It may have looked a bleak and unfriendly place from the sea, but inland and over the mountains the island is lush with wildflowers and waterfalls. Napoleon's house and the garden he designed are open to visitors, as is the site of his (empty) tomb, a particularly beautiful spot.

The islanders are friendly and open people, English speaking but an exotic ethnic mix. They delight in visitors – even an invasion of a thousand from two ships on two consecutive days.

Schoolchildren put on an impromptu performance of song and dance; the church holds a welcoming service for visitors whatever day of the week it happens to be; and taxis here have a fixed price, no haggling. The car may be a dilapidated Chevrolet pick-up or an old Ford fit for stock-car racing but with a driver-guide so proud of his island, you leave determined to return – as we did and hope to do again.

The Queen enjoys the warmest welcomes of any ship in ports around the world, yet some of her send-offs have been just as remarkable. One of them had our hosts running for cover.

We were poised to sail away in the evening after a maiden visit to Lautoka in Fiji. A thousand passengers stood at the ship's rails to witness a rousing farewell from the police band. They marched in formation in navy blue military jackets trimmed with red and gold, no hats, and calf-length white skirts with pointed hems that looked as if they'd been cut with giant pinking shears.

As six o'clock approached the band played rousing marches, show tunes, even an Elvis Presley medley. Finally, on the dot of six, the conductor announced 'our special Fijian song of farewell'. We all joined in the sentimental 'Now Is the Hour'. Scarcely a dry eye on deck.

The ship didn't move. The rain was pelting down and the bandsmen, sodden, abandoned the formation marches, packed away their electrical equipment and took shelter under a canvas canopy. Still they played. Still the ship didn't move.

The band was running out of repertoire. What they did play became more and more tentative and off-key. They turned their sheet music back to page one and repeated marches they'd played half-an-hour before. At 6.20pm the bandmaster turned to face the Queen, pointed out to sea and, arms flailing but still beaming, mimed. 'Go! Please! Just *go*'.

Finally, half an hour late, the band paused and the bandmaster raised his baton high in the air. The band played three mighty chords and a drum-roll. Right on cue, QE2's magnificent whistle sounded. The band struck one last – unrehearsed – chord. Our captain matched it once again. The Fiji police band will not forget QE2's maiden visit.

Departures brought a few personal dramas, too.

QE2 docked overnight in Laem Chabang in Thailand, about half an hour from the beach resort of Pattaya. For both days passengers were given the run of the facilities of the Royal Garden Hotel and Resort – which Ron, as former general manager of the Royal Garden Hotel in London, was unable to resist. In the business centre we were plied with iced water, coffee, pastries and exotic crystallised fruits.

The outdoor pool and tropical gardens were extensive enough to accommodate the hotel's and ship's guests with space to spare. We ate lunch at the pool bar, half-submerged (us, that is, not lunch) in cool water with the air temperature at thirty-five degrees (93F). When all that felt too much like hard work, we slipped away for a Thai massage.

We were introduced to the hotel's resident manager Bjorn Richardson, a broad-shouldered young Swede with a military background. He was a hands-on manager who clearly believed people come before paperwork, so we had much in common.

We returned to the ship for sailaway at 6pm.

At 5.15pm Eve discovered she had left an irreplaceable floppy disk in the hotel's business centre. A $12-a-minute ship-to-shore phone call to Bjorn Richardson provided just the kind of challenge he likes. 'I'll find it and put it in a taxi,' he said. 'It should get there in forty-five minutes.' Eve explained the gangway would be lifted at 5.45 but Bjorn insisted he could do it, even in the Pattaya version of the rush hour. 'Forget the taxi. I'll put it on a motor bike.'

As 6pm approached QE2's security officer stationed himself at the foot of the gangway and held off instructions to lift it. At 6.07pm as the gangway began to part company with the dock, the ship's agent ran up with an envelope grabbed from a motorcycle messenger. He in turn tossed it to our security officer who returned it to its grateful owners like a baton in some surreal relay race.

Our grateful thanks were brushed aside. All part of the QE2 service.

Trying to keep up with the demands of two homes and a small business while travelling is a complication that goes with the territory. Mail can be sent care of the ship's port agent anywhere in the world, but getting the timing right for the one day you're docked there can be a hit or miss affair. We're fortunate to have friends in most of the major ports who offer forwarding addresses for our bundles of mail and hand them over when we arrive.

For urgent correspondence QE2 has a computer learning centre with twenty PCs, and twice-daily classes. For the remainder of the twenty-four hours, passengers may use the computers for a dollar a minute, to send and receive e-mails. However, anybody serious about working while they cruise uses the ship's business center, the best-kept secret on board. We never knew quite how they managed it, but in all our years on QE2, this has been staffed by the kindest, most even-tempered, efficient team of pursers at sea. In that quiet room with just three PCs it's like having your own office complete with secretarial assistance.

Most, but by no means all, passengers who used the service are polite and appreciative, but now and again we marvelled at the staff's ability to take it on the chin when guests lost their temper. As Claire, a Yorkshire lass, put it after an angry lady shouted at her colleague:

'That woman! She went through Michael for a short-cut!'

Humour invariably saved the day, and if you read this Bernadette, Pierre, Michael and all you others, including the Information Technology officers who were called in to save more than one chapter of various manuscripts – thank you for enabling us to get this far!

Saying farewell to QE2 after a long cruise is always a wrench. The p-word is on everybody's lips. Suitcases are hauled down from the top of the wardrobe, trunks returned from the baggage master. Mouths turn down instead of up at the corners. Sunbathers lie prone on the upper decks, uncovering only those bits that can stand the cold, to eke out the last dregs of watery sunshine.

Anyone who has cruised for more than a couple of weeks knows that however many spare bags you brought, you are now up against Joneses' Second Law of Packing: *new acquisitions into old suitcases won't go*. You haul out the bulging shopping bags stashed at the top of wardrobes and confront the gifts you bought for next Christmas. Clever planning, bargains all, but who on earth were they for? And those souvenirs you haggled over in Asian or African ports and bore proudly back to the ship, as hunters must once have dragged their antelope or rhinoceros heads. Where in your already cramped home are you going to put them? Who can you give them to? What on earth possessed you?

Ah well, nothing for it. If you'll excuse us, we really must get down to that p---ing.'

Part Three

A la Carte

17

After Claridge's

A wise friend in the hospitality industry had good advice when Ron 'changed direction' after Claridge's.

You will have plenty of opportunities for consultancy', he said. 'Pick and choose. Don't feel you always have to say yes. And count on having a window of about two years in which to make your mark.'

With that in mind, we set out to

a) get our first books written and published
b) capitalise on half a century's experience
c) take on the assignments that appealed to us and would provide the challenge we need, and
d) accept as many lecturing invitations as possible, especially those involving travel.

The first of those we ticked off our list in 1997 with the publication of 'Grand Hotelier: Behind the Scenes in Britain's Best Hotels'. This was followed in 1998 by an expanded paperback edition 'Grand Hotelier: Inside the Best Hotels', and in 2000 by 'Gastromania!'.

Ron was awarded a visiting fellowship at Oxford Brookes University and an honorary doctorate from Derby University, which enabled him to maintain contact with young people and keep up to date with the academic as well as the practical aspects of their training.

The assignments that came our way varied enormously. Almost without exception, each was more enjoyable and rewarding than the last – at least in retrospect. The important thing is that they kept coming in long after our two-year 'window' might have been closed. From a starting point of finding it difficult to say 'no' lest we wouldn't be asked again, after the first year we felt comfortable turning down invitations. We became more laid-back about whether others would follow.

The trouble was, they did! If you find yourself in this position, don't assume that if you increase the price it will put people off and save you from having to say 'no'. Human psychology being what it is, that doesn't always work. The more we increased our fees, (without asking more than we considered fair) the more work was offered. Potential clients assume if you price yourself and your work high, then you must be good.

We were called in as the major building programme got under way that would transform the Priory Bay Hotel on the Isle of Wight into one of the leading country house hotels in the south, with a first-rate restaurant.

At first sight the words 'curate' and 'egg' came to mind – and the 'good' could be applied to only a few parts at that. Once you drove past the holiday camp at the bottom of the driveway and the motley collection of utilitarian outbuildings, the location was promising and the seventy acres of grounds could be impressive. On the other hand, its own previous incarnation as a holiday camp had left a legacy of crumbling mansion, self-catering accommodation in peeling, rendered cottages, an outdoor pool that looked rancid, and a nine-hole golf course below the standard of the poorest municipal course.

The owner had spent part of his childhood on the island, and after selling his company in London, invested in his dream hotel. His lawyer brother joined him as business partner, his long-time friends, neighbours, and sailing chums on the island welcomed the venture with the promise of business. A London interior designer friend worked on the rooms. There was still a long way to go.

The Brief

- To assess the projected operation and recommend consultancy input for the first year.
- To suggest the way forward to gain the highest possible hotel guide ratings.
- To train the young manager to top country-house hotel standards.
- To assist in recruiting and training a team that would provide the level of service anticipated by the owner.
- To introduce operating systems, job descriptions, appraisal schemes and manuals for each department.

The Challenges

A young local manager had been appointed. He had great charm and intelligence, but no hospitality experience or training. What he and the owners did share was boundless enthusiasm and energy and a dogged determination to succeed. Their native wit and intelligence, we knew, would see them through.

There were times when we wondered if that would be enough. There were times when we argued. The owners had their hearts set on a French chef, the most *nouvelle* of cuisine, and prices to match. We counseled a good British chef to prepare unpretentious but exciting British food. Fresh fish and seafood, prime beef, local poultry and game prepared and served simply and without the 'two ingredients too many' that mar so much fashionable cuisine designed more for the stimulation of the chef than the palate of the consumer. They argued that the local clientele already had access to the best of British and were up for something more sophisticated. We wondered if the populace was ready for French cuisine served in small portions with elaborate garnishes at London prices. We were both right as it turned out. It took a while, and we still believe the hotel would have taken off more quickly had they kept things simple, but the brothers stuck to their gastronomic guns and Priory Bay did take its place among the island's finest dining venues – many say the finest.

The chef, imported from France as was his kitchen brigade, proved the usual mix of talented and difficult. He was fortunate to be indulged as much as he was, and needed encouragement to ensure the kitchens were as pristine as his cuisine.

A deputy manager was appointed, this time with experience but little leadership ability and setting an inadequate example in standards of appearance. Friends or acquaintances without experience and often without references filled other posts. Attention was concentrated on 'top dressing', while back of house areas and equipment were neglected.

Bedrooms were decorated simply and stylishly, and priced at a level affordable by the well heeled of fashionable Fulham and their offspring. Priory Bay would be a family hotel, and with its self-catering cottage accommodation upgraded, the brothers were confident it would attract the younger stockbrokers and merchant bankers and financial analysts tired of the annual summer traipse to Tuscany or the Dordogne. With the Isle of Wight less than three hours door to door from SW3, the Cowes Regatta and other annual events to guarantee a full house during the season, and good sailing weather if not assured then always possible, their predictions proved spot on.

The Solutions

Much of our work focused on staff training; setting up workable systems and introducing operations manuals that would enable everyone involved to see the direction in which Priory Bay must go in order not only to attract the right clientele but also to ensure they returned.

The property's uniqueness came from the location, the food and, we were determined, the warmth and sincerity of the welcome backed up by impeccable personal service. Less sexy but just as essential, was the introduction of guest directories, promotional material, job descriptions and training manuals.

We were concerned that however good the food introduced by the French chef (and it *was* good) it could be let down by a slapdash or indifferent approach in the dining room. A designated member of the management team, we urged, should be on hand at all times to take overall responsibility for the restaurant, and not be afraid to make his or her presence felt.

An operations manual for the dining room attempted to set attainable standards while not imposing unrealistic demands on young and inexperienced staff:

Guest Relations and Communications

How to be a star!

Guests – customers – come to Priory Bay in the same way as an audience goes to the theatre. The 'stage' is the dining room or the bar. You have already set the stage by laying-up the tables, or setting-up the bar. Now your audience expects from you a *performance* on your 'stage', not just an *appearance*.

The difference?

An 'appearance' is when you walk diffidently into the bar, timidly say good evening, and 'Would you like to see the menu?' (Of course they'd like to see the menu – that's why they're here.)

A 'performance' is when you stride up to the customer, a smile on your face (which makes *them* feel immediately more relaxed) and confidently say 'Good evening Mr. X or Mrs. Y (because you have already found out the name, haven't you?) Let me leave the menu with you. The chef has some wonderful special dishes on tonight. They are…'

Your 'audience' comes to be entertained, to be 'sold'.

They deserve your enthusiasm and your genuine care.
- Make sure you know the guest's name.
- Use it.
- Smile!
- Let them see it matters to you that they have a wonderful evening.
- Don't be afraid to show off. If you're proud of your product – the food, the ambience, the service – then let the customer see this and encourage him or her to share in it.

Accentuate the positive – always.
Be positive in your approach, your speech and your body language. If you appear hesitant to the customer, or tentative in the way you approach them, they will not have confidence in you or be excited at the prospect of the evening ahead. They will hesitate to ask or accept your recommendations, and both you and they will be denied the opportunity to make use of your skills.
- Make positive statements rather than questions that allow a 'no' answer. 'Let me leave the menu with you' instead of 'would you like me to leave the menu?' And 'I'll bring you the wine list' or 'Here is our wine list, sir' rather than 'Would you like to see the wine list?'
- Then, 'may I take your order? Or would you like me to tell you a little more about the dishes?' or 'Are you ready to order, Madam/Mrs. Smith, or would you like a few more minutes?'
- Be observant and learn to judge the right moment to make your statement in the midst of general conversation. If somebody is approaching the punch line of a story, then of course you can hover for a moment. But there must come a time when you lean towards the host, politely say excuse me, and ask for their attention.
- When you do ask a question, make it open-ended, one that demands a response. 'How was your meal, sir?' is better than 'I

hope you enjoyed your lunch' because it requires the customer to **tell** you. 'Is there anything I can do for you?' wins hands down over 'Is everything all right?' And never, ever 'was everything OK?'

Be Pro-Active

Anticipation is everything. When you *look* around the dining room or the bar, make sure you *see* everything that is going on. Does anyone look as though they're not having a good time? Not enjoying their cocktail, neglecting their aperitif? Still waiting for food, drinks, condiments or anything they asked for earlier that might have been overlooked? Don't be afraid to catch their eye and ask if there is something you can do for them.

- If there are used glasses on an unoccupied bar table, clear them away. Now! Sounds obvious, but sometimes if you have a routine way of doing things – clearing ashtrays first, *then* wiping down the bar, *then* polishing glasses and only after that removing glasses from tables – change it! **Put yourself in the customers' shoes.** They don't want to sit and look at used glasses and they don't care *whose* job it is to clear them.
- **You** make sure tablecloths are clean, there are no crumbs, the peanuts are on the bar or the tables (in proper, hygienic containers that dispense them unhandled to every customer), the crisps replaced with fresh for each new arrival.
- If diners leave food on the plate, *always* ask if they have enjoyed their meal, and if they hesitate but you suspect a problem, ask if you might bring them something else.
- **You** suggest the things you'd like to sell: a different cocktail, a new house wine, a liqueur coffee. These don't sell themselves and customers who come out to have a good time don't object to recommendations. They can always say no. But they often say yes!
- **Make it your goal to see that every guest or customer feels they've had a little more than they paid for.**
- When you say goodbye leave them with a positive impression. Take for granted that you *will* see them again: 'Thank you for coming. We're looking forward to seeing you again soon.' That's more positive than 'I hope we'll see you again.'

There were similar exercises for other departments such as reception and housekeeping.

The young manager, with whom Ron worked closely that first year, did realise the potential he showed from the outset. The venture is a success. The historic thatched tithe barn in the grounds was transformed into a venue for weddings and smart parties. There is no better restaurant on the island. Self-catering accommodation is booked a year ahead. The golf course and the swimming pool are much improved. The sea laps the bottom of the garden with private moorings for mariner guests. All around are the poshest yacht clubs in the land.

Priory Bay is living proof that (perhaps with just a little help from your consultant friends) first-class small hotels can still be operated successfully by people who learn from the bottom up.

The commute to the Isle of Wight was replaced by an assignment closer to home, for a banqueting operation in London. The venue could accommodate up to nine hundred people for a reception, with banqueting rooms that could seat from fifty to six hundred guests at a seated luncheon or dinner.

The Brief
- To advise and guide the recently-appointed operations manager.
- To improve standards in the operations department.
- To recommend restructuring.
- To present a report based on an overview of all departments.

The Challenges
A new operations manager had been appointed. He was eager to make his mark and even more eager to change everything, especially the existing staff, and surround himself with people he had worked with before.

There was also a new sales manager whose role interfaced with that of the operations manager. The sales manager 'talked the talk', eager to impress but without the wherewithal to back it up. He organized his day around back-to-back meetings. There appeared to be little to show for it. His career with the organisation was destined to be a short one.

To the casual observer, the operation resembled the swan gliding serenely over the surface of a lake. Behind the scenes, as under the water, there was a lot of thrashing about for the perceived results.

Customers were not enjoying the benefits of continuity or linked personal service for their important occasions. Events managers took the bookings and 'nursed' clients through the planning stages. A separate team of floor managers supervised the actual events, by which time the events managers had disappeared from sight. Clients had no opportunity to meet those who would be responsible for the smooth running of their special occasion until face-to-face on the night.

It should not have taken trained observers – but it did – to see that a massive clean-up of the entire premises should take priority. If you're lucky, customers don't look in corners or behind furniture or under staircases or up at light fittings. Consultants do, and the simplest of tasks – a thorough spring clean – was overdue.

As with all new assignments, Ron set about interviewing every key member of staff, from kitchen porters to team leaders, heads of department and managers. It is the consultancy equivalent of a doctor taking the patient's pulse. After a short time with each, you can pick up on the tensions and internal politics, the concerns and the aspirations of people within the organization. You are then better equipped to assess personal potential and address problem areas. Yet you remain sufficiently detached to take a clear overview of the operation.

It was clear that heads of departments were operating in separate compartments, sometimes even in isolation. Communications between the chef and other department heads was unsatisfactory. The cooking could at best be described as ordinary. The service to guests, while efficient, bordered on the indifferent. The warmth of the welcome left a lot to be desired. Repeat business was disappointing.

The Solutions

For the operations manager Ron recommended some tried and tested management techniques, namely 'face-to-face management' and 'management by walking around'. There was no need for significant staff changes, only for bringing out the best in those already there.

'Get out of the office' we suggested, 'and take the trouble to get to know the existing personnel and their capability. Make time every day for a brief, informal chat with all department heads and as many members of staff as possible, while walking around. Look, see and *act* on what your observations tell you.' This would encourage positive response from staff, boost confidence in their leader and in themselves, and pre-empt crises.

Cleanliness front and back of house was tackled in the first instance by a massive spring-clean, improved in the longer term by appointing a chief steward to supervise the leaderless band of cleaners and forge them into a team. The operations manager should have his own weekly formal inspection inside and outside the premises.

We recommended a daily discussion between the operations manager and the chef. Ideally, in the kitchen to allow the manager to observe the work in hand, to test dishes and to encourage the chef and his brigade by showing interest.

Menus and wine lists to be reviewed and updated at regular food and beverage meetings.

The sales manager did not come within our ambit; he would need to feel the touch of a heavy hand from above to re-channel his energies from verbosity into producing positive and measurable results. Our advice would have been to curb the continuous meetings and to observe, *listen*, and learn from those around him who might know a few things he hadn't yet learned.

In the existing set-up, a team of events managers reported to the sales manager, and a team of floor managers to the operations manager. You could clearly see the two teams developing into factions – a burgeoning 'us' and 'them' situation.

The antagonistic attitude between the events managers (who take bookings) and the floor managers (who supervise the events) reminded Ron of the 'hotplate wars' of his early days in hotel kitchens. We suggested that prior to a function, the events manager should introduce the client to the floor manager/s who would be responsible for the smooth running of the event. This would provide continuity for the client and enhance confidence in the organisation.

The vitally important follow-up contact with a view to repeat business should be made with these twin themes of 'continuity' and 'confidence' in mind.

Taking a longer-term view, there was a course of action that would improve relations between the two teams of managers. Events managers and floor managers should exchange roles for one week out of six.

Overall we found pockets of dedication, enthusiasm and sound experience within the organization. Through team-building exercises and sound leadership, the various parts could come together into a cohesive and successful whole.

On a different scale, Ron was invited to look at the catering and banqueting of one of the ancient City of London Livery companies. These are very traditional institutions, the catering overseen in some instances by committee, with an in-house manager, and in others by an outside contractor. In this case, however, catering was handled by the Company via a subsidiary company. The manager of the catering operation organised banquets, in-house dining and events, but his retirement was due within the year.

The Brief

- To recommend a successor to take control of the catering operation.
- To re-appraise the role of functions manager.
- To advise on re-structuring the catering operation.

The Challenges

A decision was needed as to whether the head chef, a capable young man with ambition, was suitable for promotion to a 'chef-patron' role – something that had not been tried before in this or any other Livery Company that we know of. The chef had been working hard to improve his knowledge, taking courses ranging from management to wine studies in anticipation of an enhanced role.

There may have been an assumption that the outgoing manager would be replaced by someone from a similar position in another organisation. The chef, however, in his role as kitchen manager, had delivered an impressive performance. He had greatly improved the food, his kitchen was spotless, his brigade loyal and motivated. He had a confident approach, was keen to progress beyond his traditional role, and we believed his development was far from complete. He had also successfully taken over from the functions manager during holiday periods.

The outgoing manager's knowledge had grown with the job as the job itself had grown in scope. As often happens, he was now confronted by retirement and the imminent need to pave the way for a successor. There had been few formal briefing meetings, no cross-job training or adequate staff appraisal. The appointment and development of a replacement had become a priority.

Little effort had been made to market the Hall's facilities to outside clients; this had not been the way of city Livery companies in the past. However, gross profit was up on the previous year and above budget, even though the premises were infrequently used at weekends. There was potential for improvement.

Solutions

We put forward three options for consideration, and would work with the Company to help introduce whichever they selected.

i. Recruit a new general manager with increased responsibilities, to whom all relevant staff would report.

ii. Appoint the head chef to the new position of head of the catering department.

iii. Out-source the catering operation, with a corresponding reduction in staff costs.

The Company agreed that the second option was the way ahead. The chef would work alongside the functions manager for a trial period of six months, taking sole charge during holidays and sick leave.

To allow the Company to retain the benefit of the outgoing manager's experience, he might return on a part-time basis to help promote the Hall's facilities to a wider, carefully selected, clientele; seek to revive past business; and encourage repeat business from existing clients. There should also be efforts to promote the use of the facilities at weekends for weddings and special parties.

The chef, in his new role as head of catering, should appoint a functions manager who would report to him.

Weekly briefing meetings should be set up and strictly adhered to, along with self-assessment appraisal schemes and carefully monitored cross-job training.

At the time of writing, the chef continues to enjoy great success as Head of Catering, with a Functions Manager reporting to him. Team meetings are held at 10am on every day there is a function. Positive efforts to increase business have resulted in the premises being regularly used at weekends. And the Catering Board has a marketing sub-group.

This was a classic situation in which it might have been easier to continue to operate on the existing and more traditional basis. At the same time, younger people ambitious to progress cannot be held back if they are to be retained, and in this case the right person was waiting in the wings for his own chance to shine.

All credit to an ancient and venerable institution for looking to the future, taking a chance on promoting a very different character, and not being afraid to change its method of operating to bring 'the business side' into the twenty-first century.

✦　✦　✦

While it was Ron's expertise that was called for in the consultancy assignments, the distaff side of Jones & Jones (a temporary name we adopted pending something more creative. Like many such – it stuck.) was not allowed to be idle. We worked together at the discussion and planning stages and in preparing reports and handbooks. Eve offered a different perspective. She had hotel training, was a freelance journalist specialising in hotels, restaurants and travel, and a former hotels inspector.

She had by this time added a new skill to the blend, having 'gone back to school' to take first the Higher Certificate then the Diploma of the Wine & Spirit Education Trust. Designed as a two-year course, Eve awarded herself a sabbatical year and completed the Diploma in one. With the help and encouragement of the lecturers and trainers at the W.S.E.T. in London, she went on to lecture regularly there after she qualified, then to teach Higher Certificate courses at Morley College and Kensington and Chelsea adult education centres.

We became 'twin' visiting lecturers at the Institute of Tourism Studies in Malta. Eve tutored the polite, uniformed students through their Wine & Spirit Trust exam courses. Ron lectured the senior hospitality students on hotel subjects.

Eve was invited to tutor the wine courses at Marlborough College Summer School. For ten years, three weeks in July and August were devoted to teaching adult enthusiasts eager to improve their knowledge of wine. A fresh series of courses had to be designed each year for the students who came back for more! Ron got to join them as 'butler', assistant and chief wine pourer. We joined the Marlborough team along with the inspirational and eccentric summer school director Marek Kwiatkowski, and we left with him a decade later.

We brought granddaughters and goddaughters to participate in the children's activities, enticed students from among our friends in New Orleans and New York, Dallas and California. We each gave annual evening lectures in the College theatre. We don't think the students who shared those wonderful 'learning holidays' will ever surpass the joys of Marlborough as it was in that decade. We certainly won't.

Eve loves to teach, and was flattered and only a little apprehensive when invited to tutor the butlers-in-training at the Ivor Spencer International School for Butlers. Ivor is a legendary toastmaster and his school has been turning out the best butlers in the land for a quarter of a century.

Up to sixteen men and a few women, from widely differing nationalities, age groups, and professional backgrounds attend each course; dental surgeons from Switzerland, private yacht managers from Chile, hospitality executives from all parts of Europe, and students from Australia, Japan and the Middle East. They have been the most charming, impeccably mannered, beautifully turned out and appreciative groups Eve has ever taught.

A few take the course as a sabbatical to learn about the art of the table, how to pack a Louis Vuitton trunk, handle staff and be a perfect host. Others are sent by hotel employers and go back to train the company's in-house butlers. Some become managers of charter yachts, and many graduates secure top butler jobs around the world. The privileged few end up in Buckingham Palace and other royal households. One is a wine steward who looked after us on QE2 and was seeking a new challenge. We recommended the butler training course, he completed it with the proverbial flying colours, and has held a senior position in the cellars of the Royal Household ever since.

We promised ourselves that if and when we become millionaires, then we would hire any one of them as our personal butler!

Of all the assignments, the one that remains closest to our hearts is the Dormy House Hotel.

Ron was appointed a director in 1995, but we both knew Dormy House, its managers and its owners, for many years before Ron retired from Claridge's. We admired Ingrid Phillip-Sorensen as the second beautiful Danish lady we knew (the first is our friend Grete Hobbs, who owned Inverlochy Castle) who with no hotel background or training, simply took a property by the scruff of the neck and made it the most successful of its kind.

Under Ingrid's guidance, and the chairmanship of Phillip Sorensen, Dormy House blossomed from a Cotswold stone farmhouse adjoining a golf course, with a few Scandinavian-style cottages in the grounds, to a hugely successful business. Today, the main house and the stylish single-storey cottages, the Barn Owl bar and brasserie and the more formal dining room, provide one of the cosiest getaway locations in the Cotswolds.

Little do the guests enjoying a quiet weekend realize that behind and completely separate, are the most high-tech conference and banqueting facilities in the English countryside. Self-contained suites have a capacity from twelve, in small meeting rooms, up to 170 in the Dormy Suite with state-of-the-art stage, light and sound facilities. Busy with conferences during the week, the suite at weekends takes on a more romantic guise as the venue for weddings, often the entire 'package' of ceremony, reception and honeymoon.

Ingrid Sorensen, like Ron elected to the ranks of the Master Innholders, retired as managing director, but remains a director, involved in interior design, public relations and guest liaison. She handed over the management reins to general manager David Field, now in his late thirties, who started work at Dormy House as a teenage luggage porter and progressed through the ranks.

Few business activities have given Ron more pleasure than to spend occasional days and nights at Dormy House to keep a finger on the pulse, sit down with staff on a one-to-one basis to discuss their progress and aspirations, and assist the amiable and enthusiastic young manager in any way he can to take Dormy House on to the next stages of its development.

18

California Dreamin'

Any assignment that takes us to the United States is a double delight: an opportunity to explore places we haven't visited before, and to spend time with old friends in familiar places. Even then, new discoveries are always on the menu.

A major travel hiccup resulted in a three-week stay in sun-kissed Santa Monica instead of the eight days we had planned. The bonus time allowed us to discover one of California's best-kept winter vacation secrets and share it with the readers of the New Orleans Times Picayune.

Los Angeles has Beverly Hills, Bel Air, and nearby Westwood, the quirky 'village' close to the campus of UCLA (University of California Los Angeles). Once you've said that, you've said it all about flake city, so far as we're concerned. Santa Monica is something else. For starters, it may be the world's most familiar movie 'set'; the city gives out a thousand filming permits a year. From Santa Monica Pier to Santa Monica High School – known locally as 'Sanmohi' – you've seen it on screen. L.A.'s laid-back neighbour is hyper-cool.

Except for the weather, that is. The sun smiles on Santa Monica most of the year. We have arrived on Christmas Day to twenty-six degrees (79F), though rain and cooler weather is not unknown in January. Winter highs are generally around seventeen degrees (64F). Even in summer the air is dry, evenings balmy, and the heat seldom humid or searing

Although cheek by jowl with L.A., it is a city in its own right. Not a resort in the strictest sense of the word, rather a 'sleek and chic' residential and business community of around 95,000 souls. But it does have more leisure activities than most holiday destinations. Within the city limits is a three-and-a-half mile swathe of the wide, blonde beach that stretches twenty-six miles from Malibu to Marina del Rey. The restored pier dates back to 1909 and houses the world's only solar-powered Ferris wheel. Muscle Beach, once famous for *al fresco* workouts of Hollywood bods and wannabees, has been restored and re-opened. Once again you can stroll the boardwalk and watch the honed and toned of all sexes ripple their muscles in their municipal outdoor fitness center.

Santa Monica is only eight miles from Los Angeles International Airport, yet most visitors head for better-known Hollywood or Beverly Hills. They don't know what they're missing. Accessibility is just as easy by road; the Pacific Coast Highway makes its southern drag along the ocean front. Historic Route 66 terminates nearby. The San Diego freeway sweeps all the way south to the Mexican border.

The city itself is laid out in a simple grid pattern, so getting around is easy. We know we can always borrow or rent a car but taxis are in plentiful supply and not as expensive as elsewhere. We found Viky of the Lady Cabs company stationed outside Santa Monica Place shopping mall. When her company cabs pick up lone female passengers, they always wait outside until their passenger is safely indoors. When they call for single women they phone as they approach the pick-up address so nobody has to wait outside.

Santa Monica is, however, a walking city and everything is within reach. We cover at least four miles a day and have never missed being motorised. If it rains, the Big Blue Bus, for fifty cents, shuttles us every half-hour to the beach or downtown shopping and entertainment areas.

The local paper lists entertainment for every night of the week. There's jazz, traditional and modern; theatre, both legit and 'alternative', and a thriving stand-up comedy scene. You can find music for whatever kind of dancing your heart desires in the martini bars, hotels and restaurants dotted around town, and in clubs. In summer, romantics can even dance the night away to swing bands on the pier, and for higher brows the Santa Monica Symphony performs regularly

When you tire of feasting your eyes on the beach and the breakers it's easy to get in some action of your own. It can be as gentle as walking through the leafy 'burbs admiring gardens and mansions or, energized by the sun and the cool mornings, jogging along the promenade. You can rent in-line skates or a surfboard, but most years we hire bikes and ride part of the 26-mile cycle path along the ocean's edge from Will Rogers beach to Venice beach. Depending on the time of year and the weather, we may join the joggers or power walkers of all ages along Ocean

Avenue, enjoying Palisades Park and its outdoor art, sculptures and Chinese gardens.

The city offers added value for the female of the species when the fire-fighters of the Santa Monica Fire Department park their big red truck across two parking meters and jog their regulation mile or two along the beach-front. Our friend Linda pointed Eve in the direction of the hundred steps leading up from the beach near San Vicente Boulevard, where the cognoscenti get their daily workout. 'The scenery is great,' she enthused. 'You can't miss 'em – navy shorts, logo t-shirts, and re-markable physiques.' She was right. So Eve thinks, anyway. This is also an award-winning fire-fighting team, renowned for their swift response. In the suburbs of Santa Monica where land values are in millions of dollars, house-buyers tend to buy a half-acre plot, knock down whatever is on it, and build a mansion from scratch. The fire brigade practise on the old homes during the demolition process, trying out the latest search and rescue procedures.

The city caters for families with a range of modest motels as well as the ocean-side five-star palaces like Shutters on the Beach, Casa del Mar and the Fairmont Miramar. We are blessed by having old friends, Ron and Anita Clint, who are forty-year Santa Monica residents. At their house on Fourteenth Street we not only have the best food in the city, but the best entertainment, too. Our host has been known in Los Angeles for half a century as 'Ronnie Clint of Chasen's'. He managed the legendary restaurant until it closed its doors in 1995, unintentionally starring in an award-winning movie about its closure called 'Off the Menu'. Ronnie's immortal closing line on-camera was: 'To survive in this town, you gotta learn to make pizza...'

Liverpudlian by birth, Californian by adoption, he has regaled us over the years with tales of Hollywood's finest: Dean Martin, offered wine with dinner responding, 'Not while I'm drinking...' Elizabeth Taylor ordering Chasen's chili flown by private jet to wherever in the world she was on location. Alfred Hitchcock taking vociferous offence at a starlet showing too much cleavage at the dinner table. Ronnie knew them all, catered for them all, and has been photographed with them all – *and* five US Presidents into the bargain. He is also an ace cook, throws the best parties in town, and his house may be the only place in California where you can still get a decent Hobo Steak! His family has become part of our family: the expression *mi casa es su casa* might have been invented for and by them.

With a little help from Anita, Ronnie's wife, and their daughter Linda Moritz, the distaff side of the Jones duo found herself in shoppers' heaven. We felt right at home on Montana Avenue, a European-style half-mile of pavement cafes, boutiques, gourmet food stores and relaxed, outdoorsy 'cappuccino culture'.

From Seventh to Seventeenth Street we promenaded, stopping for coffee and gossip at Peet's, lunching at Le Marmiton on excellent, bistro-style French food. At another favourite just down the road, great food is served deli-style at Marmalade, where you can eavesdrop on the city's beau monde ordering their party food. Once we lunched at Wolfgang Puck's Café, where glossy wannabee-in-movies waiters are so intent on comparing casting couch notes that we couldn't get our bill. We got up to leave and the manager who seated us in the almost-empty restaurant half an hour before flashed the full-beam smile for a nano-second and thrust menus at us.

'Hi! Table for two for you guys?'

The city's last remaining neighbourhood movie theatre, the single-screen Ariel, is on Montana. A couple of hours in there might have saved the fortune Eve spent on suede evening boots and elegant high-buckled shoes at the Peter Fox boutique. Worse, Neiman Marcus, Saks and the St. John store are but a short taxi ride away in Beverly Hills. Ronnie Clint found this very funny, the women in his household being St. John addicts, too.

'Those sales clerks,' he told Ron, 'have the best training in the world – in opening wallets. When the sales come around you spend a fortune to get a bargain.

'While you and Eve were in Beverly Hills the smell of burning plastic wafted all the way to Fourteenth Street!'

A rainy afternoon was devoted to a wash, wax and paint job (for Eve, that is. No car, remember?) Montana Avenue's beauty salon, her favourite Zaine *coiffeur* and walk-in manicure shop are all between Fourteenth and Seventeenth streets. Three hours and a hundred dollars later she emerged with curled hair, bald legs and acrylic thrills (or was it 'acrylic fills'?). She managed to persuade her ultra-conservative consort to venture in for a manicure and pedicure. He emerged with feathers ruffled and face red. One of the oriental manicurists had looked at him from under lowered eyelashes and asked if he would care for 'extended massage, sir?' Only when Eve waved the printed price list under his nose did he believe the poor manicurist had offered nothing more than the 'intensive arm, neck and shoulder massage' for an extra ten bucks! Memories of Thailand die hard.

A mustn't-miss for shopaholics is *the* most stylish interiors store at 11922 San Vicente. 'Terra Cotta' is an Aladdin's cave of imported antiques and works of art, fabulous furnishings and ornaments, laid out with such exquisite good taste we could move right in and live there. If we ever get our stately pile or our Chateau on the Loire, then only interior designer Deborah Parsons, owner of Terra Cotta, will be let loose on the decor.

At the other end of the spectrum the Third Street Promenade is a pedestrian zone with funky stores, bookstores, street entertainment, and an array of cafes and restaurants. On different days we heard hot jazz, watched mime artists, eavesdropped as people had tarot card readings, and listened to a beautiful Chinese girl in traditional cheongsam playing classical dulcimer.

There are 450 eating places within the city limits from five-star to wine bar, fuelled by four weekly farmers markets. All-time favourite restaurants for us are The Lobster, at the Santa Monica pier, and Ocean Avenue Seafood. Melisse, on Wilshire, for exquisite and expensive modern French cuisine.

Foodies make a pilgrimage to Santa Monica Seafood on Colorado Avenue, the most appetising, fragrant and well-organised indoor fish market we've seen anywhere in the world, just to see what's on offer for self-cook supper. And to 'Sur La Table' at Wilshire and Third, *the* kitchen and cookware store for stars and stargazers. There are regular demonstrations by celebrity chefs and writers like Julia Child, our favourite U.S. foodie.

When children tire of the beach there is a list of free things to do along the Santa Monica shoreline called 'Top Twenty Perks in Paradise', and the mid-city section is home to a range of museums and galleries.

The city's easy grid pattern has First to Twenty-sixth Streets running north to south, criss-crossed by parallel Avenues and Boulevards – some names you recognise from L.A. itself like San Vicente, Wilshire and Santa Monica. Those are the boulevards that cut through both cities as far as the ocean and tend to be twenty or more miles long. Others soon take on a familiar ring – Georgina, Idaho, Alta, Marguerita. That's where you spy the city's most flamboyant and expensive mansions. On foot, it's almost impossible to get lost.

Unlike much of L.A., the natives are friendly. Cars stop to let you cross the road even where there are no traffic lights or crossing signs. Stepping off the curb in front of a car is like witnessing the birth of polite twins: 'After you.' 'No, after you...' 'No, no – after *you!*' Later, we learned that drivers get a ticket if they *don't* let you cross. As do jaywalkers, so it pays to be careful. Fellow-walkers greeted us along the avenues. A family announced the arrival of their new baby with balloons on the front lawn and a notice proclaiming, 'it's a boy!' with birth date, name and weight. An octogenarian emerged from a Tudor-style mansion and waved his cigarette at us with a cheerful: 'You think it's gonna stunt my growth?'

Our favourite walk takes us from Montana north along Fourteenth Street then west down sleek Georgina Avenue to the ocean, an easy three miles. Carry on along Ocean Avenue to the Santa Monica Pier and you've made it almost five miles.

Along the length of Georgina Avenue modern mansions in architectural styles ranging from mock Tudor to *jazz moderne*, grand beyond our dreams, nestle cheek by jowl on quarter- and half-acre lots, barely a 'sports utility vehicle's' width between them. Where we come from, homes as grand as these would be set in acres of landscaped gardens and surrounded by high hedges. These have a mere square of green grass in front, clipped and sprinkled to within an inch of its life, bordered by the state bird-of-paradise flower (strelitza), impatiens, arum lilies the colour of clotted cream, bougainvillea, magnolia and camellia. The city's signature palm trees edging every avenue are pruned so their branches sprout at uniform height. Metal collars fail to deter regiments of squirrels but even they look well groomed.

Lots of dogs in Santa Monica, every one with plastic bag tucked into its collar like party hats, ready to be filled with conscientiously scooped poop.

A citrus tree in one front garden drooped under the weight of oranges; a lemon tree in another tantalised us with ripe fruit aching to be plucked for the good of our evening dry martinis. We tried to make a discreet pass that would shake the tree and dislodge just one little lemon. Ron, the more law-abiding of the two, pointed to one of the royal blue notices planted more profusely than any flower in every front yard:

ARMED RESPONSE. Visions of being pulled in by the citrus patrol, juice-guns at the ready, proved the ultimate deterrent.

Lest you imagine it's all too sanitised, a foray downtown around Second and Santa Monica and the Ocean Avenue parks in the early morning reveals the city has more than its share of the homeless and the indigent.

In times past Greta Garbo and Cary Grant, Shirley Temple and Joan Crawford were among the stars who called Santa Monica home. Now Steven Spielberg and Goldie Hawn, Al Pacino, Sylvester Stallone and Oliver Stone have at least a business base here. The not-so-young but still upwardly mobile are busy building their dream homes. Each time we visit we find gaping holes where last time perfectly fine houses had stood. New owners knock 'em down and build 'em up again, every time a bigger and better property. 'The smallest house north of Montana', not much more than a trailer home in a quarter-acre lot, was for sale a few years ago at $750,000. That, too, will be replaced by a Mexican hacienda or a Tudor mansion.

Santa Monica's proximity to the fleshpots of Los Angeles in general and Hollywood in particular mean you never feel hemmed in. Universal Studios is eighteen miles away, Disneyland forty-five, and the spectacular Getty Center just ten miles. You can get there by bus, but our friend had secured car park reservations for 10am on a Monday morning. All you pay for your day at the Getty is the five-dollar parking fee. You leave your car, board a cute tram that climbs the steep hill for you, and revel in the view from the top. The Getty itself is an architectural jewel. Meier's cream-coloured linked pavilions are perfectly in harmony with their hilltop site high over the city and the valley. Waterways and fountains, plantings of delicate trees, cactus gardens, even a maze, suggest design inspiration from the Alhambra in Seville. At every turn there is something for each of the senses to feed on. The collection is eclectic – from illuminated manuscripts through early photographs to religious paintings and eighteenth century French furniture and porcelain. It deserves a whole day and, like Santa Monica itself, plenty of return visits.

✦ ✦ ✦

Another California dream that sustains us on cold winter days is a four-drive or a half-hour flight up the coast to visit friends in Cambria. Mid-way between L.A. and San Francisco, this is one of the most unspoiled and spectacular regions on the California coast. Close to Hearst Castle, an hour's drive from San Luis Obispo, and paradise for lovers of ocean and marine life.

We met Bob and Sylvia Huth on their honeymoon almost thirty years ago, when they were staying at John Tovey's country house hotel Miller Howe. They lived in Marina del Rey at the time, just a few miles from Santa Monica, and flew over to London for forty-eight hours to attend our wedding. Now they have moved north to share a magnificent home built by Sylvia's parents in Cambria.

There are so many diversions on that glorious wild stretch of the California coast, we seldom make it as far as Carmel and the Monterey Peninsula. Most years, let's be honest, we seldom make it past the hundreds of wineries of the Central Coast region, grown from a few dozen just ten years ago. Most of them have tasting rooms and picnic gardens. Cambria is a charming town, not too touristy, with uncrowded streets full of antique stores and boutiques for browsing.

Walk along the cliff top paths within sight and sound of the surf crashing beneath, and be aware it is thanks entirely to the local community. In a rare gesture of common purpose, the townsfolk of Cambria raised sufficient funds to snatch the land from developers hell-bent on extending the town.

We try to hit Cambria in January, in time to visit the colonies of elephant seals. In their hundreds they flubber up on the beach to birth their pups, nurse them and wean them. Then they start to mate all over again when the giant males are horny and the poor females have lost half their weight through whelping and nursing. The creatures take no notice of the visitors that surround them. The words 'homely' and 'fat' and 'lazy' are singularly inappropriate to anybody who loves them as we do.

While the exhausted females suckle their young, a 5,000-pound alpha male will face up to any young bull that might fancy his chances of taking over the harem. They huff and they puff and they raise themselves up to their considerable height, proboscises like windsocks on an airfield. After a moment you can practically hear them shake their heads and say 'Aw what the hell – too much like hard work...' and sink back on to the sand. Smart move, because fights can be bloody and violent and leave the protagonists scarred for life.

After nature in the raw, the comforting environs of Hearst Castle are only a few minutes away. Drive there and be warned lest you think you've had a wine tasting too many. For yes, that *is* a herd of zebra grazing just off the highway. William Randolph Hearst imported them when he built his folly of a castle, and the descendents of the herd can still be glimpsed as you approach. The castle and visitors' center are open all year, and the Imax movie of Hearst and his history is good entertainment. During the season docents – including our friend's mother, Lois – dress in period costume and play the part of Hearst's house guests, so you get the feeling you're gate-crashing a private party.

Sylvia's parents John and Lois de Nicola drove the six of us on a Saturday evening to have dinner in one of their favourite small towns. An hour's drive inland from Cambria, Templeton has surprises in store for the unwary.

We stepped out of the car and thought, 'Nothing is what it seems.' It is a gem of a little railroad town, like a Wild West movie set. Main Street must have looked just the same a hundred years ago, stores with plank floors and canopies, covered sidewalks, and hitching posts for your horse.

We seemed to be the only tourists as we sauntered (Templeton is a sauntering kind of town) into Herrmann's Chocolate Lab and Ice Cream Parlor. Everything is made on the premises in full view of the lighted shop window. And it smells oh-so-tempting. One of the ladies behind the counter handed chocolate-coated strawberries to all six of us and beamed: 'Ah. Here comes the doctor!' Excellent, we thought as a kindly looking man in white coat strode in. Good to know the town doctor takes a regular dose of such good medicine.

He picked up a tray of freshly made chocolates and turned around to reveal the slogan on the back of his white 'lab coat'. It said 'Dip it and they will come'. We began to feel a little like Alice after her encounter with the White Rabbit and wondered if it was something they put into the chocolates. But it turned out 'the doctor' is the name the townsfolk bestow on the candy-store proprietor. He patrols Main Street every weekend offering samples to passers-by. 'I'm the town hooker', he explained. 'One taste and they're hooked.'

Next we moseyed into a Wild West emporium crammed with necessities and collectables. Templeton is deep in horse country and 'California Classics', according to the notice, is where locals buy

'Essentials & Accessories for Horse, Ranch & Rider'. Three rooms are piled high with neckerchiefs and antique saddles, collections of western and country music, buckaroo trappings and hand-stitched leather chaps – even 'frontier and western wedding apparel'. But hang on in there, we thought. There's something strange here, too. Dorothy Lee Rogers, the manager and, she informed us, 'horse columnist for the local press', pointed past a pile of stuff to what looked like a really good copy of a bronze cowboy statue. On closer inspection, it was no copy, but one of half a dozen original bronzes on display by local sculptor Jim Stuckenberg.

Jim, part Native American and former rodeo rider, breeds and raises horses, was born deaf, and may be one of the finest western artists of his generation. His work has been bought for the White House and the Reagan Library and by a posse of astute collectors. Bronzes sell for $13,000.00. Yet he eschews conventional galleries in favour of the local store.

Dorothy Lee invited us to visit a little longer and she'd call Jim to come over and meet us, but dinner called – another surprise. Our hosts had said we were dining 'at Penny's' but hadn't explained that the restaurant used to be a parsonage. The eponymous Penny has maintained the nineteenth-century house much as it was when the town's minister and his family lived there. Apart, that is, from the startlingly realistic life-size wax cowboy, clad in hat, boots and spurs, reclining half-submerged in a bubble bath in the ladies' room.

Food is described as 'heirloom cuisine', recipes handed down from Penny's own family as 'the basis but with improvements'. Pork loin with raspberry currant sauce came with homemade stuffing, braised red cabbage with apple, and caramelised shallots. Stuffed chicken breast had a pesto filling of fresh basil, sun-dried tomatoes, pine nuts and parmesan cheese. This was served with polenta, the pork with fresh fennel. Reasonable prices, too.

Driving back to Cambria a fog had blown in from the ocean and cloaked the hills and the highway. By next morning, it was clear again and we watched a couple of young deer nibbling lazily on the grass right outside our bedroom window. 'Two bucks for breakfast', we teased our hosts, 'and it's still a bargain!'

19

The Wizardry of Oz

Everyone should have his or her first view of Sydney from the sea. No other vista – not the Statue of Liberty and the skyline of New York, not Hong Kong or the Bay of Acapulco – can compete (though we make an exception for Venice). Sail or cruise through the natural channel of the Heads and you find yourself face to face with the city, the Harbour Bridge and the Opera House. It is every picture postcard you ever saw.

From her first glimpse through pouring rain on Oriana Eve was hooked. Ron's hook had been in place since 1945, when he spent a life-changing year in Sydney while waiting for demob from the Royal Navy. Now it is our winter retreat, the place we call home for a few weeks each year.

Drawing the line at being airborne for twenty-four hours, we break our journey overnight in Bangkok. We do splurge on business class flights. To compensate, we do not always stay in the best hotels. It's good for us, we reasoned, to eschew the pointless theatricality and even more pointless room rates of hotels like the Mandarin Oriental, on a short stopover, in favour of a little local flavour. On our first extended visit we spent a night at the three-star Hotel Asia Airport. Found, booked and pre-paid on the Internet, it all worked like magic. The shuttle bus found us; the front desk found our reservation, and we were ushered up to the requested 'quiet room on an upper floor' within minutes.

We were almost sorry, two days after Christmas, to miss the hotel's 'traditional Christmas dinner' of seafood basket with tatar sauce (sic); crabmeat soup; orange sherbet; ostrich steak with garlic sauce; and crepe suzette.

Staff greeted us with both namaste and 'a merry Christmas to you'. They took care over our 4.45am wake-up call, 5.15am porter, and 5.30am shuttle for our early check-in. We could have had breakfast in the coffee shop from five in the morning; we enjoyed the outdoor pool, checked out the fitness centre and the bowling alley. The bill? Less than our last continental breakfast at the Mandarin Oriental.

We came to Australia with a mission. Caterer & Hotelkeeper, the weekly hospitality magazine, had commissioned us to send back regular 'dispatches from the front'

Arriving in Sydney just before New Year's Eve, the first thing that struck us about the Aussies is how downright obliging they are. Not because it's good for tourism but because they are friendly and laid-back by nature. We never heard the expression 'whingeing pom'- they just wouldn't be that nasty.

Bus drivers, shop assistants, people you meet on beaches or on ferries, all seem genuinely to want you to have as good a time as they're having. Especially since they're fortunate enough to live there and you're not! Waiters and waitresses greet you warmly and look after you well. They don't introduce themselves, don't call you sir or madam, nor aspire to be your new best friend. They don't even interrupt conversations to run through their daily specials. Bravo to all that.

Nobody can throw a party like Sydneysiders and everybody was in party mood as they prepared to bring in the New Year. Bush fires raged in the outer suburbs. The smell of smoke and the pall that hung over the highest buildings cast a shadow over the city, but celebrations were under way regardless.

Whole sections of the Central Business District were cordoned off for public parties. Martin Place, the main city square, was festooned with giant screens for the New Year countdown, floors laid for dancing, mobile bars and food stalls, and DJs ready to rock. Open spaces in Hyde Park and the Domain were decked with marquees and sound systems for live bands.

Wherever crowds were expected, there were rows of Portaloos. In city streets the portables were lined up in banks of fifteen. In the park, we counted a single line of sixty-one. As Cilla Black might have said, that's 'a lorra lorra lavs.' Just as prolific were the banks of litterbins, three in a row, for plastic, paper and non-recyclable waste.

Entry to public events was strictly controlled, with 24-hour traffic diversions, security bag searches, refusal of admission to anybody under the influence, and no alcohol except that dispensed from authorised bars. We sent thought waves back to London: *Ken Livingstone – check it out.*

For our own New Year celebration we chose the revolving restaurant on the seventy-second floor of the Sydney Tower. Five-course dinner with unlimited good wines and Piper Heidseick champagne at midnight, dancing to two bands and a fabulous 380-degree view of the fireworks over Sydney Harbour Bridge for the equivalent of £100 each.

Once you recover from the shock of the fare, Australia is an economical, exciting destination. In the heart of its most expensive city, our smart serviced apartment was within easy walking distance of everything we needed, and cost less than a room at the YMCA at home. That included air conditioning, daily maid service and 24-hour concierge.

Entertainment is affordable. We make a beeline for the Opera House and book tickets for half a dozen operas, concerts and plays. Reasonable seats for six performances cost the equivalent of one good pair of tickets at our own Royal Opera House. Most performances are packed with people of all kinds and from all walks of life. No black ties, but not many corporate eventers either. A glass of champagne and a pack of smoked salmon sandwiches for the equivalent of a tenner for two make it an affordable special occasion.

We have seen a brilliant new production of Faust and a flawed one of The Merry Widow, an exquisite Marriage of Figaro, and a superb Flying Dutchman. We should have seen Magic Flute, too, but after forty minutes of waiting in the foyer with a good-natured crowd of hundreds, we were told the performance was cancelled. People queued patiently for refunds, or went home to wait for credit card amendments. Nobody lost their temper or yelled at the staff.

Next day we returned to ask what the problem was. 'Not absolutely sure,' said the lady in the ticket office. 'But we think it was gas fumes in the orchestra pit.' Personally we find the trombonist is usually to blame but … she assured us it would have come from the construction work outside the Opera House.

We have watched 'Blithe Spirit' in as 'spirited' a production as you could wish for, with Miriam Margolyes as Madame Arcati in the Opera House theatre. And the debut of Sydney Opera's new chief conductor and artistic director Gianluigi Gemelli. He chose the Verdi Requiem as his introductory performance. Full orchestra, four trombones high up in the circle, a choir of 250 from the Roma Chorus and the Sydney Chorale. For an encore we had the Hebrew Slaves chorus from Aida. For a *finale*, a whimsical sixteen-bar introduction to an unexpected and roof rousing rendering of Waltzing Matilda! With full orchestra, chorus and audience.

It might have taken Ron half a century to return to Sydney, but the important things had not changed. The homes where he and his mates, young sailors far from home, were welcomed as members of the family still stood. Sydney's Victorian heritage remained, even if much of it was overshadowed by a skyline as modern as any in the world. And the attitude and approach of the citizens was just as 'can-do' and positive as ever.

We took a walk down to the Grace Hotel. It was built in extravagant art deco style in 1930 as the headquarters of the Grace Brothers department store empire, restored and re-opened as a hotel in 1997. The brochure relates the history of its transformation from office block to civil service and military use to hotel.

'Gone', it assures readers, 'are the dingy offices where poor clerks spent their lives in semi-obscurity...'

Ron knew, dear reader, because he *was* one of those 'poor clerks'. We found the office he occupied as a Royal Navy clerk. Even then in 'the happiness business', his job was to assist the release of servicemen who had chosen to begin a new life in Australia.

The Grace Building was requisitioned as headquarters of the Supreme Commander of allied forces in the Pacific, General Douglas Macarthur. We wondered if he, too, kept his promise to return.

The menu of the hotel's Deli Café read '*SOD Pumpkin Soup*'. Quite right, we thought. The waiter explained it meant 'Soup of the Day', adding: 'But you know, nobody has ordered it since I've been here...'

We seldom had a disappointing meal or poor service in Sydney restaurants. Places like *Fish at the Rocks*, which can't be described as cheap by Australian standards, has customers forming an orderly queue outside. *Fish* has wood floors, bentwood chairs, marble-topped tables and absolutely no pretensions.

We've seldom tasted better fish – barramundi and whiting so fresh they might have been alive and flipping just minutes before. There's a modest wine list with most available by the glass, but like many Sydney restaurants, *Fish* operates a BYO or bring-your-own-wine policy with a two dollars a head corkage charge.

If we felt a 'yen' for a barbie, we didn't have far to go. Next door to our apartment was one of Sydney's quirkiest restaurants. At *Suminoya*, if you don't eat up, you pay up! Their speciality is *scichirin* a kind of Japanese barbecue they claim as the healthy traditional way of cooking meats and seafood.

Dinner comes as a series of courses – sashimi or marinated squid, then salad, soup, rice and your *yakiniku* (barbecue). Strips of raw beef, pork rib, chicken, 'beef intestine' and vegetables are brought to the table along with an individual charcoal grill for DIY cooking.

The menu asks patrons to desist from ordering 'unnecessary food' with the gentle reminder 'We may ask you to pay for substantial leftovers.'

Our friends Professor John and Verity Norman provided a birthday treat for Ron by arranging lunch with Professor Myles Gibson and his wife Ena, who were also visiting from the UK. They had on a previous visit recommended the Medina Apartments in Martin Place, where we have stayed ever since. The restaurant was the splendid '*41*', at the top of the Chiffley Tower, and the scene of a bizarre coincidence.

While he was general manager of London's Athenaeum Hotel in the 1970s, Ron had to ask disgraced Australian tycoon Alan Bond, a regular guest in the hotel, to take his feet off the (brand new) coffee tables in the Windsor Lounge. Now here Ron stood, making use of the facilities in the gents' cloakroom of Sydney's smartest restaurant, walls of glass giving stupendous views over the city from forty-one floors up. At that moment he was told that the world's most spectacular gents' was the erstwhile marbled bathroom of Bondy's penthouse, inhabited by him before his fall from grace.

Oh – and the food was great, too!

Acqua Luna, habitat of celebrity chef Darren Simpson, lived up to its reputation as one of Sydney's finest. The one with the 'wow' factor, though, was *Aria*, where the words 'exquisitely simple' apply to décor, service and food. We had watched the owner, another celebrity chef, Matthew Moran, on a TV series in which six couples were given financial backing to open their own restaurant. Matt was one of the judges and so impressed us that we couldn't wait to try his restaurant overlooking the Opera House.

Modern Australian cuisine at its best, at prices that were exactly half what we've learned to expect in London.

Sunday treat was brunch at *The Botanic*, a conservatory-style restaurant built like a tree house in the Botanic Gardens. Be warned, though: this is pretty close to the habitat of up to eight thousand fruit bats that hang in furry clusters from every tree. These are diurnal in habit and if the sight, sound or smell of them bothers you, take a detour. You might prefer the screeching yellow-crested cockatoos. They're quite likely to perch on a drinking fountain and 'ask' you by alternately pointing with their beak and looking you in the eye, to turn on the tap. We fell for it and asked a park ranger about it. 'Oh, they're just winding you up,' he retorted. 'Those buggers are quite capable of turning the tap on themselves.'

On a perfect summer Saturday (the last, as it turned out, before a week or two of torrential rain) we sat on the terrace of *Doyle's*, a Sydney institution. Facing Circular Quay and the Opera House with the Harbour Bridge over one shoulder, we could almost reach out and touch the Seabourne Sun newly docked that morning.

The oysters were plump and juicy, the barramundi grilled to perfection, the lobster almost more than we could eat.

We knew at least one member of the Doyle family would be within calling distance. The senior Doyles are the venerable Jack and Alice, whose 'Fish Cookbook' is still reprinting after several decades and royalties still go to the Seaman's Mission. Sons Tim, Jim and Peter are head chefs of the three 'branches'. Margaret and Michael Doyle produce the restaurants' own-label wines from the Southern Highlands of NSW, and Peter Doyle senior does the same from his Hunter Valley vineyards. The restaurant, under the supervision of five generations of the family, has been flourishing since 1885.

There are no lengths to which the Aussies won't go, it seems, to ensure they get it right. We return again and again to *Kingsley's* in the spectacular Wooloomooloo Finger Wharf redevelopment.

Couldn't be more appropriate because this is where Ron's battleship King George V docked on its return to Sydney from the Pacific in 1945. Then, Wooloomooloo was run-down and seedy, fit for sailors after a long spell at sea, but not much else. Today it's the smartest address in town. Kingsley's is where we go on our first nights and our last nights, where we celebrate birthdays and any other excuse we can find. We go for the best steaks we've ever tasted, or fine fish simply cooked, a relaxed ambience, and fun.

Owner Kingsley Smith practically raises his own cattle – and his own wine. In his mid-thirties he has three fashionable restaurants, one in

Central Business District opened and flourishing for a dozen years, the second in the Finger Wharf, and now Kingsley's Schnitzel and Ale House, in Wooloomooloo town.

Brought up in his parents' guesthouse Kingsley inherited a passion for good food, good wine, hard work – and risk-taking. Years working as a waiter didn't deter him from opening his own steak-house at the age of twenty-two. 'I financed it myself and my family signed some guarantees. Everybody warned me against it – east-meets-west cuisine was pretty firmly established by then, and they reckoned steak-houses were old-fashioned.'

He became so involved in selecting his beef on the hoof, he now works closely with the Australian equivalent of the Meat and Livestock Commission. Meanwhile, Kingsley's father acquired a twenty-hectare vineyard of 32-year-old semillon vines in the Hunter Valley, and, with nearby 'blockies' or smallholders supplying other varieties, now produces the restaurant's own-label wines.

Laid-back as they are, the Aussies do take their food and wine seriously. Adelaide University claimed a world first during our visit. In conjunction with the Cordon Bleu School, it was offering a full-time Master's degree course in gastronomy. The syllabus included the cultural aspects of food and cooking, history of dining, recipes and cuisine 'from Escoffier to Jamie Oliver'.

Its aim? 'To put gastronomy right up there with art and architecture where it belongs.'

Ron took his investigation of Sydney's hotels as seriously as our mission to 'dine out and tell all'.

Sydney's Central Business District has a skyline as modern as those of Dallas and Chicago, but the city has done a good job of preserving its Victorian heritage buildings. Some of these, like the architectural gem that is the Queen Victoria Building, have become shopping malls-with-a-difference. Others house Sydney's leading hotels. We didn't stay in them – several weeks demand the independence of an apartment – but we did the rounds with a critical eye.

The Intercontinental, with its own hotel school and the pick of the best staff, struts its five-star stuff in the former Treasury building. Behind the original sandstone façade is a classic courtyard atrium and wrought iron Paris-style lift. Bedrooms are in the 31-storey tower that rises from behind the Victorian building, out of sight unless you're in the street and looking up.

Our neighbour, The Westin in Martin Place, occupies part of the colonnaded General Post Office. There's an atrium with upscale shops and food and beverage outlets. The original marble staircase has been retained, with a café-bar on a raised terrace overlooking a public walkway, and passers-by enjoy goldfish-bowl views of guests. The *Mosaic* restaurant with mandatory celebrity chef is on a first-floor balcony with views over the atrium. Décor throughout the hotel is modern, not quite minimalist. Overall impression – impressive.

Once upon a time The Regent, near Circular Quay, was the best address in town. Nowadays in its livery of Four Seasons it strikes us as strictly passé. On two brief visits it failed, alone among the hotels, to fulfil the first requirement of a hotel – that is, to exude a warm welcome. Verdict? Alas, pretty charmless.

Modern 'essentialist' as we heard minimalism described here, is represented by the Quay Grand, stark and stylish with rooms overlooking Circular Quay and the Bridge from one side, the Opera House and Botanic Gardens from the other. Two smart restaurants, the informal one with inside-outside dining.

The fashionable 'W', part of the Wooloomooloo Finger Wharf development is 'something completely different', within the interior of the historic wood buildings of the old wharf. The 'W' shares super-cool premises with apartments, many of them owned by household name movie stars, half a dozen fashionable indoor/outdoor restaurants, and club-bars.

Two hotels stood out, for quite different reasons. One is the Sir Stamford, which we nicknamed The Connaught of Sydney. Formerly a Ritz Carlton property, it's boutique-size with 106 rooms (including eleven suites) in Macquarie Street, Sydney's most desirable address. Stunning views, soothing French décor, public rooms intimate, welcoming, and luxurious – and the most beautiful bar in town.

The other is the Russell at The Rocks. The building dates back to 1790 and has been an inn since 1853. Not de luxe but quirky, cosy, and the place we'll choose when we need a hotel in Sydney. There are just twenty-nine rooms including a suite and an apartment. Public areas are Victorian yet light and airy with plenty of fresh flowers and decent oil paintings. Breakfast is served in a sunny roof garden looking out to sea. With charming rooms at seductively low rates, we should be keeping this one to ourselves!

Sydney has a transportation system of buses, trains and ferries that make it easy to explore, and we had been challenged *not* to rent a car. Based in the city centre, there was nowhere in the surrounding beaches, national parks or indeed in New South Wales that was not accessible quickly, cheaply and without hassle.

A train ride from Martin Place to Katoomba allowed us to spend a magical couple of days in the Blue Mountains, marvelling at the vastness of the mountains and rainforest, blue-misted and aromatic from a million gum trees. Riding the cable car down the mountainside to the rainforest walkway, we also discovered the remains of the region's nineteenth-century mining industry. Eve refused the almost-vertical miniature railway down the mountainside, but was persuaded to ride it back up again, strapped in securely as the carriages are hauled mechanically up the sheer slope. 'What happens,' asked a fellow-passenger, 'if the rope breaks?' 'Well then,' said the operator laconically, 'You get to the bottom in four seconds.'

From Echo Point we gazed out to the Three Sisters rock formation and recalled the legend of the father who turned his three beautiful daughters into stone to save them from the evil Bunyip. Alas, father lost his magic stick and couldn't turn them back again.

After a couple of hours' sightseeing we looked for a cold drink in the one-street Blue Mountains 'capital' of Katoomba. It was Saturday and the temperature had soared to twenty-nine degrees (84F) by mid-day – and rising. Our first stop, the Crush Café, was closed. In the window was a hand-written sign:

We couldn't stand the heat, so we got out of the kitchen. Sorry guys. See you Monday. Kerren.

Further along, pinned to the open door of a boutique was another notice, printed by somebody who was clearly cross but too nice to be nasty.

To the man (sic) who stole a cream beaded vintage cardigan from my shop on 31st January. Just want you to know I hope you enjoy wearing it. And... that we have you on video surveillance. Please feel free to return it any time.

Wherever we travel, if it's a Saturday we can count on a wedding. The Blue Mountains were no exception. In the little town of Leura we stood in the shade of a galleried shop and gazed across the road as a beautiful bride entered the church. A whiskery pair of bushwhackers gazed right along with us. 'Whew,' said one. 'Ain't she a beaut?' The other shook his head slowly from side to side and sighed. 'Yeah, mate. A real corker.'

Eve was so touched that these macho old Aussie males were not afraid to show their feminine side, she couldn't resist remarking; 'Why, I think that's really nice of you. She *is* a gorgeous bride, isn't she?'

The men looked at each other, then at Eve, as though she was clearly lacking in the nous department.

'Yeah,' the first man drawled. 'The Bentley – she's a bit of orright. But that vintage Holden ... *that's* what I call a car...'

On a tranquil day in Koo Ring Gai national park, a two-hour bus and boat-ride from the city, we hiked (or rather, 'took a bush walk') on a nature trail for four hours without seeing another soul. Just us, magnificent views down to the sea, the odd goanna waddling slowly into the bush, and a small kangaroo that hopped across the path in front of us.

An overnight visit to Australia's capital city allowed an overview of Canberra and a few of the art and architectural treasures to be enjoyed there. It's not a late-night city but the Parliament Buildings, old and new, art gallery, and the magnificent avenue of war memorials justify a visit of at least a couple of days. The planning and layout of the Australian capital are impressive, and a total contrast to the earlier architecture of the other principal cities.

Before leaving New South Wales we usually aim to decamp on the Manly ferry for a week or two at the beach. If we're lucky we not only catch the last of the summer sunshine, but time it to coincide with Australia Day, when once again the whole of Sydney is en fete. Any excuse for a summer party! We had already shared the tail end of Christmas then the New Year's Eve celebrations. Soon there would be Valentine's Day, the waterfront area decked out for the Azure Party, when five thousand gays and lesbians were expected for the opening event, a morning parade through the city of 'Dikes on Bikes'.

On Manly Beach Australia Day weekend signals the annual Surf Carnival. We never dreamed we'd see for ourselves those legions of lifeguards built like brick dunnies, clad in neck-to-knee swimsuits topped by tight rubber caps with chinstraps.

They showed off their life-saving skills in more ways than you'd think possible – in boats, on boards, swimming, rope-winding and resuscitating from early morning until dusk. On the last day the teams, in day-glo Lycra club colours, marched with military precision, club banners raised aloft, in the annual march-past along the beach. Accompanied by a full pipe band in kilts and solar topees.

Taking stock of the things that best sum up the Sydneysiders' approach to life, we decide:

It's the signs in the Botanic Gardens that urge 'Please walk on the grass. And hug the trees. And smell the roses'.

It's the bus terminus in Woy Woy where commuters are urged to 'Kiss n' Ride'. And the world's friendliest bus driver, Brian Riley, who explained it to us.

It's the sign in the window of a walk-in medical centre 'Endoscopy Centre. Bulk Billing.'

It's the dog-grooming parlour called 'Rover the Rainbow'.

It's the men in suits who board the evening commuter ferry to the northern beaches and pluck from their briefcases a few 'stubbies' carefully masked in brown paper bags. On the outside decks they turn their backs to the 'strictly no smoking' and 'alcohol-free zone' signs, face into the breeze, huddle in a matey circle, loosen ties, light up, drink up, and no doubt anticipate the thought of a t-bone sizzling on the barbie.

Those same guys, knowing Sydney has the slowest-changing traffic lights in the world (we always said the only way to get to the other side is to be born there) wouldn't be seen dead jay-walking though there isn't a car in sight.

20

'Wait Awhile...'

Smiling ground staff in Sydney's ritzy departures terminal showed real eagerness to find the seats we wanted. Quantas flight attendants were friendly, attentive and patient. Whoever trains them deserves congratulations.

The 747 had generous legroom. The captain left us alone – didn't interrupt conversation or in-flight movies with pointless observations on the weather. Or scare us with a blow-by-blow account of how many empty miles lay between us and the ground. We got talking with the chief stewardess about wine. We confessed how much we enjoyed wines from the Margaret River region of Western Australia. Her brother-in-law was a winemaker in Margaret River, she told us. It was quite a small winery, she doubted we'd have heard of it. Turned out to be Capel Vale. It was, we were happy to report, the Australian wine we bought most regularly. Especially the verdelho. She gave us an introduction to our favourite winemaker, even explained the duck logo was 'Frederick' (there must have been several Fredericks over the years we'd been buying the label...)

Five-and-a-half hours from one state capital to another were, in fact, remarkably unstressful.

A foretaste of things to come?

We thought Sydney was laid-back. In Perth they reckon Sydneysiders are stressed-out and work-obsessed, notorious for rushing everywhere. It's too hot and too tranquil here even to think of rushing. They say W.A. stands not for Western Australia but for 'wait awhile'.

Our friend Gerty Ewen met us at the airport. When we got to her car, parked an hour before, her expensive camera was sitting on the bonnet just as she'd absent-mindedly left it.

In our salubrious suburb of South Perth where we rented an apartment with a pool for two weeks, public transport seemed to run only between 9am and 5pm. The bus didn't go anywhere we needed to go. Our apartment block was on the banks of the Swan River, with miles of towpaths, lush green parks, cycle paths and scenic walks. The city centre, with the businesses, stores, hotels and restaurants, theatres and cinemas was a five-minute ferry ride across the river. The last ferry to the city departed at 9pm.

In Sydney life revolves around the ocean and the beaches; Perth's is river-based and gentler. This is The Wind in the Willows.

After two days we realised we had been spoiled for public transport in Sydney. Perth is different. We still did not want to give in and rent a car. We found bicycles instead.

The citizens in Western Australia's capital are so untroubled they can afford to be nice to each other even where competition is involved. A sign outside one of many coffee bars almost boasted 'The Best Cappuccino on This Side of Town.' Over a newsagents' magazine rack, 'Please feel free to purchase if you wish to read'. We're still trying to work out another notice, on the grass near Government House that informed us: 'Bore water used for reticulation.'

Optimism is rife even in the press. Under a display ad in The Sunday Times (W.A.) for a new treatment for impotence, another box heralded a sale of maternity clothes.

Anticipating a wine-tasting trip to the Margaret River region, we telephoned a highly recommended B&B Rosewood Cottage. An answering machine recorded our message. Two hours later came an apologetic return call from the owners, *from their boat*. They were out fishing, they explained, and our phone call should have been diverted to their mobile. Only when they called home to pick up messages did they get ours. They were still on the boat, quite far out to sea, and the line was breaking up. They'd be home in about an hour. Could they call us then?

W.A. enabled us to visit friends we seldom got to see. This part of Australia is so vast, so remote from other states and from other countries, let alone the UK, that visits in either direction are rare and expensive.

Our apartment was just around the corner from the home of the friend who welcomed us at the airport, psychotherapist Gerty Ewen. She introduced us to her favourite pastime and her favourite place to spend an evening – and a little money.

We were surprised to learn that while Las Vegas it ain't, Perth has more casino to the square mile than most other capital cities. And it all belongs to Burswood, or to give it its proper name, Burswood International Resort Casino. Nowhere else in the State of W.A. will you find so much as a pokie (slot machine to you). Burswood sits in solitary splendour in several hundred acres of manicured gardens and an eighteen-hole golf course on the banks of the Swan River. Opened in 1987, it had just completed a £35.6million refurbishment.

The Casino's main gaming floor covers 4,686 square metres, with ninety-one tables and 1,145 computerised video gaming machines with jackpots worth up to a thousand dollars. These are not slots, we were corrected. No mere games of chance but of 'skill' (that is, punters must make a decision, even if it's only choosing numbers for keno). The resort has nine restaurants and six bars and a no-smoking policy throughout.

A free bus service whisks tourists from city hotels out to Burswood a few minutes away and within view of the city centre. For ten Australian dollars local senior citizens, sometimes called 'aged pensioners' get transport, lunch and gaming vouchers. The Casino is open twenty-four hours a day with no membership requirement.

For non-gamblers, Burswood is a 374-bedroom resort hotel, with state-of-the-art convention centre, 2,300-seat theatre and separate concert venue, The Dome, with a capacity of 20,000. Headliners within a few weeks of our visit included President Clinton, Rod Stewart, the Red Army Choir and the Hopman Cup tennis tournament.

We decided even the 'pokies' were beyond our gambling expertise – couldn't make head nor tail of them – and sloped off instead for dinner with Gerty at the Hyatt Regency Hotel. We first met Gerty when she stayed at the Athenaeum Hotel in 1978. That night, in another of those strange and happy coincidences that seem to occur wherever we travel, dining at a table nearby we spotted Dr. and Mrs. Wally Gould, old friends of Gerty and fellow- Athenaeum guests from the 1970s.

The Hyatt Regency provided a prime example of the good nature of Australians. We had had problems with our laptop and it was starting to feel like excess baggage. Three Internet centres had been unable to assist. On the off chance we called in at the hotel's business center to seek emergency advice, and the receptionist tried her best but couldn't make sense of the misbehaving machine. Andre Diaz, the duty manager, overheard us discussing it and volunteered to help.

We explained we were not residents, but he insisted, rather than waiting in the business centre while he attempted to correct the fault, that we take a seat in the lounge and talk to our friends over after-dinner coffee. In an hour the problem was solved.

Back home I fear we'd have wasted our time even asking.

Another joyful reunion in Perth with Sharman and Barry Samuels and their two daughters at their stunning home in South Perth. The family had been shipmates on Oriana in 2000. Between Sharman's formidable cooking, Barry's enviable wine collection, and the sizzling company of the two lovely girls and their pets, the evening seemed to melt away.

We had difficulty understanding a fellow-guest who feared an incipient 'wine like' in W.A. until he explained that local growers faced quite serious over-production. Swan River vineyards were offering wine grapes for sale to amateur wine-makers straight off the vine – a press-your-own rather than pick-your-own service. One grower with four hectares and a thirteen-tonne over-production was offering his grapes at sixty to eighty cents a kilo.

We hadn't seen Ruby and Cliff Booth since the 1980s. Ruby is the sister of our friend Ronnie Clint in Santa Monica, so we had kept in touch by proxy with major events in their life. Both great cooks, Ruby makes an English trifle worth crossing continents for. The Booths, fellow Liverpudlians, had their own catering business in Perth for years, and they know their wines as well as their onions. It was typical of Cliff, knowing we were running out of time and anxious to see the Margaret River wine region, to offer to accompany us.

At the end of a long, hard day's wine tasting (and an even longer, harder day's driving for Cliff) we had managed to visit a dozen of the sixty-two wineries. As we waved goodbye to the last one, we resolved 'God willing, we'll be back, guys.' Just then, who should step over the threshold of the tasting room but ... Barry and Sharman Samuels, our hosts from three nights before and, like us, three hundred kilometres from home. Talk about 'of all the wine joints in all the world...' All we needed was Dooley Wilson, a piano and 'As Time Goes By.'

The wine harvest in the southwest of the continent was five weeks behind the Hunter Valley in New South Wales. After a warm dry spell, they aimed to get the chardonnay, sauvignon and semillon in by the middle of March. White grapes were already covered with acres of netting. Public vineyard enemy number one in this region are silvereyes, tiny birds that bore holes in the grapes and suck out the juice. Then there are the parakeets that peck their pick before their favourite sport – knocking the undamaged grapes off the vine. Four-legged animals, too, from rabbits to 'roos, are eager to picnic among the ripening grapes.

When the whites are safely gathered in, the nets are transferred to the shiraz and cabernets which ripen a week or two later.

In our opinion many of the wines of the Margaret River region are the best in Australia – crisp, true fruit flavours that nevertheless remain subtle and worth savouring at leisure, with or without food. None of the in-your-face or over-ripe flavours too often found in New World wines. Pierr'o and Cullens, Evans & Tate, Voyager and Vasse-Felix are high on our list, but they're not alone.

We found the tasting rooms vary from de luxe, like Voyager's, to the older and intimate at Amberley Estate. Unlike many of the California wineries, tastings are mostly free, and producers occasionally show their older, rarer wines. Many have restaurants that could hold their own in any city.

Winery staff are, in the main, patient with cellar-door visitors. In every coach party, every carload there are those who know zilch and more who know it all. So we forgive the ill-tempered pourer at Cullens, and the others who asked 'What wine do you like, red or white, sweet or dry?' when we're up for some serious sniff-swirl-slurp-and-spit.

Except the nice girls at Vasse-Felix. Eve quietly suggested that the 2000 Shiraz was out of condition (it was more than slightly corked). Our pourer took it to her colleague at the other tasting table, who sniffed it, shrugged, gave her another opened bottle – then placed ours on her own table for the next visitors to taste!

Before leaving W.A. we thought it might be fun to take our bikes, don our helmets, and cycle to Fremantle (we never did learn to call it 'Freo'). We fortified ourselves with giant cappuccinos and home-baked muffins sitting outside in the sun at our favourite riverside restaurant, Plantation. The Italian owner Ian ('nobody here can pronounce my name. Ian they remember!') greeted us warmly as he did whenever we went in for breakfast, lunch or dinner. A fifty-kilometre round trip? Were we sure? Easy peasy, we laughed. There are cycle paths most of the way. Hah!

The cycle paths leading out of Perth along the river were superb, and despite almost sweltering heat we relished the fresh air, the exercise, and the breeze in our face when we pedaled fast enough. Until, that is, we noticed the outskirts of Fremantle began to *swell*. Instead of flat paths, the landscape began to undulate, then to climb. And climb. And climb. The last few miles, and never mind what the map says, were uphill. The temperature had reached thirty degrees (86F). Shame-faced we walked and pushed the last two or three miles straight on to the train homeward bound for Perth.

Later that day we read in the newspaper that the latest euphemism-mnemonic here for the elderly but not yet incapacitated is SWELS – 'seniors with energetic lifestyles'. Guess if the cycle helmet fits...

One day, when time allows, we will venture farther north to Broome, where our Sydney friends John and Verity have built a beautiful home in the place where John's ancestors helped establish the pearling industry. That, however, is a journey for another day. We have seen only the merest fraction of the country and everything we see only whets our appetite for more.

In Perth, you can walk along the banks of the Swan River and see families enjoying an evening picnic or cooking on the communal barbies. Retrace your tracks early next morning and you won't find as much as a lolly-wrapper on the grass. We haven't had a disappointing or overpriced meal. Nor found a single public convenience – and there seems to be one every hundred yards in the cities we visited – unfit for use.

Waiters and shop assistants look you in the eye and listen when you speak.

The Australians have so much to be proud of. They are the proudest, friendliest, kindest, most isolated and cleanest people we've ever met. Their care for the environment, their country and each other is a lesson to us all. Pity they can't be nicer to New Zealand!

Skirtless in Switzerland

After Ron gave a talk to the Hull Literary and Philosophical Society, he received a letter from a friend of the president. It came from Switzerland, and the friend was secretary of the Federation of Anglo Swiss Clubs. Would Ron, or Eve, or both, she asked, consider a two-week lecture tour of Switzerland to address the individual clubs in a dozen cities?

Delighted! We had spent very little time in Switzerland. This would give us an opportunity to explore the country, travelling from city to city for five days of each week, leaving weekends free to spend wherever we wished. Ron agreed to deliver the first series of talks the following year, and Eve would be the speaker two years later.

The Federation of Anglo Swiss Clubs has a branch in most major and many smaller cities throughout Switzerland. Half the members are British expatriates or speak English as their first language, and the other half are Swiss nationals keen to improve their English.

We decided to see Switzerland by train; driving from city to city every day would put us under too much time pressure. The efficiency of Swissrail was legendary (a reputation that was to prove fully justified). The Federation would pay lecture fees plus return flight and first-class fifteen-day Swissrail pass for one, plus overnight accommodation in modest hotels. The other would pay their own fare, thus making it an inexpensive two-week 'working holiday' that would allow us access to people and places we'd never otherwise have known. Occasionally we would be invited to stay as guests in Club members' homes, and always to dine with our hosts before or after the presentation.

Our first visit was in spring, and the country was as beautiful in its greenery as it would be later veiled in white.

We made a number of discoveries. For example, only the cows graze in Switzerland. The Swiss take mealtimes as they take most other things – seriously and precisely. On our first two-week tour of ten cities, moving to a new destination every day, we'd arrive around 2.30 in the afternoon having learned not to expect lunch.

Once we mastered the timing, though, we dined royally all the way. The Swiss are hearty trenchermen, and in local restaurants we feasted on regional specialities, washing down the air-dried venison, beef or cheese fondue, *raclette* (Swiss cheese melted over tiny new potatoes), with spritzy local wine or surprisingly fulsome, soft fruity reds. That they produce wine at all is a credit to Swiss husbandry. Imagine growing grape vines at three thousand feet, on precipitous granite slopes, which are snow covered for months of the year. The Swiss not only do it, but also produce higher yields of good quality grapes than most other nations.

They are unsentimental in their approach to viticulture, as to most things. They will fertilise, irrigate, chaptalise (that is, add sugar before fermentation to increase the alcohol content) and de-acidify, to produce quaffable –sometimes-delectable – wine. Some years they wrestle 140 million litres from their snowy slopes, from the spritzy, fresh-scented Dezaley to the gentle, not-quite-dry Fendant and crisp, fruity Chasselas. Red wines tend to appetisingly moderate alcohol, in a softly fruity style from gamay and pinot noir grapes. Being primarily a wine-importing country, they get to keep most of it to themselves.

Villagers in Champagne, not far from Lake Neuchatel, were up in arms over one of the conditions of Switzerland's possible entry into the European Community. Minute quantities of their dry, rustic white wine have been produced for generations, for strictly local consumption. It's not bubbly, it's not exported, and it ain't Dom Perignon. But if Switzerland wants to join the EC, then the wine from the Swiss village of Champagne must change its name.

As the controversy neared a climax visitors were greeted by billboards proclaiming '*Champagne est mort*'!

Theirs is a country that stops you in your tracks by the variety of its beauty – from chocolate-box prettiness to grandeur. Then sets you right back on track with the efficiency of its transport systems.

We allowed plenty of time each day for unpunctuality and mishaps. We needn't have concerned ourselves; any unpunctuality or mishaps could only be on our part. Half an hour spent with a nice lady and a computer at the *Hauptbahnhof* in Zurich equipped us with fifteen-day first-class Swissrail passes, which cost far less than we anticipated, pocket-sized print-outs of our 'ideal' train each day, departure time, platform, any changes of train including how many minutes to change platform, and final arrival time. It also told us whether there was a dining car or snack service, and gave alternative earlier and later trains.

No city is more than a couple of hours from any other, and you can see most of the country in two weeks with time to explore a little in each stopover. Our passes allowed us to travel free on buses, trams, boats, ferries and cable cars all over Switzerland. This had to be the travel bargain of Europe.

In sixteen days only one train was late, by seven minutes. There were three announcements and apologies. In other countries, when a train leaves the station you look at your watch to see if it is on time. In Switzerland, the train moves off and you look at each other and say, 'Ah. It must be 12.52.'

That's the Swiss for you. Everything works, it's spotlessly clean, and the people unfailingly polite and helpful. No litter in the streets, or on the railway lines, no rowdy kids or teenagers (where do they hide them?) We got a kick out of spotting lumber yards or recycling plants from the train window, with timber neatly stacked and equipment painstakingly cleaned and graded in rows according to size.

The working part of our bi-annual visits, taking turn to be 'lecturer on duty' was hardly arduous. An hour's talk with questions afterwards to small audiences with a wide range of interests. Some Anglo Swiss Clubs had their own premises, but most hired a room in a hotel or restaurant. Audiences could range from ten to sixty, half of them UK expatriates and the others Swiss, perhaps married to British spouses, doing jobs that demanded fluent English, or simply interested in the activities sponsored by the Clubs at their regular meetings.

Their instructions were always spot on: whereabouts of the railway station, how to find the hotel, (always within walking distance) and a map showing the venue. If this was separate from our hotel, then a club member would come along to escort us, on foot or by tram. We would be armed before we left the UK with telephone numbers of at least two people in each city in case of emergency. Truly, it's a joy to do business with the Swiss!

Even with our super-efficient hosts, there were often a few anxious moments when we arrived in a new town until we found (a) the hotel we'd be staying in, (b) the venue we'd be speaking in (not always the same place) and (c) checked out the audio-visual equipment. Sometimes this was hired for our use, sometimes it belonged to the club and a member was designated to bring it along and set it up. Best for us was when it came as part of the package in the venue and the venue was also our overnight hotel.

We took nothing for granted. We had learned from experience always to take both carousel and cartridge slide-holder, for you can never predict what equipment is going to be available. We became adept at turning plastic beer crates or cardboard cartons, covered with a cloth, into lecterns, and carried a small penlight to read notes if required in a darkened room. To speak even more slowly and clearly than usual, since some of your audiences come to improve their English language skills. And to be careful with the jokes. What might amuse a British or an American audience is not guaranteed to raise a smile from the Swiss. That varied from town to town, too. Eve nervously worked her way through a light-hearted account of our world cruise peppered with the usual anecdotes to a group that remained stony faced throughout (including the Federation president who had driven eight hours to be with us). Exactly the same talk with exactly the same tales had them laughing out loud every few minutes in a city not fifty miles away.

Language and humour pitfalls lurk whenever you drop your guard for an instant. Eve was introduced to a member of the French-speaking audience, a middle-aged lady, and was told she was the mother of nine children. Eve 'a-ah-ed' suitably and attempted a compliment.

'Vous etes bien blessée, Madame.'

A raised eyebrow, a pained silence and a quick flutter of conversation covered the dropped brick. Apparently, Eve had told the mother-of-nine, 'Ah, then you are badly wounded, Madame.'

Her worst moment, however, came the year she made 'the tour' on her own. In La Chaux de Fonds, on the western, French-speaking side of the country, she checked into her comfortable hotel room and settled down for a short nap before meeting her hosts for supper.

Refreshed and looking forward to renewing acquaintance with the Club members, she dressed in her smartest suit, which had a long jacket and shortish skirt, gathered up carousel, slides, notes and handbag and took the elevator downstairs. Eve could sense the momentary widening of the eyes of the ladies who greeted her, but thought no more about it until they walked in single file into the restaurant. Against the wall by the entrance was an antique mirrored armoire. A sideways glance to check her appearance one final time revealed something amiss. Two more steps into the room and it dawned: she had forgotten to put her skirt on.

Luckily, the jacket was three-quarter length and covered a multitude of sins. Unluckily, it stopped way too far short of her knees. No wonder the ladies looked askance. God bless restaurants that station any kind of mirror at their entrance.

People think of Switzerland as a winter destination, but our first Alpine spring was literally a breath of fresh air. Viewed from trains as we criss-crossed the country, sleek cows with bells around their necks chomped on lush green meadows speckled with buttercups and Alpine flowers. On the slopes behind them nestled farmhouses with scarlet geraniums in every window box, so perfect you half expected the farmer and his wife to pop out of little swing doors every hour.

There was snow still on the mountains, and a few dogged skiers lining up for cable cars at the weekend, but in every town it seemed a festival was under way to herald the onset of spring. The Swiss seem always to be modestly celebrating something – the end of winter, the day the cows go back on to the mountain, even Mardi Gras (though you couldn't confuse it with the New Orleans version). In Basel, oom-pah bands practise for months in rooms over restaurants, then play for three days morning to night.

Food in season is always a good excuse to celebrate. We arrived at the start of the asparagus season and the green spears featured in every course in every menu. Another year we were just in time for the game-fest that follows the hunting season. On every hotel and restaurant menu deers-r-us, the differences between roe, antelope and chamois precisely defined.

We narrowly missed the mushroom season in Biel-Bienne (German-French bi-lingual city, so bi-lingual name) but were in time for the onionfest, a weekend farmers' market with onions tied into bear-shapes, onions decorating every lamppost, and onions in everything edible served in the town's restaurants and cafes.

In Zurich we arrived for the start of *Sechsleuten*, a two-day celebration when the good Swiss burghers let down their hair (in a dignified kind of way). On Sunday the children from toddlers to adolescents, paraded through the city in costumes whose designs date from mediaeval times. It rained on their parade, and while some of the littler ones cried with the cold, their stouter-hearted brothers and sisters donned un-mediaeval see-through plastic macs and braved the elements as they followed the marching bands.

Having watched so many American parades with self-confident, sleek-thighed and orthodontically unchallenged teenagers working the crowd as they marched, we had trouble restraining ourselves from calling out to these somewhat grim and embarrassed-looking kids: 'Come on – *smile*! *Enjoy* yourselves!'

Next day it was the turn of the adults, in the costumes and liveries of the ancient craft Guilds. Descendents of silversmiths, bakers, shoemakers and weavers processed through Zurich in the wake of a giant 'snowman' which they hoist on to a bonfire and burn to signify the death of winter and the arrival of spring.

In Lucerne the stars of the spring parade were the gentle, doleful-eyed cows and their calves, newly out of winter quarters and hungry for the fresh mountain pastures. The cows were garlanded with flowers and their clanging bronze cowbells reverberated through the city streets. Inside the bars, farmers in national dress, drunk as happy skunks on litre pots of beer, grew redder-cheeked by the minute and exchanged liberal pinches of snuff. At last they rounded up a posse of sweet children to lead the parade through the twilit streets of Lucerne. Nose to tail with the last cow, this being Switzerland, came the street-cleaning machines.

The Swiss couldn't be described as gregarious, but just ask for directions, or appear to be struggling with your luggage, and somebody is at your side and eager to oblige. They will leave whatever they're doing – railway guards, passengers, passers-by – to help or advise. Eve once had her bag carried by a nun (she admits she was not looking her best).

In return they expect you to behave, to enjoy yourself, of course, but not too much. If, in your haste, you ask a question without first bidding the bus driver or the station attendant *bonjour* or *guten tag* they will gently reprimand you by pointedly saying it to *you* before they answer. On more than one occasion when one of us got excited and raised our voice a little, we were treated to disapproving glares from tightly corseted matrons and sober-suited men with briefcases. We asked a bunch of British expats what they missed. 'Eccentricity' came the reply. 'And wit. Swiss humour is no laughing matter...'

If the Swiss are predictable, their weather isn't. Our friend Amanda Green who used to be a tour guide there advised: 'Pack everything. Wear layers. Discard as you go.' There were four days, one in Zurich and three in Geneva, when Eve wished she had brought a fur coat. Twelve days when she was relieved not to have to lug it around. A Swiss spring week will bombard you with weather: sixteen degrees (61F) and sunshine today, snow tomorrow, torrential rain the next. Then t-shirt and shorts (but not *too* short) at teatime on a day that begins one degree above freezing.

Provided you don't expect anything to be open after five o'clock on a weekday and between Saturday lunchtime and Monday morning, most Swiss cities have good shops and boutiques, and plenty of diversions. We especially loved Zurich – its compactness, the ease of getting around on trams, boats and ferries. We felt thoroughly pampered at the lovely Hotel Baur au Lac, and discovered that a local restaurant, *Dezaley*, had fondue that made dieting seem downright ungrateful.

The more we visit Switzerland the more we appreciate Geneva, a sophisticated city strung like a necklace around the lake, mountains soaring protectively behind. Our refuge there is the splendid Hotel Beau Rivage, owned and run by the Mayer family, overlooking the lake and as elegant and tranquil as you could wish for. Dining at the Beau Rivage is no hardship – the food is among the finest in the city. But venturing out is fun, too, and we returned many times to *Les Armures* up in the old city for fondue or air-cured beef, and to *l'Entrecote* for steak-frites that are the best outside of Belgium.

Taxis in most towns are expensive but public transport is so good, especially the trams and buses, you seldom need cabs. Given more time and less luggage, we could have picked up bicycles at rail stations and used them to whiz around the city, confident that Swiss drivers would respect our right of way. We could even have ridden our bikes on to the next city and left them at the rail station.

In other cities we found modest railway hotels, three or occasionally four-star, clean, comfortable and affordable, sometimes surprisingly luxurious. The St. Gothard in Basel, run by the same family for three generations and refurbished to a high standard, was a real find. Neuchatel has a hotel run by the local hotel school, and the high standard of accommodation and service made their 'Eurotel' a bargain.

Lucerne, Basel and other cities have their own 'hotel school hotels' and they are worth seeking out.

It's sad that visitors neglect Switzerland's smaller towns and cities off the beaten ski track and all easily accessible by car or train. Most have an old section with cobbled streets, a market and mediaeval buildings, often a splendid cathedral or historic church. St. Gallen in the northeast of the country, an important centre for the textile industry, has a splendid baroque cathedral and an ornate *bibliotheque* whose history can be traced to the 13th century.

A few miles away is the Alpine village of Ebnat-Kappel which looks like every tourist-brochure picture you've ever seen. We have been guests there of Alison and Dieter Schwarz in their traditional Swiss chalet home at the foot of a mountain. Alison is a marvellous cook, Dieter has a superb wine cellar, and now he has retired from military reserve duty, we no longer have to be nervous about the guns propped up just outside our attic bedroom.

Switzerland's economy took a hard knock after the Japanese flooded the market with cheap digital watches. Recession bit deep, but in two decades the country was back on track with its two principal industries of money and tourism. It is as prosperous and contented, with its history of neutrality and political independence, as any nation in Europe. Citizens accept national, cantonal and local referendums as a fact of life. Hardly a month goes by without the requirement to vote for or against something, even if only the closing of your local town centre to traffic on one weekend a month.

From the Panoramic Express, one of the world's loveliest rail journeys from Montreux to Gstaad, we looked out on grassy mountain slopes. Embossed on one, in letters thirty feet high, the single word '*non*'. On others, animal shapes, faded and less easy to discern. They looked for all the world like crop circles, but these were man-made. Swiss-made, at that. Local hill farmers, incensed by some threatened legislation, were encouraged by their union to take a stance. The Swiss farmers took up their haystacks and decorated their mountainsides with giant animals, symbols – and the occasional less creative but straight-to-the-point '*non*'.

Gstaad is a storybook town. Like strolling inside a giant cuckoo clock factory. Even the civic buildings are oversized wooden chalets. Out of season the only sign of the star-studded winter to come are the sponsors' names on a bronze statue of Rosie the Calf 'drinking' realistically from the town cattle trough. Elizabeth Taylor's name is there along with philanthropists and society moguls from both sides of the Atlantic. But then the bronze *is* by her daughter Liza Todd.

Snug inside their cashmere cocoons, owners of the Valentino and Hermes and Andre Grima boutiques gossip desultorily or tidy the already impeccably arranged stock ready for the influx of the haughty and the naughty as soon as the dusting of snow on the peaks becomes a crust and Gstaad is transformed once again into the piste of choice of the stars.

One thing guaranteed to confuse the visitor is language. In a country the size of a large American shopping mall they speak *four* official languages. You never know when you step off a train which tongue you're going to hear. Until, that is, you learn to listen out for the bi- and sometimes tri-lingual station announcements.

If they say '*nächste halt*' before '*prochaine arrêt*' then prepare to say '*guten Tag*' or '*gruzie*'. The other way around, and it's going to be a '*bonjour*' kind of a day. If you're in one of the cantons where they speak Romansch, then you're on your own.

Having adjusted our ears to German the first few days, we found it disorienting to step off a train in a new city after barely an hour's journey to hear everybody speaking French or Italian or Romansch. But most people who have contact with visitors speak English well.

We left Switzerland from Geneva airport – not a bad place to find yourself around lunchtime, with a decent restaurant. The menu that day courteously suggested a starter of 'small pastry of hot goat.'

The Swiss are always polite, always on time, always predictable. The gnomes are in Zurich, all's well with the world.

22

Venetian Winter

It was something Nigella Lawson wrote when she was a columnist in one of the Sunday papers, long before her 'domestic goddess' days. She loves Venice as we do, but felt you could never truly be at home in the city until you spent time in an apartment of your own, shopping, cooking, living as the Venetians do. That thought simmered away on the back burners of our minds until one day we asked ourselves, why not?

Eve's editor on the New Orleans Times travel section agreed to publish a feature on our extended stay in Italy's most exciting city. A winter working holiday on (more or less) dry land it would be, then.

Venice welcomed us on a mid-December morning with sunshine, brittle blue skies and zero degrees. Ripples reflected off the canals cast moving shadows on to the walls of pastel-shaded palazzos. Barges tied up alongside while they unloaded the mail, the groceries and the wine for the citizens of *La Serenissima*.

We were joining them for a month. We had spent our honeymoon at the Cipriani and tried to return for a brief visit every year or so. But while Natale Rusconi may be one of the great hoteliers of the world and a generous host, none but the super-rich can contemplate more than two or three nights at the Cipriani or its twin Fortuny-clad palazzi.

Would we miss the warm welcome of the dignified Dr. Rusconi? The outdoor pool? The views from Palazzo Vendramin across to St. Mark's? The personal butler? Of course we would. But our new experience would prove every bit as seductive. We would enjoy the city at our leisure and, most serendipitous of all, would find Venice curiously devoid of tourists at year's end.

For a daily cost equivalent to that of breakfast in the grand hotels, we rented a tiny apartment in a sixteenth century palazzo, Santa Maria Nova. Most houses in Venice are 'palazetti' split up into apartments. Ours was a modest conversion in the Cannaregio district not far from the Rialto. Our host was Robert Hendrick, an affable Englishman who rents out two double bedrooms and the self-contained attic apartment, forty steps up from street level, the last twenty positively mediaeval in their steep spiral to roof level.

Not a grand apartment, but it nestled among the terracotta rooftops of the city and we soon felt at home. The bedroom and sitting-dining room had chestnut beams, forgettable furnishings, and walls painted a cheerful pale yellow. Terazzo floors called *pavimenta Veneziana* or 'Venetian pavement' helped keep the apartment cool in summer.

From the bedroom and sitting room windows we could – just – see the tip of the Campanile in St. Mark's Square. We had a clear view of our local Church, Santa Maria dei Miracoli, its marbled dome soaring over the network of canals.

As soon as our host was out of earshot we misquoted Shakespeare to each other over a quirky little Romeo and Juliet balcony inexplicably overlooking the inside staircase.

The world's smallest kitchenette had a window from which the cook could sticky-beak into the courtyards and windows of neighbouring apartments. There was a dolls-house fridge, two-burner hotplate, and enough equipment for the simple cooking we had in mind.

One floor down, a spacious but bathless bathroom sported an electric shower that dribbled rather than spouted hot water – but only on good days. All part of the fun of 'abroad', we consoled ourselves.

Our landlord explained that people who buy a palazzo in Venice don't always bother with a formal survey. 'If it's been standing for six hundred years,' he reasoned, 'you imagine it will stand for as long as you do.

'You take for granted the odd bit of rising damp or damaged walls and woodwork,' he added with, we thought, commendable English understatement.

We couldn't wait to explore 'our' neighbourhood, make friends with the local shopkeepers, and familiarise ourselves with the arcane traditions of the fish and vegetable markets over the Rialto Bridge.

Having secured seven-day *vaporetto* passes (four-week passes would have been more economical, but they run from the first to the last day of the month), an early lesson was essential if we were to follow the most basic directions. That is, Venice is divided into 'this' side of the Grand

Canal and 'that' side; the (San) Marco side and the (San) Polo side. Neither is more desirable, though Cannaregio (this side) is the district where most Venetians live. There are six *sestiere* or districts. Addresses consist of a number and a *sestiere*, 7439 Castello, or 414 San Polo for instance. No street name, no house name. Bridges aren't much help as locators either: Venice has four hundred of them. Visitors would be lost without the goodwill and polite patience of the citizenry.

They'd be even more lost without hands. Pointing, hand-signals, arm waving, gestures great and small, are indispensable. Italians must be ahead of the rest of Europe in one aspect of road safety; drivers *have* to pull off the motorway to use mobile phones because they need one hand to hold the cell phone and the other to gesticulate, without which speech is impossible.

Eve was excited to learn that our next-door neighbour was a favourite thriller writer, Donna Leon, an American University professor who lives and teaches in Venice and writes atmospheric novels set in the city. Their central character is the charismatic Commissario Guido Brunetti. We are not proud to admit that, like a couple of turkeys, we set out to track down the police headquarters building or Questura, where Brunetti has his office overlooking the *campo* or square and the church of San Silvestre. Eve insists she even identified the office, with a single cream rose in a vase on the windowsill, of the glamorous police secretary Signorina Elletra.

The little *calle* across the square from our apartment was a hive of small shops; grocers, butchers, a hardware store, pharmacy, bakery and toyshop. Plus the inevitable half dozen bars and cafes. A short walk away was the main shopping drag of Strada Nuova and *Stand*a, our closest supermarket.

The third time we were asked for directions as we emerged from our front door we felt flattered to be mistaken for locals. Eve was asked by two Japanese visitors to pose with her bunch of tulips from the market, standing in front of the Rialto Bridge while they photographed 'Very nice Venice lady…'

Two weeks before Christmas, tourists were so rare that when you did come across somebody speaking English, instant friendships were struck up and addresses exchanged (Hi! Stephen Bennett and family from Columbus, Ohio. Remember us? In the bar on the Strada Nuova? We remember you, with your four lovely children, and how surprised you were at all the attention you received. Far from being the land of the large family, as you expected, Italy has one of the lowest birth rates in Europe.)

We were drawn into that bar by a lone waiter in long white apron who beckoned us inside on a frosty morning. Ron ordered a grappa to 'correct' his *caffe* and the bartender brought half a tumbler. Ron tipped him a thousand lire, Giovanni slapped him on the shoulder, and our daily return was assured.

This is the time of year to make the most of everything cultural and historic that Venice has to offer. Major exhibitions were queue-free. We lingered in churches and galleries where in other years we've been jostled in and marched out again after a cursory glance at frescoes and pictures.

We feasted on Tintoretto, over-dosed on Titian, and sated ourselves on the paintings and sculpture at the Guggenheim. There was a special exhibition 'The Year of Her Century', which included a viewing of Peggy Guggenheim's personal visitors' books, signed by major artists, statesmen and celebrities of her day, often with a sketch or a verse.

We re-visited 'The Angel of the City' sculpture by Marini Marini that dominates the garden at the back of the house overlooking the Grand Canal. The man on the horse sports a gigantic phallus, and Peggy Guggenheim is said to have unscrewed the offending member once a year when a boat-load of nuns had to pass close by on their way to a religious festival.

One day, inevitably, a visitor succeeded in stealing the phallus and Guggenheim wired the artist: 'the bird has flown. Please send another.'

The Mayan art exhibition, newly opened, was the only one that had a half-hour queue outside. We took good advice, arrived just before opening time, and walked straight in to a spectacular array of Mayan art and artefacts, beautifully staged and lit, and with blessedly succinct written commentary. The exhibit followed us to London, but how smug we felt having had our own preview in Venice!

We lingered over a stunning display of modern glass at the Palazzo Fortuny, the centrepiece a giant's necklace of clear glass, fifteen feet high, crystalline droplets suspended from the ceiling in gradually deepening cascades. Exhibits ranged from exquisite chandeliers and delicate epergnes to far-fetched and fun 'Biotechno' sculptures that flashed, pulsated and emitted ethereal under-sea sounds.

'The World of Casanova' at the Ca' Rezonnico was the second biggest crowd-puller after the Mayans. Seldom seen works by Watteau, Canaletto and Joshua Reynolds were overshadowed – literally, since the exhibits were sadly ill lit – by sumptuous clothes, jewellery and objets d'art of the period.

What luxury to wander for hours in the near-empty rooms of the sixteenth century Scuola Grande di S. Rocco, the walls and ceilings covered with Tintoretto canvases and frescoes. A voluptuous array of Titians and Tiepolos, too, and in the Albergo Hall, what many consider to be the world's most important painting, The Crucifixion. Having the time to gaze and absorb the immense amount of detail felt like reading a contemporary account of the last hours of Christ's life.

And all the while the sun shone! We arrived with Burberrys, hats and umbrellas, yet in a month it rained only three or four times. Eve was pleased, though, that she'd brought her 'long service award' after twenty years of marriage, a mink coat. Venice was freezing. While in London the anti-fur brigade make for uncomfortable daytime outings for expensive skins, Venetians have no such problems. Women wear mink and sables, foxes and small animals of indeterminate origin to the supermarket, the launderette, for a visit to McDonalds (yes, alas, there are three) and for fetching the fresh-baked bread twice a day. When you live through a scorching Venetian summer, the bitter winter cold and the damp from the Lagoon chill to the bone. Furs are a fact of life.

It took a while to attempt the rapid-fire technique required for buying often unidentifiable fish and seafood in the open-air market. We should have armed ourselves with the Italian names of the fish we like, and be sure we could recognise them on the slab. As it was, for the first day or two we didn't know our *san pietro* from our *dorado*, couldn't distinguish our *trota* from our *rombo*.

In our neighbourhood stores the food was fresh, local and of outstanding quality. The shopkeepers cut it up or measured it out and packaged it in little parcels of waxed paper and string, presenting it like a gift.

Our local butcher cut ham in wafer-thin slices, interleaving each one with greaseproof paper. He counted out six or eight ready-to-cook veal meatballs only after asking how hungry we were. Then instructed us to make sure the oil in the pan was good and hot, fry them quickly and serve with spaghetti, tomato salsa and a little salad.

Diplomacy demanded we split our custom between the two delis in our shopping alley, Salizade Canizan. *Langio Gualtiero* was run by the man we called The Professor. Tall and ascetic, he regarded us over half-moon spectacles and told us the provenance of salami and cheese before he cut them. Explained with a disdainful shrug that the *finocchiona* (salami with fennel) we asked for was a speciality of Tuscany and would therefore not be called for in his shop. No V8 juice either. 'We have such beautiful fresh vegetables. Why would we need vegetable juice?'

We found both in the shop next door but one. *Barreton* was run by 'Rasputin' and his brother. Rasputin was square, built like a tank, with full black beard and cherubic smile. His brother contented himself with a luxuriant moustache. He carved San Danieli ham and doled out chunks of good cheese and samples of local wine in a back room while Rasputin starred front of house. He made his own 'mustard marmalade', a local New Year's tradition, and it was a sign of his persuasiveness that he talked us into trying some, ladled out of a marble basin on the counter. Only the once, though.

Our favourite provisioner, visited almost daily, was the fresh pasta shop in Strada Nuova. Smiling girls sold home made pasta in dozens of shapes, colours and flavours. We tried the lemon tagliatelli, the smoked salmon gnocchi, pasta flavoured with squid ink, with basil, with tomato, with spinach. In the back room they cooked the sauces, two or three different kinds each day. The aroma of roasting duck for the *salsa anatra* drew us in from the cold. We stood in the shop and inhaled deeply and the boss came over to apologise. 'The smell. It is troubling you? It is too much?' 'Too much?' we sighed. 'Never!' And bought a container big enough to feed four hungry navvies.

Their lobster and truffle sauce had a flavour so pervasive that when Eve tipped the contents into a saucepan that evening, she cracked a couple of eggs into the empty container and used them to whip up truffled scrambled eggs for breakfast.

The ladies in the pasta shop spoke no English, but managed to instruct us on how to handle the goods. Our Italian could just about keep up.

'Don't overcook the pasta,' they warned. '*Al dente*. Always *al dente*. A few minutes only.' And the gnocchi? 'Two minutes. Watch for the gnocchi to rise to the top of the pan. That means they are ready. No more or they will be ruined.'

The saddest thing Venice ever threw at us was to discover on our return in 2003 that the pasta shop had closed.

When we travel we try to stick to local wines. Our neighbourhood *enoteca* (literally, 'library') *Boldrin* was just around the corner. The family produced a selection of *ciachetti*, little snacks of meatballs, sandwiches, baby squid, anchovies and deep fried rice to accompany tankards of local beer or drafts of wine from the Veneto. The walls were lined, book-case style, with fine wines for sale, but the cask Merlot and Cabernet, newly arrived from the autumn harvest, were so easy to drink we followed local custom and took our empty two-litre water bottles to be filled every few days for the equivalent of a pound or two.

Our most memorable meals were taken in two of our favourite restaurants in the world. *Osteria da Fiori* and *Harry's Bar*, truly a legend in its own lunchtime.

We first felt like true Venetians when we were able to find our way to da Fiori without asking for directions. Now we head for Campo San Polo on 'that' side of the Rialto Bridge and exit the square to our right. You can easily walk past da Fiori, so unobtrusive is the entrance. Inside there is a small bar and a modest back room laid up with crisp linen and sparkling silver.

The welcome is courteous, not effusive, typically Venetian. These are not heart-on-sleeve, extrovert people in the way of Neapolitans, but more restrained in the Northern Italian manner. The food at da Fiori is fish or seafood, usually a little appetiser of tiny shrimp, main courses of turbot, cod, bream, sea bass and squid or octopus – all depends on what has been caught that morning. House wine comes in Venetian glass jugs, good soave, cabernet, merlot rose or foaming *prosecco*, Italy's light and mood enhancing answer to champagne.

Harry's Bar by contrast is eccentric, cramped, noisy; a cabaret for people-watchers. Well-heeled tourists make a beeline for it, yet the place still manages to be full of Venetians. We learned not to accept a table in the upstairs room (though we had fun the one time we did). Locals take lunch or dinner in the same room as the bar; no matter that proximity forces intimacy and too bad if you dislike cigarette smoke.

Best fun is to be had at the bar, watching the bartender, hands moving faster than you can see, preparing trademark *bellinis* or *negroni* cocktails by the dozen. The complimentary snacks disappear from the plate almost before they're put down. You can tell the Venetians – they're the slick, sleek and cashmered ones who don't touch the nibbles. The Americans are easy to spot, too. The ladies are sorority members of the same school of cosmetic surgery, faces taut, foreheads immobile. Black Chanel and diamonds are de rigeur. Husbands sport Turnbull and Asser shirts and Cartier watches.

As the evening progresses, the bartender may reach up to the art deco clock on the wall behind the bar to move the big hand back by fifteen or twenty minutes. When visitors come in to claim their 8.30pm table, still occupied by a party of four halfway through their main course, the bartender can point to the clock and say regretfully: 'But Signor, it is still only ten after eight...'

We eventually get to tuck into the risotto we'd looked forward to for days. It is especially good in springtime, when the *risotto primavera* is spiked with baby vegetables. And in the truffle season, when the waiter shaves seductively aromatic white truffles over the *risotto con funghi*. As an appetiser all you need is a little deep-fried shrimp or fresh scampi. Harry's Bar does most things, even the simplest, with unusual flair. At a price. We've never managed even a simple supper with aperitifs and house wine without contemplating a mortgage.

Harry's Dolci, on the island of Guidecca, has the same owner, but offers a more affordable experience. The restaurant is panelled and mirrored in traditional manner but outside there are tables looking across the canal to the Zattere. The set lunch menu draws us back during summer visits, when we sit outside and watch the daily parade of Venetian life on the Grand Canal. Once we spotted a commercial boatman cruising down the canal past our table, reading a newspaper he'd spread out on the hatch, both arms outstretched for page turning, and the tiller wedged firmly between the cheeks of his bottom. Way to go!

Most of our lunches and dinners were enjoyed in less salubrious surroundings. *Tre Spiedi*, a minute's walk from our apartment, run by two brothers and their wives, served fresh fish and homemade pasta. We seldom looked at a menu, just asked *il padrone's* advice. With local wine and two courses, our bill was usually the price of cocktails at Harry's Bar, the total scribbled on the paper tablecloth.

Two young men at the next table one evening offered to take our photograph. 'Sir,' one said politely in halting English. 'I would like to propose a different position for you and your woman...' It took us a moment to figure out he was merely suggesting we make a better photograph by sitting closer together.

We stopped feeling like visitors when we understood the differences between a *trattoria* (serves the simplest food); *osteria* (originally an inn serving no-frills food and drink); *rosticeria* (a middle range restaurant specialising in roasted and grilled meats); and *ristorante* (usually the most formal and often the most expensive).

Wintertime aromas are gentle on the nostrils. The occasional whiff of decay from a canal, the mouth-watering fragrance of the afternoon bread baking, the satisfyingly musty odour of a church crypt.

You dare not stop *looking* with real concentration lest you miss something – like your footing on some of the narrower *fondamenta*, and go crashing into a canal. You could miss the one church you haven't yet explored; the lighted window allowing a glimpse of a chandeliered salon overlooking the canal as you pass by on the vaporetto. Or the haunting sight of a Venetian funeral gondola. We stood with a small knot of people with heads bowed while two white-shirted gondoliers with black armbands removed the deceased from the water gate of an ancient palazzo.

Later, the funeral barge, poled by four strong *gondolieri*, would lead a stately procession of mourners over to the island of San Michele, where the Venetians lay their dead to rest.

One aspect of the Venetian way of death bemused us. Outside every neighbourhood church were notices of recent deaths accompanied by passport-size photographs of the newly deceased, usually elderly. What we want to know is: *when do they take the photographs?*

There is always music in Venice. Usually Vivaldi's Four Seasons, it's true, or the popular medleys played by the orchestras outside the Piazza's rival cafes Florian and Quadro. But you *can* with a little application find other music. La Fenice had not yet arisen from its ashes, but there was operetta at the Teatro Goldoni, the cheerful *Sogno di un Valzer* (Waltz Dream) by Oscar Strauss.

Over a swift *espresso* one frosty morning Robert reminded us that in the glory days of Venice the population was almost a quarter of a million. By the middle of the last century it had decreased to 155,000, and at the end of the millennium, to 67,000. 'When I arrived here three years ago,' he said, 'there were 68,000. People are leaving now at the rate of fifty a week.' Only the tourist population is expanding, to a worrying ten million a year.

Robert discovered from personal experience that reconstruction or refurbishment in Venice requires a whole new mindset even for someone experienced in renovating property in the UK. Every scaffolding pipe, every floorboard, every concrete mixer, every stick of furniture is delivered, slowly, on canal barges. Builders' rubble is taken away, after tumbling down a chute on to a small skip, on canal barges. Your fridge, television, microwave oven or new dishwasher arrive the same way, trundled to your door on a luggage trolley by one of the freelance porters who meet the canal boats.

Other differences brought smiles to our faces.

'The builders arrived at 7.30am,' Robert told us. 'They insisted on the use of a bedroom and bathroom to change out of their designer clothes and into immaculate blue overalls. They worked hard until the bells clanged at noon.

'That was their signal to wash and change clothes again and disappear for lunch. Some went home, the others just down to Boldrin, the local wine bar.

'Two hours later to the minute they were back, giggling merrily, to sweep up the morning's mess until six o'clock, when they would again wash, change, and go home.'

A Sunday morning lie-in is not to be expected in Venice. Nobody sleeps through *the bells*. Hundreds of them. Near and far, tuneful and monotone. LOUD, since most of them rang close to the level of our attic bedroom.

Long walks on cold, clear days were high on our agenda. We set out on a Sunday morning to cover about four miles from our apartment via the Ghetto, the original area settled by the Jews in the 1400s. By the sixteenth century they were not allowed to live anyplace else, or to build outwards, so they built upwards. Their legacy is Venice's only 'high rise' apartment buildings, five and in one case seven, storeys high.

The first Church on our itinerary, San Marcuolo, was closed. It is the unfinished church – its exposed red brick exterior never did get its marble overcoat. Inside there is a Tintoretto, but we knew there would be others. Santa Maria del' Orta, restored after the floods of 1966, made up for it. There, we feasted on a dozen 'Tintoretti' and viewed the tombs of the painter and his son and daughter.

Our route took us along the Fondamenta della Misericordia, inaptly named site of the city's nightclubs, jazz and blues venues. Venice is an early-to-bed city, but such nightlife as there is, is here. A brief diversion to take in the old Arab quarter. Later, our walk led us to the church of St. Georgio dei Grechi and the Greek district.

First, after passing the beautiful Ca' d'Oro, a stop at our favourite bar for *caffe coretto*. We were greeted like long-lost relatives by the bartender who had seen us only two days before. He called Eve 'Madonna' and Ron 'Dottore' and this time the 'correcting' grappa almost filled the small tumblers.

Fortified, we gazed at the immense church of Ss. Giovanni y Paolo and the public hospital alongside it, a former monastery. We made it on feet that were growing numb with the cold as far as the Arsenale, site of Venice's maritime past. Not, it has to be admitted to the lion-guarded gates of the main entrance. In fact, we made a pig's ear of the dog's-leg we had planned and found ourselves around the back, taking a half-mile walkway with derelict Arsenale buildings on our right and the Lagoon underneath and to our left. Our only companions on this grim stretch were legions of feral cats.

In the distance we could hear what sounded like a soccer match. Hallucinating? Cold can do that to you. We had no choice but to turn back (and it was a *long* way) or keep going. Up ahead, when we felt we could trudge no further, the walkway petered out and we found the football pitch at the end of the world.

Two spectators advised, one in Italian the other in English, that we go thataway and in a few minutes we'd find the vaporetto. We think it was their polite way of telling us women were not welcome, for there wasn't another in sight. It took a moment to realise the man who spoke to us in English was the moustachioed brother of 'Rasputin' at our local deli.

Our walks confirmed that Venice's principal hazards come from above and below. Dogs and pigeons. Pigeons and dogs. The birds are scabrous and a damn nuisance. They targeted Ron's new raincoat and scored direct hits on the shoulder, over the sleeve and halfway down the back. The mess had dried before either of us noticed it. To quote the elegant French gentleman who *did* notice as he passed, head shaking in sympathy, '*Ils crottent, les pigeons, comme ils crottent...*'

Venetians love their dogs. Not what you'd call proper dogs either. These are small, yappy, tattered dogs, like rats on a string. Yorkshire terriers, daschunds, papillons or chihuahuas. Often fed from little silver dishes fished from a Louis Vuitton handbag. Restaurant staff play along and bring food and water without cracking a smile. Only the occasional yelp gives away a deftly placed kick when a waiter sees his chance. Besotted owners clutch these pampered pooches like precious accessories but with full pavement privileges. The pooper-scooper had not yet reached Venice. You must look where you walk. That's when you're not focusing skyward to avoid the pigeons.

Despite the unsettling advent of McDonalds lunchtime is still sacrosanct. Businesses close for two hours, and most people, schoolchildren included, join their families for a cooked mid-day meal and a rest. Alcohol is incorporated into Italians' lives in such a manner that you rarely see anybody the worse for drink. Workmen knock back their early-morning grappa or 'correct' their coffee; young women with babies on their laps enjoy a grappa after lunch in a café; and it's not unusual to see elderly ladies of utmost respectability smacking their lips over a glass of *vino rosso* or a quarter-litre of beer with a half-sandwich in the late afternoon.

Officially a city, Venice is essentially a small town. It doesn't have much crime. It can be traversed entirely on foot. And despite its undoubted mystique and atmosphere of 'otherness', we have never felt threatened or uncomfortable. Easy as it is to get lost, you can never be far from where you want to be. Carry a map, look up, and locate the nearest church tower.

Payback for the lack of traffic and noise is that you *walk*. Everywhere. Whatever the weather. When you go to dinner. To visit friends. Shop. Have tickets for the theatre or a concert. Umbrellas and sensible shoes stand by the door of every apartment.

For distances, there is the vaporetto, Venice's efficient public transportation. (Water taxis are expensive.) The number one route is the 'hop-on-hop-off service for sightseeing, and stops at landing stages close to most major venues. Other routes take you to the 'near' islands of Burano and Murano, Torcello and the Lido, though not to all of the hundred-and-eighteen islands of the Lagoon.

On honeymoon in Venice we took a gondola ride, naturally. Now, as honorary Venetians we use the *traghetti* or public gondolas that ply back and forth across the Grand Canal. These take about a dozen passengers (six too many!) and cost pennies. Eve regards with abject terror the notion of standing upright in a swaying boat in mid-canal with nothing but a wooden plank between her and the water. Only wimps, we were assured, attempt to sit down. Eve made it across only by clinging to her husband in front and a bewildered Venetian businessman behind.

December 24th, Christmas Eve to us, is the Italians' Christmas Day – the feast of San Stefano. The shops remain open during the day, and after dark Venice glowed with colourful arts and crafts markets, decorations and tiny white lights strung like necklaces across narrow streets and over bridges. She was the Grand Duchess flaunting the family jewels.

After Christmas Eve supper in Harry's Bar, booked for 9.30pm, seated at 10.30, we attended midnight Mass in St. Mark's Basilica. In the half-hour leading up to midnight the atmosphere was sombre, expectant. No music, almost no lights, priests and helpers bustling about like stage managers, checking props and watches for the theatrical production that was to come. At midnight the Basilica was slowly illuminated, the golden mosaics on walls and roof glowing progressively brighter until 'the Light of the World' was proclaimed. The Mass and the readings were in three languages.

Next day we woke to find our rooftops vista veiled in frost. Too cold to walk for long, we slipped inside the Frari Church and spent an hour, almost the only visitors, amidst the most beautiful interiors of Venice. Recently restored, the Church seemed bathed in a light of its own. The choir, carved and gilded to within an inch of its life, is set in the middle. The perspective from the back of the church to the Altar and the jewelled stained glass windows beyond is breathtaking.

Our favourite painting in all Venice is here, the Bellini triptych showing the Madonna and Child flanked by saints. Four hundred years old it is vivid with colour, light and the individuality of the characters.

In the Piazza Ron found unaccustomed pleasure in sketching undisturbed in and around the Basilica before visiting the three splendid horses of St. Mark's; not the reproductions outside the cathedral but the originals, now safely stabled in the loggia.

The handsome arches and architecture of the fish market, devoid of traders, stalls, merchandise and customers could be admired without interruption. Ron stood for almost two hours sketching in near-zero temperatures, oblivious to the cold, fingerless mittens the only concession to frost and ice.

As New Year approaches Venice presents a different face. Christmas market traders de-rig their stalls, citizens and tourists take to the streets around San Marco and prepare to party. We had done our research, visiting the major hotels and over coffee or a cocktail, garnering details of their New Year's Eve plans. The Cipriani was closed for the winter, so we could check out the competition with a clear conscience. We decided only the Danieli would do.

Dinner was superb, and at midnight we strolled on to the roof terrace overlooking the Grand Canal to watch a half-hour display of mind-blowing pyrotechnics – volley after volley of golden rain, Catherine wheels, multi-coloured set-pieces of hearts and roses, fired into the sky from barges on the Lagoon.

As we toasted each other and our neighbours and the New Year bells tolled all around, we thought 'Life doesn't get much better than this.'